THROUGH THE BRAZILIAN WILDERNESS

Colonel Roosevelt and Colonel Rondon
At Navaïté on the River of Doubt
From a photograph by Cherrie

THROUGH THE BRAZILIAN WILDERNESS

BY

THEODORE ROOSEVELT

WITH ILLUSTRATIONS FROM PHOTOGRAPHS BY KERMIT ROOSEVELT
AND OTHER MEMBERS OF THE EXPEDITION

KALPAZ

ISBN: 978-93-5128-778-0(PB)

First Published in 1914
Indian Reprint in 2017

Published by

Kalpaz Publications
C-30, Satyawati Nagar,
Delhi – 110052
E-mail: kalpaz@hotmail.com
Website: kalpazpublications.com
Ph.: +91-9212142040

Cataloging in Publication Data—DK
Courtesy: D.K. Agencies (P) Ltd. <docinfo@dkagencies.com>

Roosevelt, Theodore, 1858-1919, **author.**
Through the Brazilian wilderness / by Theodore Roosevelt ; with illustrations from photographs by Kermit Roosevelt and other members of the expedition.
pages cm
"First published in 1914"—Title page verso.
Includes index.
ISBN 9789351287780

1. Roosevelt-Rondon Scientific Expedition (1913-1914) 2. Animals—Brazil. 3. Brazil—Description and travel. 4. Roosevelt River (Brazil) I. Roosevelt, Kermit, 1889-1943, photographer. II. Title.

F2515.R78 2017 DDC 508.81 23

Map showing the entire South American journey of Colonel Roosevelt and members of the expedition

PREFACE

THIS is an account of a zoogeographic reconnoissance through the Brazilian hinterland.

The official and proper title of the expedition is that given it by the Brazilian Government: Expedicão Scientifica Roosevelt-Rondon. When I started from the United States, it was to make an expedition, primarily concerned with mammalogy and ornithology, for the American Museum of Natural History of New York. This was undertaken under the auspices of Messrs. Osborn and Chapman, acting on behalf of the Museum. In the body of this work I describe how the scope of the expedition was enlarged, and how it was given a geographic as well as a zoological character, in consequence of the kind proposal of the Brazilian Secretary of State for Foreign Affairs, General Lauro Müller. In its altered and enlarged form the expedition was rendered possible only by the generous assistance of the Brazilian Government. Throughout the body of the work will be found reference after reference to my colleagues and companions of the expedition, whose services to science I have endeavored to set forth, and for whom I shall always feel the most cordial friendship and regard.

THEODORE ROOSEVELT.

SAGAMORE HILL,
September 1, 1914.

CONTENTS

CHAPTER		PAGE
I.	The Start	1
II.	Up the Paraguay	38
III.	A Jaguar-Hunt on the Taquary	62
IV.	The Headwaters of the Paraguay	95
V.	Up the River of Tapirs	132
VI.	Through The Highland Wilderness of Western Brazil	167
VII.	With a Mule-Train Across Nhambiquara Land	203
VIII.	The River of Doubt	243
IX.	Down an Unknown River into the Equatorial Forest	282
X.	To the Amazon and Home; Zoological and Geographical Results of the Expedition	321
	Appendices—	
	A. The Work of the Field Zoologist and Field Geographer in South America	343
	B. The Outfit for Travelling in the South American Wilderness	353
	C. My Letter of May 1 to General Lauro Müller	370
	Index	373

ILLUSTRATIONS

Colonel Roosevelt and Colonel Rondon at Navaïté on the River of Doubt . . . . *Frontispiece*
Photogravure from a photograph by Cherrie.

FACING PAGE

Group—The mussurama swallowing the jararaca or fer-de-lance, after having just killed it. Method of the mussurama's attack upon the jararaca 24

Man-eating fish, piranha 42

Group—Indian boy with coati (coon-like animal) and parakeet. Tupi girl with young ostrich. Indian girl at cooking-pot 48

Group—Indians rolling logs at wood station. Palms along the bank of the river 50

Cattle on the upper Paraguay River 58

Group—Nips with the marsh deer. Returning to the *fazenda* (ranch) with the marsh deer on the saddle 76

Group—The brown boy on the long-horned trotting steer, which he managed by a string through its nostril and lip. Colonel Roosevelt and the first jaguar 80

Group—A South American puma. A South American jaguar 84

Group—Nine-banded armadillo. Capybaras. Collared peccary . . . 88

The entire party on the way back to the ranch 92

An Indian village 102
We passed an Indian fishing village on the edge of the river, with huts, scaffoldings for drying the fish, hammocks, and rude tables.

Group—Wood ibis. South American jabiru. Sariema 106

Group—A jabiru's nest. A troupial nest 118

FACING PAGE

Snake-birds and cormorants 120
Mixed flocks of scores of cormorants and darters covered certain trees, both at sunset and after sunrise.

Group—The great ant-eater. South American tapir 134

Colonel Roosevelt and Colonel Rondon with bush deer 138
We hung the buck in a tree.

The return from a day's hunt 142
Tapir, white-lipped peccary, and bush deer.

Kermit Roosevelt 152

Two pranchas being pulled by launch with our baggage and provisions . 160
The prancha was towed at the end of a hawser and her crew poled.

Colonel Roosevelt and Colonel Rondon looking over the vast landscape . 174
The ground was sandy, covered with grass and with a sparse growth of stunted, twisted trees, never more than a few feet high.

The Salto Bello Falls 188
There is a sheer drop of forty or fifty yards, and a breadth perhaps three times as great.

Group—One woman was making a hammock. The mothers carried the child slung against their side or hip, seated in a cloth belt, or sling, which went over the opposite shoulder of the mother 192

Group—The game of headball played by Parecís Indians at Utiarity Falls 194
The kick-off: a player runs forward, throws himself flat on the ground, and butts the ball toward the opposite side. Often it will be sent to and fro a dozen times, from head to head until finally it rises.

The Falls of Utiarity 196
I doubt whether, excepting, of course, Niagara, there is a waterfall in North America which outranks this if both volume and beauty are considered.

Group—A lonely grave by the wayside. The Parecís dance 198

The dance of the Parecís Indians 200
A number carried pipes through which they blew a kind of deep stifled whistle in time to the dancing.

Group—Tres Burity. The kitchen under the ox-hide at Campos Novos . 208

At the Juruena we met a party of Nhambiquaras, very friendly and sociable, and very glad to see Colonel Rondon 216

FACING PAGE

Group—Nhambiquara child with a pet monkey. The men had holes pierced through the septum of the nose and through the upper lip, and wore a straw through each hole 218

Group—Maloca or beehive hut of the Nhambiquaras. A Nhambiquara shelter hut and utensils 220

The ant-hills were not infrequently taller than a horseman's head . . . 222

Group—A Nhambiquara family. Nhambiquara women and children. "Adam and Eve" 236

Group—Nhambiquara archer. First position. Second position . . . 240

Group—I did my writing in headnet and gauntlets. Colonel Roosevelt's canoe disappears down the River of Doubt 244

Colonel Roosevelt's and Colonel Rondon's canoes at the mouth of the Bandeira 248

In mid-afternoon we came to the mouth of a big and swift affluent. . . . It was undoubtedly the Bandeira.

The rapids of Navaïté 250

There were many curls, and one or two regular falls.

Cherrie holding a rifle to show the width of the rapids at Navaïté . . . 252

At one point it was less than two yards across.

Portaging around Navaïté Rapids 254

We spent March 3 and 4 and the morning of the 5th in portaging around the rapids.

Rapids of the Dúvida 258

Dragging the canoes over a portage by means of ropes and logs . . . 262

Group—Manner of dragging the canoes across a hilly portage. Making the big canoe which was soon afterward lost 266

Group—The Upper Dúvida. Cherrie in his canoe 284

Group—Red-and-yellow macaw. Egret. Curassow. Hyacinthine macaw. Toco toucan. Trumpeter 290

The river rushed through a wild gorge, a chasm or canyon, between two mountains 300

Group—Rapids at the chasm. We bathed and swam in the river although in it we caught piranhas 308

FACING PAGE

Group—Castanho-tree (Brazil-nut). Pacova-tree 314

Group—At the rubber-man's house. The canoe rigged with a cover under which Colonel Roosevelt travelled when sick 324

The camaradas, gathered around the monument erected by Colonel Rondon 332

MAPS

FACING PAGE

Map showing the entire South American journey of Colonel Roosevelt and members of the expedition vii

Map of the River of Doubt (Dúvida), christened Rio Roosevelt and subsequently Rio Téodoro by direction of the Brazilian Government . 338

THROUGH THE BRAZILIAN WILDERNESS

THROUGH THE BRAZILIAN WILDERNESS

CHAPTER I

THE START

ONE day in 1908, when my presidential term was coming to a close, Father Zahm, a priest whom I knew, came in to call on me. Father Zahm and I had been cronies for some time, because we were both of us fond of Dante and of history and of science—I had always commended to theologians his book, "Evolution and Dogma." He was an Ohio boy, and his early schooling had been obtained in old-time American fashion in a little log school; where, by the way, one of the other boys was Januarius Aloysius MacGahan, afterward the famous war correspondent and friend of Skobeloff. Father Zahm told me that MacGahan even at that time added an utter fearlessness to chivalric tenderness for the weak, and was the defender of any small boy who was oppressed by a larger one. Later Father Zahm was at Notre Dame University, in Indiana, with Maurice Egan, whom, when I was President, I appointed minister to Denmark.

On the occasion in question Father Zahm had just returned from a trip across the Andes and down the Amazon, and came in to propose that after I left the presidency he and I should go up the Paraguay into the interior of

South America. At the time I wished to go to Africa, and so the subject was dropped; but from time to time afterward we talked it over. Five years later, in the spring of 1913, I accepted invitations conveyed through the governments of Argentina and Brazil to address certain learned bodies in these countries. Then it occurred to me that, instead of making the conventional tourist trip purely by sea round South America, after I had finished my lectures I would come north through the middle of the continent into the valley of the Amazon; and I decided to write Father Zahm and tell him my intentions. Before doing so, however, I desired to see the authorities of the American Museum of Natural History, in New York City, to find out whether they cared to have me take a couple of naturalists with me into Brazil and make a collecting trip for the museum.

Accordingly, I wrote to Frank Chapman, the curator of ornithology of the museum, and accepted his invitation to lunch at the museum one day early in June. At the lunch, in addition to various naturalists, to my astonishment I also found Father Zahm; and as soon as I saw him I told him I was now intending to make the South American trip. It appeared that he had made up his mind that he would take it himself, and had actually come on to see Mr. Chapman to find out if the latter could recommend a naturalist to go with him; and he at once said he would accompany me. Chapman was pleased when he found out that we intended to go up the Paraguay and across into the valley of the Amazon, because much of the ground over which we were to pass had not been covered by collectors. He saw Henry Fairfield Osborn, the president of the museum, who wrote me that the museum would be pleased to send under me a couple of naturalists, whom, with my approval, Chapman would choose.

The men whom Chapman recommended were Messrs. George K. Cherrie and Leo E. Miller. I gladly accepted both. The former was to attend chiefly to the ornithology and the latter to the mammalogy of the expedition; but each was to help out the other. No two better men for such a trip could have been found. Both were veterans of the tropical American forests. Miller was a young man, born in Indiana, an enthusiastic naturalist with good literary as well as scientific training. He was at the time in the Guiana forests, and joined us at Barbados. Cherrie was an older man, born in Iowa, but now a farmer in Vermont. He had a wife and six children. Mrs. Cherrie had accompanied him during two or three years of their early married life in his collecting trips along the Orinoco. Their second child was born when they were in camp a couple of hundred miles from any white man or woman. One night a few weeks later they were obliged to leave a camping-place, where they had intended to spend the night, because the baby was fretful, and its cries attracted a jaguar, which prowled nearer and nearer in the twilight until they thought it safest once more to put out into the open river and seek a new resting-place. Cherrie had spent about twenty-two years collecting in the American tropics. Like most of the field-naturalists I have met, he was an unusually efficient and fearless man; and willy-nilly he had been forced at times to vary his career by taking part in insurrections. Twice he had been behind the bars in consequence, on one occasion spending three months in a prison of a certain

South American state, expecting each day to be taken out and shot. In another state he had, as an interlude to his ornithological pursuits, followed the career of a gun-runner, acting as such off and on for two and a half years. The particular revolutionary chief whose fortunes he was following finally came into power, and Cherrie immortalized his name by naming a new species of ant-thrush after him—a delightful touch, in its practical combination of those not normally kindred pursuits, ornithology and gun-running.

In Anthony Fiala, a former arctic explorer, we found an excellent man for assembling equipment and taking charge of its handling and shipment. In addition to his four years in the arctic regions, Fiala had served in the New York Squadron in Porto Rico during the Spanish War, and through his service in the squadron had been brought into contact with his little Tennessee wife. She came down with her four children to say good-by to him when the steamer left. My secretary, Mr. Frank Harper, went with us. Jacob Sigg, who had served three years in the United States Army, and was both a hospital nurse and a cook, as well as having a natural taste for adventure, went as the personal attendant of Father Zahm. In southern Brazil my son Kermit joined me. He had been bridge building, and a couple of months previously, while on top of a long steel span, something went wrong with the derrick, he and the steel span coming down together on the rocky bed beneath. He escaped with two broken ribs, two teeth knocked out, and a knee partially dislocated, but was practically all right again when he started with us.

In its composition ours was a typical American expedition. Kermit and I were of the old Revolutionary stock, and in our veins ran about every strain of blood that there was on this side of the water during colonial times. Cherrie's father was born in Ireland, and his mother in Scotland; they came here when very young, and his father served throughout the Civil War in an Iowa cavalry regiment. His wife was of old Revolutionary stock. Father Zahm's father was an Alsacian immigrant, and his mother was partly of Irish and partly of old American stock, a descendant of a niece of General Braddock. Miller's father came from Germany, and his mother from France. Fiala's father and mother were both from Bohemia, being Czechs, and his father had served four years in the Civil War in the Union Army—his Tennessee wife was of old Revolutionary stock. Harper was born in England, and Sigg in Switzerland. We were as varied in religious creed as in ethnic origin. Father Zahm and Miller were Catholics, Kermit and Harper Episcopalians, Cherrie a Presbyterian, Fiala a Baptist, Sigg a Lutheran, while I belonged to the Dutch Reformed Church.

For arms the naturalists took 16-bore shotguns, one of Cherrie's having a rifle barrel underneath. The firearms for the rest of the party were supplied by Kermit and myself, including my Springfield rifle, Kermit's two Winchesters, a 405 and 30–40, the Fox 12-gauge shotgun, and another 16-gauge gun, and a couple of revolvers, a Colt and a Smith & Wesson. We took from New York a couple of canvas canoes, tents, mosquito-bars, plenty of cheesecloth, including nets for the hats, and both light cots and hammocks. We took ropes and pulleys which proved invaluable on our canoe trip. Each equipped himself with the clothing he fancied. Mine consisted of khaki, such as

I wore in Africa, with a couple of United States Army flannel shirts and a couple of silk shirts, one pair of hob-nailed shoes with leggings, and one pair of laced leather boots coming nearly to the knee. Both the naturalists told me that it was well to have either the boots or leggings as a protection against snake-bites, and I also had gauntlets because of the mosquitoes and sand-flies. We intended where possible to live on what we could get from time to time in the country, but we took some United States Army emergency rations, and also ninety cans, each containing a day's provisions for five men, made up by Fiala.

The trip I proposed to take can be understood only if there is a slight knowledge of South American topography. The great mountain chain of the Andes extends down the entire length of the western coast, so close to the Pacific Ocean that no rivers of any importance enter it. The rivers of South America drain into the Atlantic. Southernmost South America, including over half of the territory of the Argentine Republic, consists chiefly of a cool, open plains country. Northward of this country, and eastward of the Andes, lies the great bulk of the South American continent, which is included in the tropical and the subtropical regions. Most of this territory is Brazilian. Aside from certain relatively small stretches drained by coast rivers, this immense region of tropical and subtropical America east of the Andes is drained by the three great river systems of the Plate, the Amazon, and the Orinoco. At their headwaters the Amazon and the Orinoco systems are actually connected by a sluggish natural canal. The headwaters of the northern affluents of the Paraguay and the southern affluents of the Amazon are sundered by a stretch of high land, which toward the east broadens out into the central plateau of Brazil. Geologically this is a very ancient region, having appeared above the waters before the dawning of the age of reptiles, or, indeed, of any true land vertebrates on the globe. This plateau is a region partly of healthy, rather dry and sandy, open prairie, partly of forest. The great and low-lying basin of the Paraguay, which borders it on the south, is one of the largest, and the still greater basin of the Amazon, which borders it on the north, is the very largest of all the river basins of the earth.

In these basins, but especially in the basin of the Amazon, and thence in most places northward to the Caribbean Sea, lie the most extensive stretches of tropical forest to be found anywhere. The forests of tropical West Africa, and of portions of the Farther-Indian region, are the only ones that can be compared with them. Much difficulty has been experienced in exploring these forests, because under the torrential rains and steaming heat the rank growth of vegetation becomes almost impenetrable, and the streams difficult of navigation; while white men suffer much from the terrible insect scourges and the deadly diseases which modern science has discovered to be due very largely to insect bites. The fauna and flora, however, are of great interest. The American museum was particularly anxious to obtain collections from the divide between the headwaters of the Paraguay and the Amazon, and from the southern affluents of the Amazon. Our purpose was to ascend the Paraguay as nearly as possible to the head of navigation, thence cross to the sources of one of the affluents of the Amazon, and if possible descend it in canoes built on the spot. The Paraguay is regularly navigated as high as boats can go. The starting-point for our trip was to be Asuncion, in the state of Paraguay.

My exact plan of operations was necessarily a little indefinite, but on reaching Rio de Janeiro the minister of foreign affairs, Mr. Lauro Müller, who had been kind enough to take great personal interest in my trip, informed me that he had arranged that on the headwaters of the Paraguay, at the town of Cáceres, I would be met by a Brazilian Army colonel, himself chiefly Indian by blood, Colonel Rondon. Colonel Rondon has been for a quarter of a century the foremost explorer of the Brazilian hinterland. He was at the time in Manaos, but his lieutenants were in Cáceres and had been notified that we were coming.

More important still, Mr. Lauro Müller—who is not only an efficient public servant but a man of wide cultivation, with a quality about him that reminded me of John Hay—offered to help me make my trip of much more consequence than I had originally intended. He has taken a keen interest in the exploration and development of the interior of Brazil, and he believed that my expedition could be used as a means toward spreading abroad a more general knowledge of the country. He told me that he would co-operate with me in every way if I cared to undertake the leadership of a serious expedition into the unexplored portion of western Matto Grosso, and to attempt the descent of a river which flowed nobody knew whither, but which the best-informed men believed would prove to be a very big river, utterly unknown to geographers. I eagerly and gladly accepted, for I felt that with such help the trip could be made of much scientific value, and that a substantial addition could be made to the geographical knowledge of one of the least-known parts of South America. Accordingly, it was arranged that Colonel Rondon and some assistants and scientists should meet me at or below Corumbá, and that we should attempt the descent of the river, of which they had already come across the head-waters.

I had to travel through Brazil, Uruguay, the Argentine, and Chile for six weeks to fulfil my speaking engagements. Fiala, Cherrie, Miller, and Sigg left me at Rio, continuing to Buenos Aires in the boat in which we had all come down from New York. From Buenos Aires they went up the Paraguay to Corumbá, where they awaited me. The two naturalists went first, to do all the collecting that was possible; Fiala and Sigg travelled more leisurely, with the heavy baggage.

Before I followed them I witnessed an incident worthy of note from the standpoint of a naturalist, and of possible importance to us because of the trip we were about to take. South America even more than Australia and Africa, and almost as much as India, is a country of poisonous snakes. As in India, although not to the same degree, these snakes are responsible for a very serious mortality among human beings. One of the most interesting evidences of the modern advance in Brazil is the establishment near São Paulo of an institution especially for the study of these poisonous snakes, so as to secure antidotes to the poison and to develop enemies to the snakes themselves. We wished to take into the interior with us some bottles of the anti-venom serum, for on such an expedition there is always a certain danger from snakes. On one of his trips Cherrie had lost a native follower by snake-bite. The man was bitten while out alone in the forest, and, although he reached camp, the poison was already working in him, so that he could give no intelligible account of what had occurred, and he died in a short time.

Poisonous snakes are of several different families, but the most poisonous ones, those which are dangerous to man, belong to the two great families of the colubrine snakes and the vipers. Most of the colubrine snakes are entirely harmless, and are the common snakes that we meet everywhere. But some of them, the cobras for instance, develop into what are on the whole perhaps the most formidable of all snakes. The only poisonous colubrine snakes in the New World are the ring-snakes, the coral-snakes of the genus *elaps*, which are found from the extreme southern United States southward to the Argentine. These coral-snakes are not vicious and have small teeth which cannot penetrate even ordinary clothing. They are only dangerous if actually trodden on by some one with bare feet or if seized in the hand. There are harmless snakes very like them in color which are sometimes kept as pets; but it behooves every man who keeps such a pet or who handles such a snake to be very sure as to the genus to which it belongs.

The great bulk of the poisonous snakes of America, including all the really dangerous ones, belong to a division of the widely spread family of vipers which is known as the pit-vipers. In South America these include two distinct subfamilies or genera—whether they are called families, subfamilies, or genera would depend, I suppose, largely upon the varying personal views of the individual describer on the subject of herpetological nomenclature. One genus includes the rattlesnakes, of which the big Brazilian species is as dangerous as those of the southern United States. But the large majority of the species and individuals of dangerous snakes in tropical America are included in the genus lachecis. These are active, vicious, aggressive snakes without rattles. They are exceedingly poisonous. Some of them grow to a very large size, being indeed among the largest poisonous snakes in the world —their only rivals in this respect being the diamond rattlesnake of Florida, one of the African mambas, and the Indian hamadryad, or snake-eating cobra. The fer-de-lance, so dreaded in Martinique, and the equally dangerous bushmaster of Guiana are included in this genus. A dozen species are known in Brazil, the biggest one being identical with the Guiana bushmaster, and the most common one, the jararaca, being identical or practically identical with the fer-de-lance. The snakes of this genus, like the rattlesnakes and the Old-World vipers and puff-adders, possess long poison-fangs which strike through clothes or any other human garment except stout leather. Moreover, they are very aggressive, more so than any other snakes in the world, except possibly some of the cobras. As, in addition, they are numerous, they are a source of really frightful danger to scantily clad men who work in the fields and forests, or who for any reason are abroad at night.

The poison of venomous serpents is not in the least uniform in its quality. On the contrary, the natural forces

—to use a term which is vague, but which is as exact as our present-day knowledge permits—that have developed in so many different families of snakes these poisoned fangs have worked in two or three totally different fashions. Unlike the vipers, the colubrine poisonous snakes have small fangs, and their poison, though on the whole even more deadly, has entirely different effects, and owes its deadliness to entirely different qualities. Even within the same family there are wide differences. In the jararaca an extraordinary quantity of yellow venom is spurted from the long poison-fangs. This poison is secreted in large glands which, among vipers, give the head its peculiar ace-of-spades shape. The rattlesnake yields a much smaller quantity of white venom, but, quantity for quantity, this white venom is more deadly. It is the great quantity of venom injected by the long fangs of the jararaca, the bush-master, and their fellows that renders their bite so generally fatal. Moreover, even between these two allied genera of pit-vipers, the differences in the action of the poison are sufficiently marked to be easily recognizable, and to render the most effective anti-venomous serum for each slightly different from the other. However, they are near enough alike to make this difference, in practice, of comparatively small consequence. In practice the same serum can be used to neutralize the effect of either, and, as will be seen later on, the snake that is immune to one kind of venom is also immune to the other.

But the effect of the venom of the poisonous colubrine snakes is totally different from, although to the full as deadly as, the effect of the poison of the rattlesnake or jararaca. The serum that is an antidote as regards the pit-viper is wholly or well-nigh useless as regards the colubrines. The animal that is immune to the bite of one may not be immune to the bite of the other. The bite of a cobra or other colubrine poisonous snake is more painful in its immediate effects than is the bite of one of the big vipers. The victim suffers more. There is a greater effect on the nerve-centres, but less swelling of the wound itself, and, whereas the blood of the rattlesnake's victim coagulates, the blood of the victim of an elapine snake—that is, of one of the only poisonous American colubrines—becomes watery and incapable of coagulation.

Snakes are highly specialized in every way, including their prey. Some live exclusively on warm-blooded animals, on mammals, or birds. Some live exclusively on batrachians, others only on lizards, a few only on insects. A very few species live exclusively on other snakes. These include one very formidable venomous snake, the Indian hamadryad, or giant cobra, and several non-poisonous snakes. In Africa I killed a small cobra which contained within it a snake but a few inches shorter than itself; but, as far as I could find out, snakes were not the habitual diet of the African cobras.

The poisonous snakes use their venom to kill their victims, and also to kill any possible foe which they think menaces them. Some of them are good-tempered, and only fight if injured or seriously alarmed. Others are excessively irritable, and on rare occasions will even attack of their own accord when entirely unprovoked and unthreatened.

On reaching São Paulo on our southward journey from Rio to Montevideo, we drove out to the "Instituto Serum-thérapico," designed for the study of the effects of the venom of poisonous Brazilian snakes. Its director is Doctor Vital Brazil, who has performed a most extraordinary work and whose experiments and investigations are not only of the utmost value to Brazil but will ultimately be recognized as of the utmost value for humanity at large. I know of no institution of similar kind anywhere. It has a fine modern building, with all the best appliances, in which experiments are carried on with all kinds of serpents, living and dead, with the object of discovering all the properties of their several kinds of venom, and of developing various anti-venom serums which nullify the effects of the different venoms. Every effort is made to teach the people at large by practical demonstration in the open field the lessons thus learned in the laboratory. One notable result has been the diminution in the mortality from snake-bites in the province of São Paulo.

In connection with his institute, and right by the laboratory, the doctor has a large serpentarium, in which quantities of the common poisonous and non-poisonous snakes are kept, and some of the rarer ones. He has devoted considerable time to the effort to find out if there are any natural enemies of the poisonous snakes of his country, and he has discovered that the most formidable enemy of the many dangerous Brazilian snakes is a non-poisonous, entirely harmless, rather uncommon Brazilian snake, the mussurama. Of all the interesting things the doctor showed us, by far the most interesting was the opportunity of witnessing for ourselves the action of the mussurama toward a dangerous snake.

The doctor first showed us specimens of the various

important snakes, poisonous and non-poisonous, in alcohol. Then he showed us preparations of the different kinds of venom and of the different anti-venom serums, presenting us with some of the latter for our use on the journey. He has been able to produce two distinct kinds of anti-venom serum, one to neutralize the virulent poison of the rattlesnake's bite, the other to neutralize the poison of the different snakes of the lachecis genus. These poisons are somewhat different and moreover there appear to be some differences between the poisons of the different species of lachecis; in some cases the poison is nearly colorless, and in others, as in that of the jararaca, whose poison I saw, it is yellow.

But the vital difference is that between all these poisons of the pit-vipers and the poisons of the colubrine snakes, such as the cobra and the coral-snake. As yet the doctor has not been able to develop an anti-venom serum which will neutralize the poison of these colubrine snakes. Practically this is a matter of little consequence in Brazil, for the Brazilian coral-snakes are dangerous only when mishandled by some one whose bare skin is exposed to the bite. The numerous accidents and fatalities continually occurring in Brazil are almost always to be laid to the account of the several species of lachecis and the single species of rattlesnake.

Finally, the doctor took us into his lecture-room to show us how he conducted his experiments. The various snakes were in boxes, on one side of the room, under the care of a skilful and impassive assistant, who handled them with the cool and fearless caution of the doctor himself. The poisonous ones were taken out by means of a long-handled steel hook. All that is necessary to do is to insert this under the snake and lift him off the ground. He is not only unable to escape, but he is unable to strike, for he cannot strike unless coiled so as to give himself support and leverage. The table on which the snakes are laid is fairly large and smooth, differing in no way from an ordinary table.

There were a number of us in the room, including two or three photographers. The doctor first put on the table a non-poisonous but very vicious and truculent colubrine snake. It struck right and left at us. Then the doctor picked it up, opened its mouth, and showed that it had no fangs, and handed it to me. I also opened its mouth and examined its teeth, and then put it down, whereupon, its temper having been much ruffled, it struck violently at me two or three times. In its action and temper this snake was quite as vicious as the most irritable poisonous snakes. Yet it is entirely harmless. One of the innumerable mysteries of nature which are at present absolutely insoluble is why some snakes should be so vicious and others absolutely placid and good-tempered.

After removing the vicious harmless snake, the doctor warned us to get away from the table, and his attendant put on it, in succession, a very big lachecis—of the kind called bushmaster—and a big rattlesnake. Each coiled menacingly, a formidable brute ready to attack anything that approached. Then the attendant adroitly dropped his iron crook on the neck of each in succession, seized it right behind the head, and held it toward the doctor. The snake's mouth was in each case wide open, and the great fangs erect and very evident. It would not have been possible to have held an African ring-necked cobra in such fashion, because the ring-neck would have ejected its venom through the fangs into the eyes of the onlookers. There was no danger in this case, and the doctor inserted a shallow glass saucer into the mouth of the snake behind the fangs, permitted it to eject its poison, and then himself squeezed out the remaining poison from the poison-bags through the fangs. From the big lachecis came a large quantity of yellow venom, a liquid which speedily crystallized into a number of minute crystals. The rattlesnake yielded a much less quantity of white venom, which the doctor assured us was far more active than the yellow lachecis venom. Then each snake was returned to its box unharmed.

After this the doctor took out of a box and presented to me a fine, handsome, nearly black snake, an individual of the species called the mussurama. This is in my eyes perhaps the most interesting serpent in the world. It is a big snake, four or five feet long, sometimes even longer, nearly black, lighter below, with a friendly, placid temper. It lives exclusively on other snakes, and is completely immune to the poison of the lachecis and rattlesnake groups, which contain all the really dangerous snakes of America. Doctor Brazil told me that he had conducted many experiments with this interesting snake. It is not very common, and prefers wet places in which to live. It lays eggs, and the female remains coiled above the eggs, the object being apparently not to warm them, but to prevent too great evaporation. It will not eat when moulting, nor in cold weather. Otherwise it will eat a small snake every five or six days, or a big one every fortnight.

There is the widest difference, both among poisonous and non-poisonous snakes, not alone in nervousness and irascibility but also in ability to accustom themselves to out-of-the-way surroundings. Many species of non-poisonous snakes which are entirely harmless, to man or to any other animal except their small prey, are nevertheless very vicious and truculent, striking right and left and biting freely on the smallest provocation—this is the case with the species of which the doctor had previously placed a specimen on the table. Moreover, many snakes, some entirely harmless and some vicious ones, are so nervous and uneasy that it is with the greatest difficulty they can be induced to eat in captivity, and the slightest disturbance or interference will prevent their eating. There are other snakes, however, of which the mussurama is perhaps the best example, which are very good captives, and at the same time very fearless, showing a complete indifference not only to being observed but to being handled when they are feeding.

There is in the United States a beautiful and attractive snake, the king-snake, with much the same habits as the mussurama. It is friendly toward mankind, and not poisonous, so that it can be handled freely. It feeds on other serpents, and will kill a rattlesnake as big as itself, being immune to the rattlesnake venom. Mr. Ditmars, of the Bronx Zoo, has made many interesting experiments with these king-snakes. I have had them in my own possession. They are good-natured and can generally be handled with impunity, but I have known them to bite, whereas Doctor Brazil informed me that it was almost impossible to make the mussurama bite a man. The king-snake will feed greedily on other snakes in the presence of man—I knew of one case where it partly swallowed another snake while both were in a small boy's pocket. It is immune to viper poison but it is not immune to colubrine poison. A couple of years ago I was informed of a case where one of these king-snakes was put into an enclosure with an Indian snake-eating cobra or hamadryad of about the same size. It killed the cobra but made no effort to swallow it, and very soon showed the effects of the cobra poison. I believe it afterward died, but unfortunately I have mislaid my notes and cannot now remember the details of the incident.

Doctor Brazil informed me that the mussurama, like the king-snake, was not immune to the colubrine poison. A mussurama in his possession, which had with impunity killed and eaten several rattlesnakes and representatives of the lachecis genus, also killed and ate a venomous coral-snake, but shortly afterward itself died from the effects of the poison. It is one of the many puzzles of nature that these American serpents which kill poisonous serpents should only have grown immune to the poison of the most dangerous American poisonous serpents, the pit-vipers, and should not have become immune to the poison of the coral-snakes which are commonly distributed throughout their range. Yet, judging by the one instance mentioned by Doctor Brazil, they attack and master these coral-snakes, although the conflict in the end results in their death. It would be interesting to find out whether this attack was exceptional, that is, whether the mussurama has or has not as a species learned to avoid the coral-snake. If it was not exceptional, then not only is the instance highly curious in itself, but it would also go far to explain the failure of the mussurama to become plentiful.

For the benefit of those who are not acquainted with the subject, I may mention that the poison of a poisonous snake is not dangerous to its own species unless injected in very large doses, about ten times what would normally be injected by a bite; but that it is deadly to all other snakes, poisonous or non-poisonous, save as regards the very few species which themselves eat poisonous snakes. The Indian hamadryad, or giant cobra, is exclusively a snake-eater. It evidently draws a sharp distinction between poisonous and non-poisonous snakes, for Mr. Ditmars has recorded that two individuals in the Bronx Zoo which are habitually fed on harmless snakes, and attack them eagerly, refused to attack a copperhead which was thrown into their cage, being evidently afraid of this pit-viper. It would be interesting to find out if the hamadryad is afraid to prey on all pit-vipers, and also whether, it will prey on its small relative, the true cobra—for it may well be that, even if not immune to the viper poison, it is immune to the poison of its close ally, the smaller cobra.

All these and many other questions would be speedily settled by Doctor Brazil if he were given the opportunity to test them. It must be remembered, moreover, that not only have his researches been of absorbing value from the standpoint of pure science but that they also have a real utilitarian worth. He is now collecting and breeding the mussurama. The favorite prey of the mussurama is the most common and therefore the most dangerous poisonous snake of Brazil, the jararaca, which is known in Martinique as the fer-de-lance. In Martinique and elsewhere this snake is such an object of terror as to be at times a genuine scourge. Surely it would be worth while for the authorities of Martinique to import specimens of the mussurama to that island. The mortality from snake-bite in British India is very great. Surely it would be well worth while for the able Indian Government to copy Brazil and create such an institute as that over which Doctor Vital Brazil is the curator.

At first sight it seems extraordinary that poisonous serpents, so dreaded by and so irresistible to most animals, should be so utterly helpless before the few creatures that prey on them. But the explanation is easy. Any highly specialized creature, the higher its specialization, is apt to be proportionately helpless when once its peculiar specialized traits are effectively nullified by an opponent. This is eminently the case with the most dangerous poisonous snakes. In them a highly peculiar specialization has been carried to the highest point. They rely for attack and defence purely on their poison-fangs. All other means and methods of attack and defence have atrophied. They neither crush nor tear with their teeth nor constrict with their bodies. The poison-fangs are slender and delicate, and, save for the poison, the wound inflicted is of a trivial character. In consequence they are utterly helpless in the presence of any animal which the poison does not affect. There are several mammals immune to snake-bite, including various species of hedgehog, pig, and mongoose—the other mammals which kill them do so by pouncing on them unawares or by avoiding their stroke through sheer quickness of movement; and probably this is the case with most snake-eating birds. The mongoose is very quick, but in some cases at least—I have mentioned one in the "African Game Trails"—it permits itself to be bitten by poisonous snakes, treating the bite with utter indifference. There should be extensive experiments made to determine if there are species of mongoose immune to both cobra and viper poison. Hedgehogs, as determined by actual experiments, pay no heed at all to viper poison even when bitten on such tender places as the tongue and lips and eat the snake as if it were a radish. Even among animals which are not immune to the poison different species are very differently affected by the different kinds of snake poisons. Not only are some species more resistant than others to all poisons, but there is a wide variation in the amount of immunity each displays to any given venom. One species will be quickly killed by the poison from one species of snake, and be fairly resistant to the poison of another; whereas in another species the conditions may be directly reversed.

The mussurama which Doctor Brazil handed me was a fine specimen, perhaps four and a half feet long. I lifted the smooth, lithe bulk in my hands, and then let it twist its coils so that it rested at ease in my arms; it glided to and fro, on its own length, with the sinuous grace of its kind, and showed not the slightest trace of either nervousness or bad temper. Meanwhile the doctor bade his attendant put on the table a big jararaca, or fer-de-lance, which was accordingly done. The jararaca was about three feet and a half or perhaps nearly four feet long—that is, it was about nine inches shorter than the mussurama. The latter, which I continued to hold in my arms, behaved with friendly and impassive indifference, moving easily to and fro through my hands, and once or twice hiding its head between the sleeve and the body of my coat. The doctor was not quite sure how the mussurama would behave, for it had recently eaten a small snake, and unless hungry it pays no attention whatever to venomous snakes, even when they attack and bite it. However, it fortunately proved still to have a good appetite.

The jararaca was alert and vicious. It partly coiled itself on the table, threatening the bystanders. I put the big black serpent down on the table four or five feet from the enemy and headed in its direction. As soon as I let go with my hands it glided toward where the threatening, formidable-looking lance-head lay stretched in a half coil. The mussurama displayed not the slightest sign of excitement. Apparently it trusted little to its eyes, for it began to run its head along the body of the jararaca, darting out its flickering tongue to feel just where it was, as it nosed its way up toward the head of its antagonist. So placid were its actions that I did not at first suppose that it meant to attack, for there was not the slightest exhibition of anger or excitement.

It was the jararaca that began the fight. It showed no fear whatever of its foe, but its irritable temper was aroused by the proximity and actions of the other, and like a flash it drew back its head and struck, burying its fangs in the forward part of the mussurama's body. Immediately the latter struck in return, and the counter-attack was so instantaneous that it was difficult to see just what had happened. There was tremendous writhing and struggling on the part of the jararaca; and then, leaning over the knot into which the two serpents were twisted, I saw that the mussurama had seized the jararaca by the lower jaw, putting its own head completely into the wide-gaping mouth of the poisonous snake. The long fangs were just above the top of the mussurama's head; and it appeared, as well as I could see, that they were once again driven into the mussurama; but without the slightest effect. Then the fangs were curved back in the jaw, a fact which I particularly noted, and all effort at the offensive was abandoned by the poisonous snake.

Meanwhile the mussurama was chewing hard, and gradually shifted its grip, little by little, until it got the top of the head of the jararaca in its mouth, the lower jaw of the jararaca being spread out to one side. The venomous serpent was helpless; the fearsome master of the wild life of the forest, the deadly foe of humankind, was itself held in the grip of death. Its cold, baleful serpent's eyes shone, as evil as ever. But it was dying. In vain it writhed and struggled. Nothing availed it.

Once or twice the mussurama took a turn round the middle of the body of its opponent, but it did not seem to press hard, and apparently used its coils chiefly in order to get a better grip so as to crush the head of its antagonist, or to hold the latter in place. This crushing was done by its teeth; and the repeated bites were made with such effort that the muscles stood out on the mussurama's neck. Then it took two coils round the neck of the jararaca and proceeded deliberately to try to break the backbone of its opponent by twisting the head round. With this purpose it twisted its own head and neck round so that the lighter-colored surface was uppermost; and indeed at one

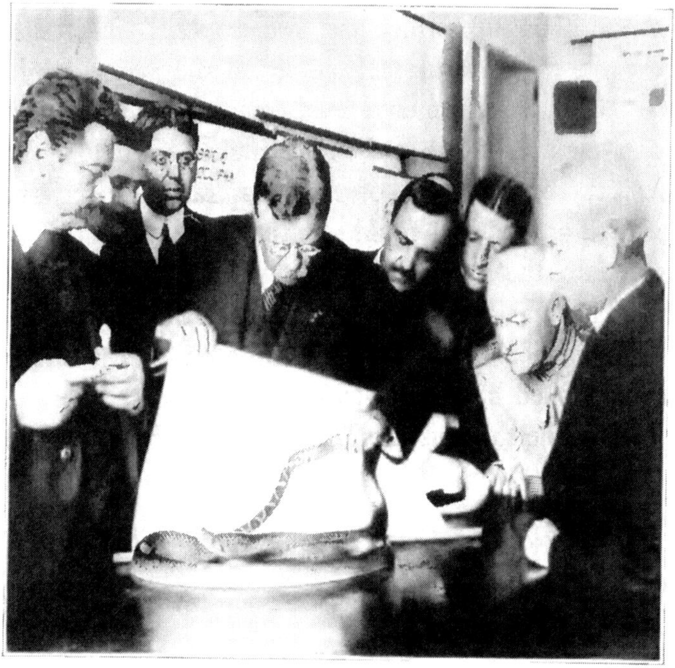

The mussurama swallowing the jararaca, or fer-de-lance, after having just killed it

From a photograph by [illegible]

Method of the mussurama's attack upon the jararaca

Reproduced by courtesy of Dr. Vital Brazil

time it looked as if it had made almost a complete single spiral revolution of its own body. It never for a moment relaxed its grip except to shift slightly the jaws.

In a few minutes the jararaca was dead, its head crushed in, although the body continued to move convulsively. When satisfied that its opponent was dead, the mussurama began to try to get the head in its mouth. This was a process of some difficulty on account of the angle at which the lower jaw of the jararaca stuck out. But finally the head was taken completely inside and then swallowed. After this, the mussurama proceeded deliberately, but with unbroken speed, to devour its opponent by the simple process of crawling outside it, the body and tail of the jararaca writhing and struggling until the last. During the early portion of the meal, the mussurama put a stop to this writhing and struggling by resting its own body on that of its prey; but toward the last the part of the body that remained outside was left free to wriggle as it wished.

Not only was the mussurama totally indifferent to our presence, but it was totally indifferent to being handled while the meal was going on. Several times I replaced the combatants in the middle of the table when they had writhed to the edge, and finally, when the photographers found that they could not get good pictures, I held the mussurama up against a white background with the partially swallowed snake in its mouth; and the feast went on uninterruptedly. I never saw cooler or more utterly unconcerned conduct; and the ease and certainty with which the terrible poisonous snake was mastered gave me the heartiest respect and liking for the easy-going, good-natured, and exceedingly efficient serpent which I had been holding in my arms.

Our trip was not intended as a hunting-trip but as a scientific expedition. Before starting on the trip itself, while travelling in the Argentine, I received certain pieces of first-hand information concerning the natural history of the jaguar, and of the cougar, or puma, which are worth recording. The facts about the jaguar are not new in the sense of casting new light on its character, although they are interesting; but the facts about the behavior of the puma in one district of Patagonia are of great interest, because they give an entirely new side of its life-history.

There was travelling with me at the time Doctor Francisco P. Moreno, of Buenos Aires. Doctor Moreno is at the present day a member of the National Board of Education of the Argentine, a man who has worked in every way for the benefit of his country, perhaps especially for the benefit of the children, so that when he was first introduced to me it was as the "Jacob Riis of the Argentine" —for they know my deep and affectionate intimacy with Jacob Riis. He is also an eminent man of science, who has done admirable work as a geologist and a geographer. At one period, in connection with his duties as a boundary commissioner on the survey between Chile and the Argentine, he worked for years in Patagonia. It was he who made the extraordinary discovery in a Patagonian cave of the still fresh fragments of skin and other remains of the mylodon, the aberrant horse known as the onohipidium, the huge South American tiger, and the macrauchenia, all of them extinct animals. This discovery showed that some of the strange representatives of the giant South American pleistocene fauna had lasted down to within a comparatively few thousand years, down to the time when man, substantially as the Spaniards found him, flourished on the continent. Incidentally the discovery tended to show that this fauna had lasted much later in South America than was the case with the corresponding faunas in other parts of the world; and therefore it tended to disprove the claims advanced by Doctor Ameghino for the extreme age, geologically, of this fauna, and for the extreme antiquity of man on the American continent.

One day Doctor Moreno handed me a copy of *The Outlook* containing my account of a cougar-hunt in Arizona, saying that he noticed that I had very little faith in cougars attacking men, although I had explicitly stated that such attacks sometimes occurred. I told him, Yes, that I had found that the cougar was practically harmless to man, the undoubtedly authentic instances of attacks on men being so exceptional that they could in practice be wholly disregarded. Thereupon Doctor Moreno showed me a scar on his face, and told me that he had himself been attacked and badly mauled by a puma which was undoubtedly trying to prey on him; that is, which had started on a career as a man-eater. This was to me most interesting. I had often met men who knew other men who had seen other men who said that they had been attacked by pumas, but this was the first time that I had ever come across a man who had himself been attacked. Doctor Moreno, as I have said, is not only an eminent citizen, but an eminent scientific man, and his account of what occurred is unquestionably a scientifically accurate statement of the facts.

I give it exactly as the doctor told it; paraphrasing a letter he sent me, and including one or two answers to questions I put to him. The doctor, by the way, stated to me that he had known Mr. Hudson, the author of the "Naturalist on the Plata," and that the latter knew nothing whatever of pumas from personal experience and had accepted as facts utterly wild fables.

Undoubtedly, said the doctor, the puma in South America, like the puma in North America, is as a general rule a cowardly animal which not only never attacks man but rarely makes any efficient defence when attacked. The Indian and white hunters have no fear of it in most parts of the country, and its harmlessness to man is proverbial. But there is one particular spot in southern Patagonia where cougars, to the doctor's own personal knowledge, have for years been dangerous foes of man. This curious local change in habits, by the way, is nothing unprecedented as regards wild animals. In portions of its range, as I am informed by Mr. Lord Smith, the Asiatic tiger can hardly be forced to fight man, and never preys on him, while throughout most of its range it is a most dangerous beast, and often turns man-eater. So there are waters in which sharks are habitual man-eaters, and others where they never touch men; and there are rivers and lakes where crocodiles or caymans are very dangerous, and others where they are practically harmless—I have myself seen this in Africa.

In March, 1877, Doctor Moreno with a party of men working on the boundary commission, and with a number of Patagonian horse-Indians, was encamped for some weeks beside Lake Viedma, which had not before been visited by white men for a century, and which was rarely visited even by Indians. One morning, just before sunrise, he left his camp by the south shore of the lake, to make a topographical sketch of the lake. He was unarmed, but carried a prismatic compass in a leather case with a strap. It was cold, and he wrapped his poncho of guanaco-hide round his neck and head. He had walked a few hundred yards, when a puma, a female, sprang on him from behind and knocked him down. As she sprang on him she tried to seize his head with one paw, striking him on the shoulder with the other. She lacerated his mouth and also his back, but tumbled over with him, and in the scuffle they separated before she could bite him. He sprang to his feet, and, as he said, was forced to think quickly. She had recovered herself, and sat on her haunches like a cat, looking at him, and then crouched to spring again; whereupon he whipped off his poncho, and as she sprang at him he opened it, and at the same moment hit her head with the prismatic compass in its case which he held by the strap. She struck the poncho and was evidently puzzled by it, for, turning, she slunk off to one side, under a bush, and then proceeded to try to get round behind him. He faced her, keeping his eyes upon her, and backed off. She followed him for three or four hundred yards. At least twice she came up to attack him, but each time he opened his poncho and yelled, and at the last moment she shrank back. She continually, however, tried, by taking advantage of cover, to sneak up to one side, or behind, to attack him. Finally, when he got near camp, she abandoned the pursuit and went into a small patch of bushes. He raised the alarm; an Indian rode up and set fire to the bushes from the windward side. When the cougar broke from the bushes, the Indian rode after her, and threw his bolas, which twisted around her hind legs; and while she was struggling to free herself, he brained her with his second bolas. The doctor's injuries were rather painful, but not serious.

Twenty-one years later, in April, 1898, he was camped on the same lake, but on the north shore, at the foot of a basaltic cliff. He was in company with four soldiers, with whom he had travelled from the Strait of Magellan. In the night he was aroused by the shriek of a man and the barking of his dogs. As the men sprang up from where they were lying asleep they saw a large puma run off out of the firelight into the darkness. It had sprung on a soldier named Marcelino Huquen while he was asleep, and had tried to carry him off. Fortunately, the man was so wrapped up in his blanket, as the night was cold, that he was not injured. The puma was never found or killed.

About the same time a surveyor of Doctor Moreno's party, a Swede named Arneberg, was attacked in similar fashion. The doctor was not with him at the time. Mr. Arneberg was asleep in the forest near Lake San Martín. The cougar both bit and clawed him, and tore his mouth, breaking out three teeth. The man was rescued; but this puma also escaped.

The doctor stated that in this particular locality the Indians, who elsewhere paid no heed whatever to the puma, never let their women go out after wood for fuel unless two or three were together. This was because on several occasions women who had gone out alone were killed by pumas. Evidently in this one locality the habit of at least occasional man-eating has become chronic with a species which elsewhere is the most cowardly, and to man the least dangerous, of all the big cats.

These observations of Doctor Moreno have a peculiar value, because, as far as I know, they are the first trustworthy accounts of a cougar's having attacked man save under circumstances so exceptional as to make the attack signify little more than the similar exceptional instances of attack by various other species of wild animals that are not normally dangerous to man.

The jaguar, however, has long been known not only to be a dangerous foe when itself attacked, but also now and then to become a man-eater. Therefore the instances of such attacks furnished me are of merely corroborative value.

In the excellent zoological gardens at Buenos Aires the curator, Doctor Onelli, a naturalist of note, showed us a big male jaguar which had been trapped in the Chaco, where it had already begun a career as a man-eater, having killed three persons. They were killed, and two of them were eaten; the animal was trapped, in consequence of the alarm excited by the death of his third victim. This jaguar was very savage; whereas a young jaguar, which was in a cage with a young tiger, was playful and friendly, as was also the case with the young tiger. On my trip to visit La Plata Museum I was accompanied by Captain Vicente Montes, of the Argentine Navy, an accomplished officer of scientific attainments. He had at one time been engaged on a survey of the boundary between the Argentine and Paraná and Brazil. They had a quantity of dried beef in camp. On several occasions a jaguar came into camp after this dried beef. Finally they succeeded in protecting it so that he could not reach it. The result, however, was disastrous. On the next occasion that he visited camp, at midnight, he seized a man. Everybody was asleep at the time, and the jaguar came in so noiselessly as to elude the vigilance of the dogs. As he seized the man, the latter gave one yell, but the next moment was killed, the jaguar driving his fangs through the man's skull into the brain. There was a scene of uproar and confusion, and the jaguar was forced to drop his prey and flee into the woods. Next morning they followed him with the dogs, and finally killed him. He was a large male, in first-class condition. The only feature of note about these two incidents was that in each case the man-eater was a powerful animal in the prime of life; whereas it frequently happens that the jaguars that turn man-eaters are old animals, and have become too inactive or too feeble to catch their ordinary prey.

During the two months before starting from Asuncion, in Paraguay, for our journey into the interior, I was kept so busy that I had scant time to think of natural history. But in a strange land a man who cares for wild birds and wild beasts always sees and hears something that is new to him and interests him. In the dense tropical woods near Rio Janeiro I heard in late October—springtime, near the southern tropic—the songs of many birds that I could not identify. But the most beautiful music was from a shy woodland thrush, sombre-colored, which lived near the ground in the thick timber, but sang high among the branches. At a great distance we could hear the ringing, musical, bell-like note, long-drawn and of piercing sweetness, which occurs at intervals in the song; at first I thought this was the song, but when it was possible to approach the singer I found that these far-sounding notes were scattered through a continuous song of great melody. I never listened to one that impressed me more. In different places in Argentina I heard and saw the Argentine mocking-bird, which is not very unlike our own, and is also a delightful and remarkable singer. But I never heard the wonderful white-banded mocking-bird, which is said by Hudson, who knew well the birds of both South America and Europe, to be the song-king of them all.

Most of the birds I thus noticed while hurriedly passing through the country were, of course, the conspicuous ones. The spurred lapwings, big, tame, boldly marked plover, were everywhere; they were very noisy and active and both inquisitive and daring, and they have a very curious dance custom. No man need look for them. They will look for him, and when they find him they will fairly yell the discovery to the universe. In the marshes of the lower Paraná I saw flocks of scarlet-headed blackbirds on the tops of the reeds; the females are as strikingly colored as the males, and their jet-black bodies and brilliant red heads make it impossible for them to escape observation among their natural surroundings. On the plains to the west I saw flocks of the beautiful rose-breasted starlings; unlike the red-headed blackbirds, which seemed fairly to court attention, these starlings sought to escape observation by crouching on the ground so that their red breasts were hidden. There were yellow-shouldered blackbirds in wet places, and cow-buntings abounded.

But the most conspicuous birds I saw were members of the family of tyrant flycatchers, of which our own king-bird is the most familiar example. This family is very numerously represented in Argentina, both in species and individuals. Some of the species are so striking, both in color and habits, and in one case also in shape, as to attract the attention of even the unobservant. The least conspicuous, and nevertheless very conspicuous, among those that I saw was the bientevido, which is brown above, yellow beneath, with a boldly marked black and white head, and a yellow crest. It is very noisy, is common in the neighborhood of houses, and builds a big domed nest. It is really a big, heavy king-bird, fiercer and more powerful than any northern king-bird. I saw them assail not only the big but the small hawks with fearlessness, driving them in headlong flight. They not only capture insects, but pounce on mice, small frogs, lizards, and little snakes, rob birds' nests of the fledgling young, and catch tadpoles and even small fish.

Two of the tyrants which I observed are like two with which I grew fairly familiar in Texas. The scissor-tail is common throughout the open country, and the long tail feathers, which seem at times to hamper its flight, attract attention whether the bird is in flight or perched on a tree. It has a habit of occasionally soaring into the air and descending in loops and spirals. The scarlet tyrant I saw in the orchards and gardens. The male is a fascinating little bird, coal-black above, while his crested head and the body beneath are brilliant scarlet. He utters his rapid, low-voiced musical trill in the air, rising with fluttering wings to a height of a hundred feet, hovering while he sings, and then falling back to earth. The color of the bird and the character of his performance attract the attention of every observer, bird, beast, or man, within reach of vision.

The red-backed tyrant is utterly unlike any of his kind in the United States, and until I looked him up in Sclater and Hudson's ornithology I never dreamed that he belonged to this family. He—for only the male is so brightly colored—is coal-black with a dull-red back. I saw these birds on December 1 near Barilloche, out on the bare Patagonian plains. They behaved like pipits or longspurs, running actively over the ground in the same manner and showing the same restlessness and the same kind of flight. But whereas pipits are inconspicuous, the red-backs at once attracted attention by the contrast between their bold coloring and the grayish or yellowish tones of the ground along which they ran. The silver-bill tyrant, however, is much more conspicuous; I saw it in the same neighborhood as the red-back and also in many other places. The male is jet-black, with white bill and wings. He runs about on the ground like a pipit, but also frequently perches on some bush to go through a strange flight-song performance. He perches motionless, bolt upright, and even then his black coloring advertises him for a quarter of a mile round about. But every few minutes he springs up into the air to the height of twenty or thirty feet, the white wings flashing in contrast to the black body, screams and gyrates, and then instantly returns to his former post and resumes his erect pose of waiting. It is hard to imagine a more conspicuous bird than the silver-bill; but the next and last tyrant flycatcher of which I shall speak possesses on the whole the most advertising coloration of any small bird I have ever seen in the open country, and moreover this advertising coloration exists in both sexes and throughout the year. It is a brilliant white, all over, except the long wing-quills and the ends of the tail-feathers, which are black. The first one I saw, at a very long distance, I thought must be an albino. It perches on the top of a bush or tree watching for its prey, and it shines in the sun like a silver mirror. Every hawk, cat, or man must see it; no one can help seeing it.

These common Argentine birds, most of them of the open country, and all of them with a strikingly advertising coloration, are interesting because of their beauty and their habits. They are also interesting because they offer such illuminating examples of the truth that many of the most common and successful birds not merely lack a concealing coloration, but possess a coloration which is in the highest degree revealing. The coloration and the habits of most of these birds are such that every hawk or other foe that can see at all must have its attention attracted to them. Evidently in their cases neither the coloration nor any habit of concealment based on the coloration is a survival factor, and this although they live in a land teeming with bird-eating hawks. Among the higher vertebrates there are many known factors which have influence, some in one set of cases, some in another set of cases, in the development and preservation of species. Courage, intelligence, adaptability, prowess, bodily vigor, speed, alertness, ability to hide, ability to build structures which will protect the young while they are helpless, fecundity—all, and many more like them, have their several places; and behind all these visible causes there are at work other and often more potent causes of which as yet science can say nothing. Some species owe much to a given attribute which may be wholly lacking in influence on other species; and every one of the attributes above enumerated is a survival factor in some species, while in others it has no survival value whatever, and in yet others, although of benefit, it is not of sufficient benefit to offset the benefit conferred on foes or rivals by totally different attributes. Intelligence, for instance, is of course a survival factor; but to-day there exist multitudes of animals with very little intelligence which have persisted through immense periods of geologic time either unchanged or else without any change in the direction of increased intelligence; and during their species-life they have witnessed the death of countless other species of far greater intelligence but in other ways less adapted to succeed in the environmental complex. The same statement can be made of all the many, many other known factors in development, from fecundity to concealing coloration; and behind them lie forces as to which we veil our ignorance by the use of high-sounding nomenclature—as when we use such a convenient but far from satisfactory term as orthogenesis.

CHAPTER II

UP THE PARAGUAY

On the afternoon of December 9 we left the attractive and picturesque city of Asuncion to ascend the Paraguay. With generous courtesy the Paraguayan Government had put at my disposal the gunboat-yacht of the President himself, a most comfortable river steamer, and so the opening days of our trip were pleasant in every way. The food was good, our quarters were clean, we slept well, below or on deck, usually without our mosquito-nettings, and in daytime the deck was pleasant under the awnings. It was hot, of course, but we were dressed suitably in our exploring and hunting clothes and did not mind the heat. The river was low, for there had been dry weather for some weeks—judging from the vague and contradictory information I received there is much elasticity to the terms wet season and dry season at this part of the Paraguay. Under the brilliant sky we steamed steadily up the mighty river; the sunset was glorious as we leaned on the port railing; and after nightfall the moon, nearly full and hanging high in the heavens, turned the water to shimmering radiance. On the mud-flats and sand-bars, and among the green rushes of the bays and inlets, were stately water-fowl; crimson flamingoes and rosy spoonbills, dark-colored ibis and white storks with black wings. Darters, with snakelike necks and pointed bills, perched in the trees on the brink of the river. Snowy egrets flapped across the marshes. Caymans were common, and differed from the crocodiles we had seen in Africa in two points: they were not alarmed by the report of a rifle when fired at, and they lay with the head raised instead of stretched along the sand.

For three days, as we steamed northward toward the Tropic of Capricorn, and then passed it, we were within the Republic of Paraguay. On our right, to the east, there was a fairly well-settled country, where bananas and oranges were cultivated and other crops of hot countries raised. On the banks we passed an occasional small town, or saw a ranch-house close to the river's brink, or stopped for wood at some little settlement. Across the river to the west lay the level, swampy, fertile wastes known as the Chaco, still given over either to the wild Indians or to cattle-ranching on a gigantic scale. The broad river ran in curves between mud-banks where terraces marked successive periods of flood. A belt of forest stood on each bank, but it was only a couple of hundred yards wide. Back of it was the open country; on the Chaco side this was a vast plain of grass dotted with tall, graceful palms. In places the belt of forest vanished and the palm-dotted prairie came to the river's edge. The Chaco is an ideal cattle country, and not really unhealthy. It will be covered with ranches at a not distant day. But mosquitoes and many other winged insect pests swarm over it. Cherrie and Miller had spent a week there collecting mammals and birds prior to my arrival at Asuncion. They were veterans of the tropics, hardened to the insect plagues of Guiana and the Orinoco. But they reported that never had they been so tortured as in the Chaco. The sand-flies crawled through the meshes in the mosquito-nets, and forbade them to sleep; if in their sleep a knee touched the net the mosquitoes fell on it so that it looked as if riddled by birdshot; and the nights were a torment, although they had done well in their work, collecting some two hundred and fifty specimens of birds and mammals.

Nevertheless for some as yet inscrutable reason the river served as a barrier to certain insects which are menaces to the cattlemen. With me on the gunboat was an old Western friend, Tex Rickard, of the Panhandle and Alaska and various places in between. He now has a large tract of land and some thirty-five thousand head of cattle in the Chaco, opposite Concepcion, at which city he was to stop. He told me that horses did not do well in the Chaco but that cattle throve, and that while ticks swarmed on the east bank of the great river, they would not live on the west bank. Again and again he had crossed herds of cattle which were covered with the loathsome bloodsuckers; and in a couple of months every tick would be dead. The worst animal foes of man, indeed the only dangerous foes, are insects; and this is especially true in the tropics. Fortunately, exactly as certain differences too minute for us as yet to explain render some insects deadly to man or domestic animals, while closely allied forms are harmless, so, for other reasons, which also we are not as yet able to fathom, these insects are for the most part strictly limited by geographical and other considerations. The war against what Sir Harry Johnston calls the really material devil, the devil of evil wild nature in the tropics, has been waged with marked success only during the last two decades. The men, in the United States, in

England, France, Germany, Italy—the men like Doctor Cruz in Rio Janeiro and Doctor Vital Brazil in São Paulo—who work experimentally within and without the laboratory in their warfare against the disease and death bearing insects and microbes, are the true leaders in the fight to make the tropics the home of civilized man.

Late on the evening of the second day of our trip, just before midnight, we reached Concepcion. On this day, when we stopped for wood or to get provisions—at picturesque places, where the women from rough mud and thatched cabins were washing clothes in the river, or where ragged horsemen stood gazing at us from the bank, or where dark, well-dressed ranchmen stood in front of red-roofed houses—we caught many fish. They belonged to one of the most formidable genera of fish in the world, the piranha or cannibal fish, the fish that eats men when it can get the chance. Farther north there are species of small piranha that go in schools. At this point on the Paraguay the piranha do not seem to go in regular schools, but they swarm in all the waters and attain a length of eighteen inches or over. They are the most ferocious fish in the world. Even the most formidable fish, the sharks or the barracudas, usually attack things smaller than themselves. But the piranhas habitually attack things much larger than themselves. They will snap a finger off a hand incautiously trailed in the water; they mutilate swimmers—in every river town in Paraguay there are men who have been thus mutilated; they will rend and devour alive any wounded man or beast; for blood in the water excites them to madness. They will tear wounded wild fowl to pieces; and bite off the tails of big fish as they grow exhausted when fighting after being hooked. Miller, before I reached Asuncion, had been badly bitten by one. Those that we caught sometimes bit through the hooks, or the double strands of copper wire that served as leaders, and got away. Those that we hauled on deck lived for many minutes. Most predatory fish are long and slim, like the alligator-gar and pickerel. But the piranha is a short, deep-bodied fish, with a blunt face and a heavily undershot or projecting lower jaw which gapes widely. The razor-edged teeth are wedge-shaped like a shark's, and the jaw muscles possess great power. The rabid, furious snaps drive the teeth through flesh and bone. The head with its short muzzle, staring malignant eyes, and gaping, cruelly armed jaws, is the embodiment of evil ferocity; and the actions of the fish exactly match its looks. I never witnessed an exhibition of such impotent, savage fury as was shown by the piranhas as they flapped on deck. When fresh from the water and thrown on the boards they uttered an extraordinary squealing sound. As they flapped about they bit with vicious eagerness at whatever presented itself. One of them flapped into a cloth and seized it with a bulldog grip. Another grasped one of its fellows; another snapped at a piece of wood, and left the teeth-marks deep therein. They are the pests of the waters, and it is necessary to be exceedingly cautious about either swimming or wading where they are found. If cattle are driven into, or of their own accord enter, the water, they are commonly not molested; but if by chance some unusually big or ferocious specimen of these fearsome fishes does bite an animal—taking off part of an ear, or perhaps of a teat from the udder of a cow—the blood brings up every

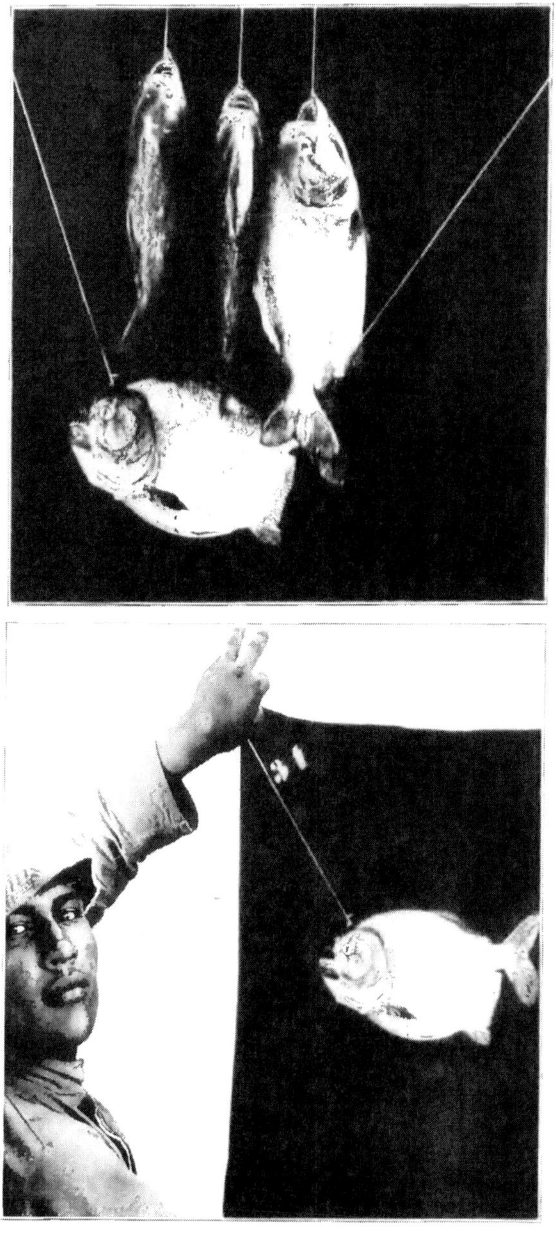

Man-eating fish, piranha

Note the razor-edged teeth

From photographs by Harper

member of the ravenous throng which is anywhere near, and unless the attacked animal can immediately make its escape from the water it is devoured alive. Here on the Paraguay the natives hold them in much respect, whereas the caymans are not feared at all. The only redeeming feature about them is that they are themselves fairly good to eat, although with too many bones.

At daybreak of the third day, finding we were still moored off Concepcion, we were rowed ashore and strolled off through the streets of the quaint, picturesque old town; a town which, like Asuncion, was founded by the conquistadores three-quarters of a century before our own English and Dutch forefathers landed in what is now the United States. The Jesuits then took practically complete possession of what is now Paraguay, controlling and Christianizing the Indians, and raising their flourishing missions to a pitch of prosperity they never elsewhere achieved. They were expelled by the civil authorities (backed by the other representatives of ecclesiastical authority) some fifty years before Spanish South America became independent. But they had already made the language of the Indians, Guaranÿ, a culture-tongue, reducing it to writing, and printing religious books in it. Guaranÿ is one of the most wide-spread of the Indian tongues, being originally found in various closely allied forms not only in Paraguay but in Uruguay and over the major part of Brazil. It remains here and there, as a *lingua geral* at least, and doubtless in cases as an original tongue, among the wild tribes. In most of Brazil, as around Para and around São Paulo, it has left its traces in place-names, but has been completely superseded as a language by Portuguese. In Paraguay it still exists side by side with Spanish as the common language of the lower people and as a familiar tongue among the upper classes. The blood of the people is mixed, their language dual; the lower classes are chiefly of Indian blood but with a white admixture; while the upper classes are predominantly white, with a strong infusion of Indian. There is no other case quite parallel to this in the annals of European colonization, although the Goanese in India have a native tongue and a Portuguese creed, while in several of the Spanish-American states the Indian blood is dominant and the majority of the population speak an Indian tongue, perhaps itself, as with the Quichuas, once a culture-tongue of the archaic type. Whether in Paraguay one tongue will ultimately drive out the other, and, if so, which will be the victor, it is yet too early to prophesy. The English missionaries and the Bible Society have recently published parts of the Scriptures in Guaraný; and in Asuncion a daily paper is published with the text in parallel columns, Spanish and Guaraný—just as in Oklahoma there is a similar paper published in English and in the tongue which the extraordinary Cherokee chief Sequoia, a veritable Cadmus, made a literary language.

The Guaraný-speaking Paraguayan is a Christian, and as much an inheritor of our common culture as most of the peasant populations of Europe. He has no kinship with the wild Indian, who hates and fears him. The Indian of the Chaco, a pure savage, a bow-bearing savage, will never come east of the Paraguay, and the Paraguayan is only beginning to venture into the western interior, away from the banks of the river—under the lead of pioneer settlers like Rickard, whom, by the way, the wild Indians thoroughly trust, and for whom they work eagerly and faithfully. There is a great development ahead for Paraguay, as soon as they can definitely shake off the revolutionary habit and establish an orderly permanence of government. The people are a fine people; the strains of blood—white and Indian—are good.

We walked up the streets of Concepcion, and interestedly looked at everything of interest: at the one-story houses, their windows covered with gratings of fretted ironwork, and their occasional open doors giving us glimpses into cool inner courtyards, with trees and flowers; at the two-wheel carts, drawn by mules or oxen; at an occasional rider, with spurs on his bare feet, and his big toes thrust into the small stirrup-rings; at the little stores, and the warehouses for matté and hides. Then we came to a pleasant little inn, kept by a Frenchman and his wife, of old Spanish style, with its *patio*, or inner court, but as neat as an inn in Normandy or Brittany. We were sitting at coffee, around a little table, when in came the colonel of the garrison—for Concepcion is the second city in Paraguay. He told me that they had prepared a reception for me! I was in my rough hunting-clothes, but there was nothing to do but to accompany my kind hosts and trust to their good nature to pardon my shortcomings in the matter of dress. The colonel drove me about in a smart open carriage, with two good horses and a liveried driver. It was a much more fashionable turnout than would be seen in any of our cities save the largest, and even in them probably not in the service of a public official. In all the South American countries there is more pomp and ceremony in connection with public functions than with us, and at these functions the liveried servants, often with knee-breeches and powdered hair, are like those seen at similar European functions; there is not the democratic simplicity which better suits our own habits of life and ways of thought. But the South Americans often surpass us, not merely in pomp and ceremony but in what is of real importance, courtesy; in civility and courtesy we can well afford to take lessons from them.

We first visited the barracks, saw the troops in the setting-up exercises, and inspected the arms, the artillery, the equipment. There was a German lieutenant with the Paraguayan officers; one of several German officers who are now engaged in helping the Paraguayans with their army. The equipments and arms were in good condition; the enlisted men evidently offered fine material; and the officers were doing hard work. It is worth while for anti-militarists to ponder the fact that in every South American country where a really efficient army is developed, the increase in military efficiency goes hand in hand with a decrease in lawlessness and disorder, and a growing reluctance to settle internal disagreements by violence. They are introducing universal military service in Paraguay; the officers, many of whom have studied abroad, are growing to feel an increased *esprit de corps*, an increased pride in the army, and therefore a desire to see the army made the servant of the nation as a whole and not the tool of any faction or individual. If these feelings grow strong enough they will be powerful factors in giving Paraguay what she most needs, freedom from revolutionary disturbance and therefore the chance to achieve the material prosperity without which as a basis there can be no advance in other and even more important matters.

Then I was driven to the City Hall, accompanied by the intendente, or mayor, a German long settled in the country and one of the leading men of the city. There was a breakfast. When I had to speak I impressed into my service as interpreter a young Paraguayan who was a graduate of the University of Pennsylvania. He was able to render into Spanish my ideas—on such subjects as orderly liberty and the far-reaching mischief done by the revolutionary habit—with clearness and vigor, because he thoroughly understood not only how I felt but also the American way of looking at such things. My hosts were hospitality itself, and I enjoyed the unexpected greeting.

We steamed on up the river. Now and then we passed another boat—a steamer, or, to my surprise, perhaps a barkentine or schooner. The Paraguay is a highway of traffic. Once we passed a big beef-canning factory. Ranches stood on either bank a few leagues apart, and we stopped at wood-yards on the west bank. Indians worked around them. At one such yard the Indians were evidently part of the regular force. Their squaws were with them, cooking at queer open-air ovens. One small child had as pets a parrot and a young coati—a kind of long-nosed raccoon. Loading wood, the Indians stood in a line, tossing the logs from one to the other. These Indians wore clothes.

On this day we got into the tropics. Even in the heat of the day the deck was pleasant under the awnings; the sun rose and set in crimson splendor; and the nights, with the moon at the full, were wonderful. At night Orion blazed overhead; and the Southern Cross hung in the star-brilliant heavens behind us. But after the moon rose the constellations paled; and clear in her light the tree-clad banks stood on either hand as we steamed steadily against the swirling current of the great river.

At noon on the twelfth we were at the Brazilian boundary. On this day we here and there came on low, conical hills close to the river. In places the palm groves broke through the belts of deciduous trees and stretched for a mile or so right along the river's bank. At times we passed cattle on the banks or sand-bars, followed by their herders; or a handsome ranch-house, under a cluster of shady trees, some bearing a wealth of red and some a wealth of yellow blossoms; or we saw a horse-corral among the trees close to the brink, with the horses in it and a barefooted man in shirt and trousers leaning against the fence; or a herd of cattle among the palms; or a big tannery or factory or a little native hamlet came in sight. We stopped at one tannery. The owner was a Spaniard, the manager an "Orientál," as he called himself, a Uruguayan, of German parentage. The peons, or workers, who lived in a long line of wooden cabins back of the main building, were mostly Paraguayans, with a few Brazilians, and a dozen German and Argentine foremen. There were also some wild Indians, who were camped in the usual squalid fashion of Indians who are hangers-on round the white man but have not yet adopted his ways. Most of the men were at work cutting wood for the tannery. The women and children were in camp. Some individuals of both sexes were naked to the waist. One little girl had a young ostrich as a pet.

Indian boy with coati (coon-like animal) and parakeet

Tupi girl with young ostrich

From photographs by Kermit Roosevelt

Indian girl at cooking-pot

Water-fowl were plentiful. We saw large flocks of wild muscovy ducks. Our tame birds come from this wild species and its absurd misnaming dates back to the period when the turkey and guinea-pig were misnamed in similar fashion—our European forefathers taking a large and hazy view of geography, and including Turkey, Guinea, India, and Muscovy as places which, in their capacity of being outlandish, could be comprehensively used as including America. The muscovy ducks were very good eating. Darters and cormorants swarmed. They waddled on the sand-bars in big flocks and crowded the trees by the water's edge. Beautiful snow-white egrets also lit in the trees, often well back from the river. A full-foliaged tree of vivid green, its round surface crowded with these birds, as if it had suddenly blossomed with huge white flowers, is a sight worth seeing. Here and there on the sand-bars we saw huge jabiru storks, and once a flock of white wood-ibis among the trees on the bank.

On the Brazilian boundary we met a shallow river steamer carrying Colonel Candido Mariano da Silva Rondon and several other Brazilian members of the expedition. Colonel Rondon immediately showed that he was all, and more than all, that could be desired. It was evident that he knew his business thoroughly, and it was equally evident that he would be a pleasant companion. He was a classmate of Mr. Lauro Müller at the Brazilian Military Academy. He is of almost pure Indian blood, and is a Positivist—the Positivists are a really strong body in Brazil, as they are in France and indeed in Chile. The colonel's seven children have all been formally made members of the Positivist Church in Rio Janeiro. Brazil possesses the same complete liberty in matters religious, spiritual, and intellectual as we, for our great good fortune, do in the United States, and my Brazilian companions included Catholics and equally sincere men who described themselves as "libres penseurs." Colonel Rondon has spent the last twenty-four years in exploring the western highlands of Brazil, pioneering the way for telegraph-lines and railroads. During that time he has travelled some fourteen thousand miles, on territory most of which had not previously been traversed by civilized man, and has built three thousand miles of telegraph. He has an exceptional knowledge of the Indian tribes and has always zealously endeavored to serve them and indeed to serve the cause of humanity wherever and whenever he was able. Thanks mainly to his efforts, four of the wild tribes of the region he has explored have begun to tread the road of civilization. They have taken the first steps toward becoming Christians. It may seem strange that among the first-fruits of the efforts of a Positivist should be the conversion of those he seeks to benefit to Christianity. But in South America Christianity is at least as much a status as a theology. It represents the indispensable first step upward from savagery. In the wilder and poorer districts men are divided into the two great classes of "Christians" and "Indians." When an Indian becomes a Christian he is accepted into and becomes wholly absorbed or partly assimilated by the crude and simple neighboring civilization, and then he moves up or down like any one else among his fellows.

Among Colonel Rondon's companions were Captain Amilcar de Magalhães, Lieutenant João Lyra, Lieutenant

Indians rolling logs at wood station

From a photograph by Kermit Roosevelt

Palms along the bank of the river

From a photograph by Kermit Roosevelt

Joaquin de Mello Filho, and Doctor Euzebio de Oliveira, a geologist.

The steamers halted; Colonel Rondon and several of his officers, spick and span in their white uniforms, came aboard; and in the afternoon I visited him on his steamer to talk over our plans. When these had been fully discussed and agreed on we took tea. I happened to mention that one of our naturalists, Miller, had been bitten by a piranha, and the man-eating fish at once became the subject of conversation. Curiously enough, one of the Brazilian taxidermists had also just been severely bitten by a piranha. My new companions had story after story to tell of them. Only three weeks previously a twelve-year-old boy who had gone in swimming near Corumbá was attacked, and literally devoured alive by them. Colonel Rondon during his exploring trips had met with more than one unpleasant experience in connection with them. He had lost one of his toes by the bite of a piranha. He was about to bathe and had chosen a shallow pool at the edge of the river, which he carefully inspected until he was satisfied that none of the man-eating fish were in it; yet as soon as he put his foot into the water one of them attacked him and bit off a toe. On another occasion while wading across a narrow stream one of his party was attacked; the fish bit him on the thighs and buttocks, and when he put down his hands tore them also; he was near the bank and by a rush reached it and swung himself out of the water by means of an overhanging limb of a tree; but he was terribly injured, and it took him six months before his wounds healed and he recovered. An extraordinary incident occurred on another trip. The party were without food and very hungry. On reaching a stream they dynamited it, and waded in to seize the stunned fish as they floated on the surface. One man, Lieutenant Pyrineus, having his hands full, tried to hold one fish by putting its head into his mouth; it was a piranha and seemingly stunned, but in a moment it recovered and bit a big section out of his tongue. Such a hemorrhage followed that his life was saved with the utmost difficulty. On another occasion a member of the party was off by himself on a mule. The mule came into camp alone. Following his track back they came to a ford, where in the water they found the skeleton of the dead man, his clothes uninjured but every particle of flesh stripped from his bones. Whether he had drowned, and the fishes had then eaten his body, or whether they had killed him it was impossible to say. They had not hurt the clothes, getting in under them, which made it seem likely that there had been no struggle. These man-eating fish are a veritable scourge in the waters they frequent. But it must not be understood by this that the piranhas—or, for the matter of that, the New-World caymans and crocodiles—ever become such dreaded foes of man as for instance the man-eating crocodiles of Africa. Accidents occur, and there are certain places where swimming and bathing are dangerous; but in most places the people swim freely, although they are usually careful to find spots they believe safe or else to keep together and make a splashing in the water.

During his trips Colonel Rondon had met with various experiences with wild creatures. The Paraguayan caymans are not ordinarily dangerous to man; but they do sometimes become man-eaters and should be destroyed whenever the opportunity offers. The huge caymans and crocodiles of the Amazon are far more dangerous, and the colonel knew of repeated instances where men, women, and children had become their victims. Once while dynamiting a stream for fish for his starving party he partially stunned a giant anaconda, which he killed as it crept slowly off. He said that it was of a size that no other anaconda he had ever seen even approached, and that in his opinion such a brute if hungry would readily attack a full-grown man. Twice smaller anacondas had attacked his dogs; one was carried under water—for the anaconda is a water-loving serpent—but he rescued it. One of his men was bitten by a jararaca; he killed the venomous snake, but was not discovered and brought back to camp until it was too late to save his life. The puma Colonel Rondon had found to be as cowardly as I have always found it, but the jaguar was a formidable beast, which occasionally turned man-eater, and often charged savagely when brought to bay. He had known a hunter to be killed by a jaguar he was following in thick grass cover.

All such enemies, however, he regarded as utterly trivial compared to the real dangers of the wilderness—the torment and menace of attacks by the swarming insects, by mosquitoes and the even more intolerable tiny gnats, by the ticks, and by the vicious poisonous ants which occasionally cause villages and even whole districts to be deserted by human beings. These insects, and the fevers they cause, and dysentery and starvation and wearing hardship and accidents in rapids are what the pioneer explorers have to fear. The conversation was to me most interesting. The colonel spoke French about to the extent I did; but of course he and the others preferred Portuguese; and then Kermit was the interpreter.

In the evening, soon after moonrise, we stopped for wood at the little Brazilian town of Porto Martinho. There are about twelve hundred inhabitants. Some of the buildings were of stone; a large private house with a castellated tower was of stone; there were shops, and a post-office, stores, a restaurant and billiard-hall, and warehouses for matté, of which much is grown in the region roundabout. Most of the houses were low, with overhanging, sloping eaves; and there were gardens with high walls, inside of which trees rose, many of them fragrant. We wandered through the wide, dusty streets, and along the narrow sidewalks. It was a hot, still evening; the smell of the tropics was on the heavy December air. Through the open doors and windows we caught dim glimpses of the half-clad inmates of the poorer houses; women and young girls sat outside their thresholds in the moonlight. All whom we met were most friendly: the captain of the little Brazilian garrison; the intendente, a local trader; another trader and ranchman, a Uruguayan, who had just received his newspaper containing my speech in Montevideo, and who, as I gathered from what I understood of his rather voluble Spanish, was much impressed by my views on democracy, honesty, liberty, and order (rather well-worn topics); and a Catalan who spoke French, and who was accompanied by his pretty daughter, a dear little girl of eight or ten, who said with much pride that she spoke three languages—Brazilian, Spanish, and Catalan! Her father expressed strongly his desire for a church and for a school in the little city.

When at last the wood was aboard we resumed our journey. The river was like glass. In the white moonlight the palms on the edge of the banks stood mirrored in the still water. We sat forward and as we rounded the curves the long silver reaches of the great stream stretched ahead of us, and the ghostly outlines of hills rose in the distance. Here and there prairie fires burned, and the red glow warred with the moon's radiance.

Next morning was overcast. Occasionally we passed a wood-yard, or factory, or cabin, now on the eastern, the Brazilian, now on the western, the Paraguayan, bank. The Paraguay was known to men of European birth, bore soldiers and priests and merchants as they sailed and rowed up and down the current of its stream, and beheld little towns and forts rise on its banks, long before the Mississippi had become the white man's highway. Now, along its upper course, the settlements are much like those on the Mississippi at the end of the first quarter of the last century; and in the not distant future it will witness a burst of growth and prosperity much like that which the Mississippi saw when the old men of to-day were very young.

In the early forenoon we stopped at a little Paraguayan hamlet, nestling in the green growth under a group of low hills by the river-brink. On one of these hills stood a picturesque old stone fort, known as Fort Bourbon in the Spanish, the colonial, days. Now the Paraguayan flag floats over it, and it is garrisoned by a handful of Paraguayan soldiers. Here Father Zahm baptized two children, the youngest of a large family of fair-skinned, light-haired small people, whose father was a Paraguayan and the mother an "Orientál," or Uruguayan. No priest had visited the village for three years, and the children were respectively one and two years of age. The sponsors included the local commandante and a married couple from Austria. In answer to what was supposed to be the perfunctory question whether they were Catholics, the parents returned the unexpected answer that they were not. Further questioning elicited the fact that the father called himself a "free-thinking Catholic," and the mother said she was a "Protestant Catholic," her mother having been a Protestant, the daughter of an immigrant from Normandy. However, it appeared that the older children had been baptized by the Bishop of Asuncion, so Father Zahm at the earnest request of the parents proceeded with the ceremony. They were good people; and, although they wished liberty to think exactly as they individually pleased, they also wished to be connected and to have their children connected with some church, by preference the church of the majority of their people. A very short experience of communities where there is no church ought to convince the most heterodox of the absolute need of a church. I earnestly wish that there could be such an increase in the personnel and equipment of the Catholic Church in South America as to permit the establishment of one good and earnest priest in every village or little community in the far interior. Nor is there any inconsistency between this wish and the further wish that there could be a marked extension and development of the native Protestant churches, such as I saw established here and there in Brazil, Uruguay, and Argentina, and of the Y. M. C. Associations. The bulk of these good people who profess religion will continue to be Catholics, but the spiritual needs of a more or less considerable minority will best be met by the establishment of Protestant churches, or in places even of a Positivist Church or Ethical Culture Society. Not only is the establishment of such churches a good thing for the body politic as a whole, but a good thing for the Catholic Church itself; for their presence is a constant spur to activity and clean and honorable conduct, and a constant reflection on sloth and moral laxity. The government in each of these commonwealths is doing everything possible to further the cause of education, and the tendency is to treat education as peculiarly a function of government and to make it, where the government acts, non-sectarian, obligatory, and free—a cardinal doctrine of our own great democracy, to which we are committed by every principle of sound Americanism. There must be absolute religious liberty, for tyranny and intolerance are as abhorrent in matters intellectual and spiritual as in matters political and material; and more and more we must all realize that conduct is of infinitely greater importance than dogma. But no democracy can afford to overlook the vital importance of the ethical and spiritual, the truly religious, element in life; and in practice the average good man grows clearly to understand this, and to express the need in concrete form by saying that no community can make much headway if it does not contain both a church and a school.

We took breakfast—the eleven-o'clock Brazilian breakfast—on Colonel Rondon's boat. Caymans were becoming more plentiful. The ugly brutes lay on the sand-flats and mud-banks like logs, always with the head raised, sometimes with the jaws open. They are often dangerous to domestic animals, and are always destructive to fish, and it is good to shoot them. I killed half a dozen, and missed nearly as many more—a throbbing boat does not improve one's aim. We passed forests of palms that extended for leagues, and vast marshy meadows, where storks, herons, and ibis were gathered, with flocks of cormorants and darters on the sand-bars, and stilts, skimmers, and clouds of beautiful swaying terns in the foreground. About noon we passed the highest point which the old Spanish conquistadores and explorers, Irala and Ayolas, had reached in the course of their marvellous journeys in the first half of the sixteenth century—at a time when there was not a settlement in what is now the United States, and when hardly a single English sea captain had ventured so much as to cross the Atlantic.

By the following day the country on the east bank had become a vast marshy plain dotted here and there by tree-clad patches of higher land. The morning was rainy; a contrast to the fine weather we had hitherto encountered. We passed wood-yards and cattle-ranches. At one of the latter the owner, an Argentine of Irish parentage, who still spoke English with the accent of the land of his parents' nativity, remarked that this was the first time the American flag had been seen on the upper Paraguay; for our gunboat carried it at the masthead. Early in the afternoon, having reached the part where both banks of the river were Brazilian territory, we came to the old colonial Portuguese fort of Coimbra. It stands where two steep hills rise, one on either side of the river, and it guards the water-gorge between them. It was captured by the Paraguayans in the war of nearly half a century ago. Some

Cattle on the upper Paraguay River

From a photograph by Kermit Roosevelt

modern guns have been mounted, and there is a garrison of Brazilian troops. The white fort is perched on the hill-side, where it clings and rises, terrace above terrace, with bastion and parapet and crenellated wall. At the foot of the hill, on the riverine plain, stretches the old-time village with its roofs of palm. In the village dwell several hundred souls, almost entirely the officers and soldiers and their families. There is one long street. The one-story, daub-and-wattle houses have low eaves and steep sloping roofs of palm-leaves or of split palm-trunks. Under one or two old but small trees there are rude benches; and for a part of the length of the street there is a rough stone sidewalk. A little graveyard, some of the tombs very old, stands at one end. As we passed down the street the wives and the swarming children of the garrison were at the doors and windows; there were women and girls with skins as fair as any in the northland, and others that were predominantly negro. Most were of intervening shades. All this was paralleled among the men; and the fusion of the colors was going on steadily.

Around the village black vultures were gathered. Not long before reaching it we passed some rounded green trees, their tops covered with the showy wood-ibis; at the same time we saw behind them, farther inland, other trees crowded with the more delicate forms of the shining white egrets.

The river now widened so that in places it looked like a long lake; it wound in every direction through the endless marshy plain, whose surface was broken here and there by low mountains. The splendor of the sunset I never saw surpassed. We were steaming east toward clouds of storm. The river ran, a broad highway of molten gold, into the flaming sky; the far-off mountains loomed purple across the marshes; belts of rich green, the river banks stood out on either side against the rose-hues of the rippling water; in front, as we forged steadily onward, hung the tropic night, dim and vast.

On December 15 we reached Corumbá. For three or four miles before it is reached the west bank, on which it stands, becomes high rocky ground, falling away into cliffs. The country roundabout was evidently well peopled. We saw gauchos, cattle-herders—the equivalent of our own cowboys—riding along the bank. Women were washing clothes, and their naked children bathing, on the shore; we were told that caymans and piranhas rarely ventured near a place where so much was going on, and that accidents generally occurred in ponds or lonely stretches of the river. Several steamers came out to meet us, and accompanied us for a dozen miles, with bands playing and the passengers cheering, just as if we were nearing some town on the Hudson.

Corumbá is on a steep hillside, with wide, roughly paved streets, some of them lined with beautiful trees that bear scarlet flowers, and with well-built houses, most of them of one story, some of two or three stories. We were greeted with a reception by the municipal council, and were given a state dinner. The hotel, kept by an Italian, was as comfortable as possible—stone floors, high ceilings, big windows and doors, a cool, open courtyard, and a shower-bath. Of course Corumbá is still a frontier town. The vehicles are ox-carts and mule-carts; there are no carriages; and oxen as well as mules are used for riding. The water comes from a big central well; around it the water-carts gather, and their contents are then peddled around at the different houses. The families showed the mixture of races characteristic of Brazil; one mother, after the children had been photographed in their ordinary costume, begged that we return and take them in their Sunday clothes, which was accordingly done. In a year the railway from Rio will reach Corumbá; and then this city, and the country roundabout, will see much development.

At this point we rejoined the rest of the party, and very glad we were to see them. Cherrie and Miller had already collected some eight hundred specimens of mammals and birds.

CHAPTER III

A JAGUAR-HUNT ON THE TAQUARY

The morning after our arrival at Corumbá I asked Colonel Rondon to inspect our outfit; for his experience of what is necessary in tropical travelling has been gained through a quarter of a century of arduous exploration in the wilderness. It was Fiala who had assembled our food-tents, cooking-utensils, and supplies of all kinds, and he and Sigg, during their stay in Corumbá, had been putting everything in shape for our start. Colonel Rondon at the end of his inspection said he had nothing whatever to suggest; that it was extraordinary that Fiala, without personal knowledge of the tropics, could have gathered the things most necessary, with the minimum of bulk and maximum of usefulness.

Miller had made a special study of the piranhas, which swarmed at one of the camps he and Cherrie had made in the Chaco. So numerous were they that the members of the party had to be exceedingly careful in dipping up water. Miller did not find that they were cannibals toward their own kind; they were "cannibals" only in the sense of eating the flesh of men. When dead piranhas, and even when mortally injured piranhas, with the blood flowing, were thrown among the ravenous living, they were left unmolested. Moreover, it was Miller's experience, the direct contrary of what we had been told, that splashing and a commotion in the water attracted the piranhas, whereas they rarely attacked anything that was motionless unless it was bloody. Dead birds and mammals, thrown whole and unskinned into the water were permitted to float off unmolested, whereas the skinned carcass of a good-sized monkey was at once seized, pulled under the water, and completely devoured by the blood-crazy fish. A man who had dropped something of value waded in after it to above the knees, but went very slowly and quietly, avoiding every possibility of disturbance, and not venturing to put his hands into the water. But nobody could bathe, and even the slightest disturbance in the water, such as that made by scrubbing the hands vigorously with soap, immediately attracted the attention of the savage little creatures, who darted to the place, evidently hoping to find some animal in difficulties. Once, while Miller and some Indians were attempting to launch a boat, and were making a great commotion in the water, a piranha attacked a naked Indian who belonged to the party and mutilated him as he struggled and splashed, waist-deep in the stream. Men not making a splashing and struggling are rarely attacked; but if one is attacked by any chance, the blood in the water maddens the piranhas, and they assail the man with frightful ferocity.

At Corumbá the weather was hot. In the patio of the comfortable little hotel we heard the cicadas; but I did not hear the extraordinary screaming whistle of the locomotive cicada, which I had heard in the gardens of the house in which I stayed at Asuncion. This was as remarkable a sound as any animal sound to which I have listened, except only the batrachian-like wailing of the tree hyrax in East Africa; and like the East African mammal this South American insect has a voice, or rather utters a sound which, so far as it resembles any other animal sound, at the beginning remotely suggests batrachian affinities. The locomotive-whistle part of the utterance, however, resembles nothing so much as a small steam siren; when first heard it seems impossible that it can be produced by an insect.

On December 17 Colonel Rondon and several members of our party started on a shallow river steamer for the ranch of Senhor de Barros, "Las Palmeiras," on the Rio Taquary. We went down the Paraguay for a few miles, and then up the Taquary. It was a beautiful trip. The shallow river—we were aground several times—wound through a vast, marshy plain, with occasional spots of higher land on which trees grew. There were many water-birds. Darters swarmed. But the conspicuous and attractive bird was the stately jabiru stork. Flocks of these storks whitened the marshes and lined the river banks. They were not shy, for such big birds; before flying they had to run a few paces and then launch themselves on the air. Once, at noon, a couple soared round overhead in wide rings, rising higher and higher. On another occasion, late in the day, a flock passed by, gleaming white with black points in the long afternoon lights, and with them were spoonbills, showing rosy amid their snowy companions. Caymans, always called jacarés, swarmed; and we killed scores of the noxious creatures. They were singularly indifferent to our approach and to the sound of the shots. Sometimes they ran into the water erect on their legs, looking like miniatures of the monsters of the prime. One showed by its behavior how little an ordinary shot pains or affects these dull-nerved, cold-blooded creatures. As it lay on a sand-bank, it was hit with a long 22 bullet. It slid into the water but found itself in the midst of a school of fish. It at once forgot everything except its greedy appetite, and began catching the fish. It seized fish after fish, holding its head above water as soon as its jaws had closed on a fish; and a second bullet killed it. Some of the crocodiles when shot performed most extraordinary antics. Our weapons, by the way, were good, except Miller's shotgun. The outfit furnished by the American museum was excellent—except in guns and cartridges; this gun was so bad that Miller had to use Fiala's gun or else my Fox 12-bore.

In the late afternoon we secured a more interesting creature than the jacarés. Kermit had charge of two hounds which we owed to the courtesy of one of our Argentine friends. They were biggish, nondescript animals, obviously good fighters, and they speedily developed the utmost affection for all the members of the expedition, but especially for Kermit, who took care of them. One we named "Shenzi," the name given the wild bush natives by the Swahili, the semicivilized African porters. He was good-natured, rough, and stupid—hence his name. The other was called by a native name, "Trigueiro." The chance now came to try them. We were steaming between long stretches of coarse grass, about three feet high, when we spied from the deck a black object, very conspicuous against the vivid green. It was a giant ant-eater, or tamanduá bandeira, one of the most extraordinary creatures of the latter-day world. It is about the size of a rather small black bear. It has a very long, narrow, toothless snout, with a tongue it can project a couple of feet; it is covered with coarse, black hair, save for a couple of white stripes; it has a long, bushy tail and very powerful claws on its fore feet. It walks on the sides of its fore feet with these claws curved in under the foot. The claws are used in digging out ant-hills; but the beast has courage, and in a grapple is a rather unpleasant enemy, in spite of its toothless mouth, for it can strike a formidable blow with these claws. It sometimes hugs a foe, gripping him tight; but its ordinary method of defending itself is to strike with its long, stout, curved claws, which, driven by its muscular forearm, can rip open man or beast. Several of our companions had had dogs killed by these ant-eaters; and we came across one man with a very ugly scar down his back, where he had been hit by one, which charged him when he came up to kill it at close quarters.

As soon as we saw the giant tamanduá we pushed off in a rowboat, and landed only a couple of hundred yards distant from our clumsy quarry. The tamanduá throughout most of its habitat rarely leaves the forest, and it is a helpless animal in the open plain. The two dogs ran ahead, followed by Colonel Rondon and Kermit, with me behind carrying the rifle. In a minute or two the hounds overtook the cantering, shuffling creature, and promptly began a fight with it; the combatants were so mixed up that I had to wait another minute or so before I could fire without risk of hitting a dog. We carried our prize back to the bank and hoisted it aboard the steamer. The sun was just about to set, behind dim mountains, many miles distant across the marsh.

Soon afterward we reached one of the outstations of

the huge ranch we were about to visit, and hauled up alongside the bank for the night. There was a landing-place, and sheds and corrals. Several of the peons or gauchos had come to meet us. After dark they kindled fires, and sat beside them singing songs in a strange minor key and strumming guitars. The red firelight flickered over their wild figures as they squatted away from the blaze, where the light and the shadow met. It was still and hot. There were mosquitoes, of course, and other insects of all kinds swarmed round every light; but the steamboat was comfortable, and we passed a pleasant night.

At sunrise we were off for the "fazenda," the ranch of M. de Barros. The baggage went in an ox-cart—which had to make two trips, so that all of my belongings reached the ranch a day later than I did. We rode small, tough ranch horses. The distance was some twenty miles. The whole country was marsh, varied by stretches of higher ground; and, although these stretches rose only three or four feet above the marsh, they were covered with thick jungle, largely palmetto scrub, or else with open palm forest. For three or four miles we splashed through the marsh, now and then crossing boggy pools where the little horses labored hard not to mire down. Our dusky guide was clad in a shirt, trousers, and fringed leather apron, and wore spurs on his bare feet; he had a rope for a bridle, and two or three toes of each foot were thrust into little iron stirrups.

The pools in the marsh were drying. They were filled with fish, most of them dead or dying; and the birds had gathered to the banquet. The most notable dinner guests were the great jabiru storks; the stately creatures dotted the marsh. But ibis and herons abounded; the former uttered queer, querulous cries when they discovered our presence. The spurred lapwings were as noisy as they always are. The ibis and plover did not pay any heed to the fish; but the black carrion vultures feasted on them in the mud; and in the pools that were not dry small alligators, the jacaré-tinga, were feasting also. In many places the stench from the dead fish was unpleasant.

Then for miles we rode through a beautiful open forest of tall, slender carandá palms, with other trees scattered among them. Green parakeets with black heads chattered as they flew; noisy green and red parrots climbed among the palms; and huge macaws, some entirely blue, others almost entirely red, screamed loudly as they perched in the trees or took wing at our approach. If one was wounded its cries kept its companions circling around overhead. The naturalists found the bird fauna totally different from that which they had been collecting in the hill country near Corumbá, seventy or eighty miles distant; and birds swarmed, both species and individuals. South America has the most extensive and most varied avifauna of all the continents. On the other hand, its mammalian fauna, although very interesting, is rather poor in number of species and individuals and in the size of the beasts. It possesses more mammals that are unique and distinctive in type than does any other continent save Australia; and they are of higher and much more varied types than in Australia. But there is nothing approaching the majesty, beauty, and swarming mass of the great mammalian life of Africa and, in a less degree, of tropical Asia; indeed, it does not even approach the similar mammalian life of North America and northern Eurasia, poor though this is compared with the seething vitality of tropical life in the Old World. During a geologically recent period, a period extending into that which saw man spread over the world in substantially the physical and cultural stage of many existing savages, South America possessed a varied and striking fauna of enormous beasts—sabre-tooth tigers, huge lions, mastodons, horses of many kinds, camel-like pachyderms, giant ground-sloths, mylodons the size of the rhinoceros, and many, many other strange and wonderful creatures. From some cause, concerning the nature of which we cannot at present even hazard a guess, this vast and giant fauna vanished completely, the tremendous catastrophe (the duration of which is unknown) not being consummated until within a few thousand or a few score thousand years. When the white man reached South America he found the same weak and impoverished mammalian fauna that exists practically unchanged to-day. Elsewhere civilized man has been even more destructive than his very destructive uncivilized brothers of the magnificent mammalian life of the wilderness; for ages he has been rooting out the higher forms of beast life in Europe, Asia, and North Africa; and in our own day he has repeated the feat, on a very large scale, in the rest of Africa and in North America. But in South America, although he is in places responsible for the wanton slaughter of the most interesting and the largest, or the most beautiful, birds, his advent has meant a positive enrichment of the wild mammalian fauna. None of the native grass-eating mammals, the graminivores, approach in size and beauty the herds of wild or half-wild cattle and horses, or so add to the interest of the landscape. There is every reason why the good people of South America should waken, as we of North America, very late in the day, are beginning to waken, and as the peoples of northern Europe—not southern Europe—have already partially wakened, to the duty of preserving from impoverishment and extinction the wild life which is an asset of such interest and value in our several lands; but the case against civilized man in this matter is grewsomely heavy anyhow, when the plain truth is told, and it is harmed by exaggeration.

After five or six hours' travelling through this country of marsh and of palm forest we reached the ranch for which we were heading. In the neighborhood stood giant fig-trees, singly or in groups, with dense, dark-green foliage. Ponds, overgrown with water-plants, lay about; wet meadow, and drier pastureland, open or dotted with palms and varied with tree jungle, stretched for many miles on every hand. There are some thirty thousand head of cattle on the ranch, besides herds of horses and droves of swine, and a few flocks of sheep and goats. The home buildings of the ranch stood in a quadrangle, surrounded by a fence or low stockade. One end of the quadrangle was formed by the ranch-house itself, one story high, with whitewashed walls and red-tiled roof. Inside, the rooms were bare, with clean, whitewashed walls and palm-trunk rafters. There were solid wooden shutters on the unglazed windows. We slept in hammocks or on cots, and we feasted royally on delicious native Brazilian dishes. On another side of the quadrangle stood another long, low white building with a red-tiled roof; this held the kitchen and the living-rooms of the upper-grade peons, the headmen, the cook, and jaguar-hunters, with their families: dark-skinned men, their wives showing varied strains of white, Indian, and negro blood. The children tumbled merrily in the dust, and were fondly tended by their mothers. Opposite the kitchen stood a row of buildings, some whitewashed daub and wattle, with tin roofs, others of erect palm-logs with palm-leaf thatch. These were the saddle-room, storehouse, chicken-house, and stable. The chicken-house was allotted to Kermit and Miller for the preparation of the specimens; and there they worked industriously. With a big skin, like that of the giant ant-eater, they had to squat on the ground; while the ducklings and wee chickens scuffled not only round the skin but all over it, grabbing the shreds and scraps of meat and catching flies. The fourth end of the quadrangle was formed by a corral and a big wooden scaffolding on which hung hides and strips of drying meat. Extraordinary to relate, there were no mosquitoes at the ranch; why I cannot say, as they ought to swarm in these vast "pantanals," or swamps. Therefore, in spite of the heat, it was very pleasant. Near by stood other buildings: sheds, and thatched huts of palm-logs in which the ordinary peons lived, and big corrals. In the quadrangle were flamboyant trees, with their masses of brilliant red flowers and delicately cut, vivid-green foliage. Noisy oven-birds haunted these trees. In a high palm in the garden a family of green parakeets had taken up their abode and were preparing to build nests. They chattered incessantly both when they flew and when they sat or crawled among the branches. Ibis and plover, crying and wailing, passed immediately overhead. Jacanas frequented the ponds near by; the peons, with a familiarity which to us seems sacrilegious, but to them was entirely inoffensive and matter of course, called them "the Jesus Christ birds," because they walked on the water. There was a wealth of strange bird life in the neighborhood. There were large papyrus-marshes, the papyrus not being a fifth, perhaps not a tenth, as high as in Africa. In these swamps were many blackbirds. Some uttered notes that reminded me of our own redwings. Others, with crimson heads and necks and thighs, fairly blazed; often a dozen sat together on a swaying papyrus-stem which their weight bent over. There were all kinds of extraordinary bird's-nests in the trees. There is still need for the work of the collector in South America. But I believe that already, so far as birds are concerned, there is infinitely more need for the work of the careful observer, who to the power of appreciation and observation adds the power of vivid, truthful, *and interesting* narration—which means, as scientists no less than historians should note, that training in the writing of good English is indispensable to any learned man who expects to make his learning count for what it ought to count in the effect on his fellow men. The outdoor naturalist, the faunal naturalist, who devotes himself primarily to a study of the habits and of the life-histories of birds, beasts, fish, and reptiles, and who can portray truthfully and vividly what he has seen, could do work of more usefulness than any mere collector, in this upper Paraguay country. The work of the collector is indispensable; but it is only a small part of the work that ought to be done; and after collecting has reached a certain point the work of the field observer with the gift for recording what he has seen becomes of far more importance.

The long days spent riding through the swamp, the "pantanal," were pleasant and interesting. Several times we saw the tamanduá bandeira, the giant ant-bear. Kermit shot one, because the naturalists eagerly wished for a second specimen; afterward we were relieved of all necessity to molest the strange, out-of-date creatures. It was a surprise to us to find them habitually frequenting the open marsh. They were always on muddy ground, and in the papyrus-swamp we found them in several inches of water. The stomach is thick-walled, like a gizzard; the stomachs of those we shot contained adult and larval ants, chiefly termites, together with plenty of black mould and fragments of leaves, both green and dry. Doubtless the earth and the vegetable matter had merely been taken incidentally, adhering to the viscid tongue when it was thrust into the ant masses. Out in the open marsh the tamanduá could neither avoid observation, nor fight effectively, nor make good its escape by flight. It was curious to see one lumbering off at a rocking canter, the big bushy tail held aloft. One, while fighting the dogs, suddenly threw itself on its back, evidently hoping to grasp a dog with its paws; and it now and then reared, in order to strike at its assailants. In one patch of thick jungle we saw a black howler monkey sitting motionless in a tree top. We also saw the swamp-deer, about the size of our blacktail. It is a real swamp animal, for we found it often in the papyrus-swamps, and out in the open marsh, knee-deep in the water, among the aquatic plants.

The tough little horses bore us well through the marsh.

Often in crossing bayous and ponds the water rose almost to their backs; but they splashed and waded and if necessary swam through. The dogs were a wild-looking set. Some were of distinctly wolfish appearance. These, we were assured, were descended in part from the big red wolf of the neighborhood, a tall, lank animal, with much smaller teeth than a big northern wolf. The domestic dog is undoubtedly descended from at least a dozen different species of wild dogs, wolves, and jackals, some of them probably belonging to what we style different genera. The degree of fecundity or lack of fecundity between different species varies in extraordinary and inexplicable fashion in different families of mammals. In the horse family, for instance, the species are not fertile *inter se;* whereas among the oxen, species seemingly at least as widely separated as the horse, ass, and zebra—species such as the domestic ox, bison, yak, and gaur—breed freely together and their offspring are fertile; the lion and tiger also breed together, and produce offspring which will breed with either parent stock; and tame dogs in different quarters of the world, although all of them fertile *inter se*, are in many cases obviously blood kin to the neighboring wild, wolf-like or jackal-like creatures which are specifically, and possibly even generically, distinct from one another. The big red wolf of the South American plains is not closely related to the northern wolves; and it was to me unexpected to find it interbreeding with ordinary domestic dogs.

In the evenings after dinner we sat in the bare ranch dining-room, or out under the trees in the hot darkness, and talked of many things: natural history with the naturalists, and all kinds of other subjects both with them and with our Brazilian friends. Colonel Rondon is not simply "an officer and a gentleman" in the sense that is honorably true of the best army officers in every good military service. He is also a peculiarly hardy and competent explorer, a good field naturalist and scientific man, a student and a philosopher. With him the conversation ranged from jaguar-hunting and the perils of exploration in the "matto grosso," the great wilderness, to Indian anthropology, to the dangers of a purely materialistic industrial civilization, and to Positivist morality. The colonel's Positivism was in very fact to him a religion of humanity, a creed which bade him be just and kindly and useful to his fellow men, to live his life bravely, and no less bravely to face death, without reference to what he believed, or did not believe, or to what the unknown hereafter might hold for him.

The native hunters who accompanied us were swarthy men of mixed blood. They were barefooted and scantily clad, and each carried a long, clumsy spear and a keen machete, in the use of which he was an expert. Now and then, in thick jungle, we had to cut out a path, and it was interesting to see one of them, although cumbered by his unwieldy spear, handling his half-broken little horse with complete ease while he hacked at limbs and branches. Of the two ordinarily with us one was much the younger; and whenever we came to an unusually doubtful-looking ford or piece of boggy ground the elder man always sent the younger one on and sat on the bank until he saw what befell the experimenter. In that rather preposterous book of our youth, the "Swiss Family Robinson," mention is made of a tame monkey called Nips, which was used to test all edible-looking things as to the healthfulness of which the adventurers felt doubtful; and because of the obvious resemblance of function we christened this younger hunter Nips. Our guides were not only hunters but cattle-herders. The coarse dead grass is burned to make room for the green young grass on which the cattle thrive. Every now and then one of the men, as he rode ahead of us, without leaving the saddle, would drop a lighted match into a tussock of tall dead blades; and even as we who were behind rode by tongues of hot flame would be shooting up and a local prairie fire would have started.

Kermit took Nips off with him for a solitary hunt one day. He shot two of the big marsh-deer, a buck and a doe, and preserved them as museum specimens. They were in the papyrus growth, but their stomachs contained only the fine marsh-grass which grows in the water and on the land along the edges of the swamps; the papyrus was used only for cover, not for food. The buck had two big scent-glands beside the nostrils; in the doe these were rudimentary. On this day Kermit also came across a herd of the big, fierce white-lipped peccary; at the sound of their grunting Nips promptly spurred his horse and took to his heels, explaining that the peccaries would charge them, hamstring the horses, and kill the riders. Kermit went into the jungle after the truculent little wild hogs on foot and followed them for an hour, but never was able to catch sight of them.

In the afternoon of this same day one of the jaguar-hunters—merely ranch hands, who knew something of the chase of the jaguar—who had been searching for tracks, rode in with the information that he had found fresh sign

Nips with the marsh deer

Returning to the *fazenda* (ranch) with the marsh deer on the saddle

From photographs by Kermit Roosevelt

at a spot in the swamp about nine miles distant. Next morning we rose at two, and had started on our jaguar-hunt at three. Colonel Rondon, Kermit, and I, with the two trailers or jaguar-hunters, made up the party, each on a weedy, undersized marsh pony, accustomed to traversing the vast stretches of morass; and we were accompanied by a brown boy, with saddle-bags holding our lunch, who rode a long-horned trotting steer which he managed by a string through its nostril and lip. The two trailers carried each a long, clumsy spear. We had a rather poor pack. Besides our own two dogs, neither of which was used to jaguar-hunting, there were the ranch dogs, which were well-nigh worthless, and then two jaguar hounds borrowed for the occasion from a ranch six or eight leagues distant. These were the only hounds on which we could place any trust, and they were led in leashes by the two trailers. One was a white bitch, the other, the best one we had, was a gelded black dog. They were lean, half-starved creatures with prick ears and a look of furtive wildness.

As our shabby little horses shuffled away from the ranch-house the stars were brilliant and the Southern Cross hung well up in the heavens, tilted to the right. The landscape was spectral in the light of the waning moon. At the first shallow ford, as horses and dogs splashed across, an alligator, the jacaré-tinga, some five feet long, floated unconcernedly among the splashing hoofs and paws; evidently at night it did not fear us. Hour after hour we shogged along. Then the night grew ghostly with the first dim gray of the dawn. The sky had become overcast. The sun rose red and angry through broken clouds; his disk flamed behind the tall, slender columns of the palms, and lit the waste fields of papyrus. The black monkeys howled mournfully. The birds awoke. Macaws, parrots, parakeets screamed at us and chattered at us as we rode by. Ibis called with wailing voices, and the plovers shrieked as they wheeled in the air. We waded across bayous and ponds, where white lilies floated on the water and thronging lilac-flowers splashed the green marsh with color.

At last, on the edge of a patch of jungle, in wet ground, we came on fresh jaguar tracks. Both the jaguar hounds challenged the sign. They were unleashed and galloped along the trail, while the other dogs noisily accompanied them. The hunt led right through the marsh. Evidently the jaguar had not the least distaste for water. Probably it had been hunting for capybaras or tapirs, and it had gone straight through ponds and long, winding, narrow ditches or bayous, where it must now and then have had to swim for a stroke or two. It had also wandered through the island-like stretches of tree-covered land, the trees at this point being mostly palms and tarumans; the taruman is almost as big as a live-oak, with glossy foliage and a fruit like an olive. The pace quickened, the motley pack burst into yelling and howling; and then a sudden quickening of the note showed that the game had either climbed a tree or turned to bay in a thicket. The former proved to be the case. The dogs had entered a patch of tall tree jungle, and as we cantered up through the marsh we saw the jaguar high among the forked limbs of a taruman-tree. It was a beautiful picture—the spotted coat of the big, lithe, formidable cat fairly shone as it snarled defiance at the pack below. I did not trust the pack; the dogs were not stanch, and if the jaguar came down and started I feared we might lose it. So I fired at once, from a distance of seventy yards. I was using my favorite rifle, the little Springfield with which I have killed most kinds of African game, from the lion and elephant down; the bullets were the sharp, pointed kind, with the end of naked lead. At the shot the jaguar fell like a sack of sand through the branches, and although it staggered to its feet it went but a score of yards before it sank down, and when I came up it was dead under the palms, with three or four of the bolder dogs riving at it.

The jaguar is the king of South American game, ranking on an equality with the noblest beasts of the chase of North America, and behind only the huge and fierce creatures which stand at the head of the big game of Africa and Asia. This one was an adult female. It was heavier and more powerful than a full-grown male cougar, or African panther or leopard. It was a big, powerfully built creature, giving the same effect of strength that a tiger or lion does, and that the lithe leopards and pumas do not. Its flesh, by the way, proved good eating, when we had it for supper, although it was not cooked in the way it ought to have been. I tried it because I had found cougars such good eating; I have always regretted that in Africa I did not try lion's flesh, which I am sure must be excellent.

Next day came Kermit's turn. We had the miscellaneous pack with us, all much enjoying themselves; but, although they could help in a jaguar-hunt to the extent of giving tongue and following the chase for half a mile, cowing the quarry by their clamor, they were not sufficiently stanch to be of use if there was any difficulty in the hunt.

The only two dogs we could trust were the two borrowed jaguar hounds. This was the black dog's day. About ten in the morning we came to a long, deep, winding bayou. On the opposite bank stood a capybara, looking like a blunt-nosed pig, its wet hide shining black. I killed it, and it slid into the water. Then I found that the bayou extended for a mile or two in each direction, and the two hunter-guides said they did not wish to swim across for fear of the piranhas. Just at this moment we came across fresh jaguar tracks. It was hot, we had been travelling for five hours, and the dogs were much exhausted. The black hound in particular was nearly done up, for he had been led in a leash by one of the horsemen. He lay flat on the ground, panting, unable to catch the scent. Kermit threw water over him, and when he was thoroughly drenched and freshened, thrust his nose into the jaguar's footprints. The game old hound at once and eagerly responded. As he snuffed the scent he challenged loudly, while still lying down. Then he staggered to his feet and started on the trail, going stronger with every leap. Evidently the big cat was not far distant. Soon we found where it had swum across the bayou. Piranhas or no piranhas, we now intended to get across; and we tried to force our horses in at what seemed a likely spot. The matted growth of water-plants, with their leathery, slippery stems, formed an unpleasant barrier, as the water was swimming-deep for the horses. The latter were very unwilling to attempt the passage. Kermit finally forced his horse through the tangled mass, swimming, plunging, and struggling. He left a lane of clear water, through which we swam after him. The dogs splashed and swam behind us. On the other bank

The brown boy on the long-horned trotting steer, which he managed by a string through its nostril and lip

From a photograph by Kermit Roosevelt

Colonel Roosevelt and the first jaguar

From a photograph by Kermit Roosevelt

they struck the fresh trail and followed it at a run. It led into a long belt of timber, chiefly composed of low-growing nacurý palms, with long, drooping, many-fronded branches. In silhouette they suggest coarse bamboos; the nuts hang in big clusters and look like bunches of small, unripe bananas. Among the lower palms were scattered some big ordinary trees. We cantered along outside the timber belt, listening to the dogs within; and in a moment a burst of yelling clamor from the pack told that the jaguar was afoot. These few minutes are the really exciting moments in the chase, with hounds, of any big cat that will tree. The furious baying of the pack, the shouts and cheers of encouragement from the galloping horsemen, the wilderness surroundings, the knowledge of what the quarry is—all combine to make the moment one of fierce and thrilling excitement. Besides, in this case there was the possibility the jaguar might come to bay on the ground, in which event there would be a slight element of risk, as it might need straight shooting to stop a charge. However, about as soon as the long-drawn howling and eager yelping showed that the jaguar had been overtaken, we saw him, a huge male, up in the branches of a great fig-tree. A bullet behind the shoulder, from Kermit's 405 Winchester, brought him dead to the ground. He was heavier than the very big male horse-killing cougar I shot in Colorado, whose skull Hart Merriam reported as the biggest he had ever seen; he was very nearly double the weight of any of the male African leopards we shot; he was nearly or quite the weight of the smallest of the adult African lionesses we shot while in Africa. He had the big bones, the stout frame, and the heavy muscular build of a small lion; he was not lithe and slender and long like a cougar or leopard; the tail, as with all jaguars, was short, while the girth of the body was great; his coat was beautiful, with a satiny gloss, and the dark-brown spots on the gold of his back, head, and sides were hardly as conspicuous as the black of the equally well-marked spots against his white belly.

This was a well-known jaguar. He had occasionally indulged in cattle-killing; on one occasion during the floods he had taken up his abode near the ranch-house and had killed a couple of cows and a young steer. The hunters had followed him, but he had made his escape, and for the time being had abandoned the neighborhood. In these marshes each jaguar had a wide irregular range and travelled a good deal, perhaps only passing a day or two in a given locality, perhaps spending a week where game was plentiful. Jaguars love the water. They drink greedily and swim freely. In this country they rambled through the night across the marshes and prowled along the edges of the ponds and bayous, catching the capybaras and the caymans; for these small pond caymans, the jacaré-tinga, form part of their habitual food, and a big jaguar when hungry will attack and kill large caymans and crocodiles if he can get them a few yards from the water. On these marshes the jaguars also followed the peccary herds; it is said that they always strike the hindmost of a band of the fierce little wild pigs. Elsewhere they often prey on the tapir. If in timber, however, the jaguar must kill it at once, for the squat, thick-skinned, wedge-shaped tapir has no respect for timber, as Colonel Rondon phrased it, and rushes with such blind, headlong speed through and among branches and trunks that if not immediately killed it brushes the jaguar off, the claws leaving long raking scars in the tough hide. Cattle are often killed. The jaguar will not meddle with a big bull; and is cautious about attacking a herd accompanied by a bull; but it will at times, where wild game is scarce, kill every other domestic animal. It is a thirsty brute, and if it kills far from water will often drag its victim a long distance toward a pond or stream; Colonel Rondon had once come across a horse which a jaguar had thus killed and dragged for over a mile. Jaguars also stalk and kill the deer; in this neighborhood they seemed to be less habitual deer-hunters than the cougars; whether this is generally the case I cannot say. They have been known to pounce on and devour good-sized anacondas.

In this particular neighborhood the ordinary jaguars molested the cattle and horses hardly at all except now and then to kill calves. It was only occasionally that under special circumstances some old male took to cattle-killing. There were plenty of capybaras and deer, and evidently the big spotted cats preferred the easier prey when it was available; exactly as in East Africa we found the lions living almost exclusively on zebra and antelope, and not molesting the buffalo and domestic cattle, which in other parts of Africa furnish their habitual prey. In some other neighborhoods, not far distant, our hosts informed us that the jaguars lived almost exclusively on horses and cattle. They also told us that the cougars had the same habits as the jaguars except that they did not prey on such big animals. The cougars on this ranch never molested the foals, a fact which astonished me, as in the Rockies they are the worst enemies of foals. It was interesting to find that my hosts, and the mixed-blood hunters and ranch workers, combined special knowledge of many of the habits of these big cats with a curious ignorance of other matters concerning them and a readiness to believe fables about them. This was precisely what I had found to be the case with the old-time North American hunters in discussing the puma, bear, and wolf, and with the English and Boer hunters of Africa when they spoke of the lion and rhinoceros. Until the habit of scientific accuracy in observation and record is achieved and until specimens are preserved and carefully compared, entirely truthful men, at home in the wilderness, will whole-heartedly accept, and repeat as matters of gospel faith, theories which split the grizzly and black bears of each locality in the United States, and the lions and black rhinos of South Africa, or the jaguars and pumas of any portion of South America, into several different species, all with widely different habits. They will, moreover, describe these imaginary habits with such sincerity and minuteness that they deceive most listeners; and the result sometimes is that an otherwise good naturalist will perpetuate these fables, as Hudson did when he wrote of the puma. Hudson was a capital observer and writer when he dealt with the ordinary birds and mammals of the well-settled districts near Buenos Aires and at the mouth of the Rio Negro; but he knew nothing of the wilderness. This is no reflection on him; his books are great favorites of mine, and are to a large degree models of what such books should be; I only wish that there were hundreds of such writers and observers who would give us similar books for all parts of America.

A South American puma

A South American jaguar

From photographs by Elwin R. Sanborn

But it is a mistake to accept him as an authority on that concerning which he was ignorant.

An interesting incident occurred on the day we killed our first jaguar. We took our lunch beside a small but deep and obviously permanent pond. I went to the edge to dip up some water, and something growled or bellowed at me only a few feet away. It was a jacaré-tinga or small cayman about five feet long. I paid no heed to it at the moment. But shortly afterward when our horses went down to drink it threatened them and frightened them; and then Colonel Rondon and Kermit called me to watch it. It lay on the surface of the water only a few feet distant from us and threatened us; we threw cakes of mud at it, whereupon it clashed its jaws and made short rushes at us, and when we threw sticks it seized them and crunched them. We could not drive it away. Why it should have shown such truculence and heedlessness I cannot imagine, unless perhaps it was a female, with eggs near by. In another little pond a jacaré-tinga showed no less anger when another of my companions approached. It bellowed, opened its jaws, and lashed its tail. Yet these pond jacarés never actually molested even our dogs in the ponds, far less us on our horses.

This same day others of our party had an interesting experience with the creatures in another pond. One of them was Commander da Cunha (of the Brazilian Navy), a capital sportsman and delightful companion. They found a deepish pond a hundred yards or so long and thirty or forty across. It was tenanted by the small caymans and by capybaras—the largest known rodent, a huge aquatic guinea-pig, the size of a small sheep. It also swarmed with piranhas, the ravenous fish of which I have so often spoken. Undoubtedly the caymans were subsisting largely on these piranhas. But the tables were readily turned if any caymans were injured. When a capybara was shot and sank in the water, the piranhas at once attacked it, and had eaten half the carcass ten minutes later. But much more extraordinary was the fact that when a cayman about five feet long was wounded the piranhas attacked and tore it, and actually drove it out on the bank to face its human foes. The fish first attacked the wound; then, as the blood maddened them, they attacked all the soft parts, their terrible teeth cutting out chunks of tough hide and flesh. Evidently they did not molest either cayman or capybara while it was unwounded; but blood excited them to frenzy. Their habits are in some ways inexplicable. We saw men frequently bathing unmolested; but there are places where this is never safe, and in any place if a school of the fish appear swimmers are in danger; and a wounded man or beast is in deadly peril if piranhas are in the neighborhood. Ordinarily it appears that an unwounded man is attacked only by accident. Such accidents are rare; but they happen with sufficient frequency to justify much caution in entering water where piranhas abound.

We frequently came across ponds tenanted by numbers of capybaras. The huge, pig-like rodents are said to be shy elsewhere. Here they were tame. The water was their home and refuge. They usually went ashore to feed on the grass, and made well-beaten trails in the marsh immediately around the water; but they must have travelled these at night, for we never saw them more than a few feet away from the water in the daytime. Even at midday we often came on them standing beside a bayou or pond. The dogs would rush wildly at such a standing beast, which would wait until they were only a few yards off and then dash into and under the water. The dogs would also run full tilt into the water, and it was then really funny to see their surprise and disappointment at the sudden and complete disappearance of their quarry. Often a capybara would stand or sit on its haunches in the water, with only its blunt, short-eared head above the surface, quite heedless of our presence. But if alarmed it would dive, for capybaras swim with equal facility on or below the surface; and if they wish to hide they rise gently among the rushes or water-lily leaves with only their nostrils exposed. In these waters the capybaras and small caymans paid no attention to one another, swimming and resting in close proximity. They both had the same enemy, the jaguar. The capybara is a game animal only in the sense that a hare or rabbit is. The flesh is good to eat, and its amphibious habits and queer nature and surroundings make it interesting. In some of the ponds the water had about gone, and the capybaras had become for the time being beasts of the marsh and the mud; although they could always find little slimy pools, under a mass of water-lilies, in which to lie and hide.

Our whole stay on this ranch was delightful. On the long rides we always saw something of interest, and often it was something entirely new to us. Early one morning we came across two armadillos—the big, nine-banded armadillo. We were riding with the pack through a dry, sandy pasture country, dotted with clumps of palms, round the trunks of which grew a dense jungle of thorns and Spanish bayonets. The armadillos were feeding in an open space between two of these jungle clumps, which were about a hundred yards apart. One was on all fours; the other was in a squatting position, with its fore legs off the ground. Their long ears were very prominent. The dogs raced at them. I had always supposed that armadillos merely shuffled along, and curled up for protection when menaced; and I was almost as surprised as if I had seen a turtle gallop when these two armadillos bounded off at a run, going as fast as rabbits. One headed back for the nearest patch of jungle, which it reached. The other ran at full speed—and ran really fast, too—until it nearly reached the other patch, a hundred yards distant, the dogs in full cry immediately behind it. Then it suddenly changed its mind, wheeled in its tracks, and came back like a bullet right through the pack. Dog after dog tried to seize it or stop it and turned to pursue it; but its wedge-shaped snout and armored body, joined to the speed at which it was galloping, enabled it to drive straight ahead through its pursuers, not one of which could halt it or grasp it, and it reached in safety its thorny haven of refuge. It had run at speed about a hundred and fifty yards. I was much impressed by this unexpected exhibition; evidently this species of armadillo only curls up as a last resort, and ordinarily trusts to its speed, and to the protection its build and its armor give it while running, in order to reach its burrow or other place of safety. Twice, while laying railway tracks near São Paulo, Kermit had accidentally dug up armadillos with a steam-shovel.

There were big ant-hills, some of them of huge dimen-

Nine-banded armadillo

Capybaras

Collared peccary

From photographs by Edwin R. Sanborn

sions, scattered through the country. Sometimes they were built against the stems of trees. We did not here come across any of the poisonous or biting ants which, when sufficiently numerous, render certain districts uninhabitable. They are ordinarily not very numerous. Those of them that march in large bodies kill nestling birds, and at once destroy any big animal unable to get out of their way. It has been suggested that nestlings in their nests are in some way immune from the attack of these ants. The experiments of our naturalists tended to show that this was not the case. They plundered any nest they came across and could get at.

Once we saw a small herd of peccaries, one a sow followed by three little pigs—they are said to have only two young, but we saw three, although of course it is possible one belonged to another sow. The herd galloped into a mass of thorny cover the hounds could not penetrate; and when they were in safety we heard them utter, from the depths of the jungle, a curious moaning sound.

On one ride we passed a clump of palms which were fairly ablaze with bird color. There were magnificent hyacinth macaws; green parrots with red splashes; toucans with varied plumage, black, white, red, yellow; green jacmars; flaming orioles and both blue and dark-red tanagers. It was an extraordinary collection. All were noisy. Perhaps there was a snake that had drawn them by its presence; but we could find no snake. The assembly dispersed as we rode up; the huge blue macaws departed in pairs, uttering their hoarse "ar-rah-h, ar-rah-h." It has been said that parrots in the wilderness are only noisy on the wing. They are certainly noisy on the wing; and those that we saw were quiet while they were feeding; but ordinarily when they were perched among the branches, and especially when, as in the case of the little parakeets near the house, they were gathering materials for nest-building, they were just as noisy as while flying.

The water-birds were always a delight. We shot merely the two or three specimens the naturalists needed for the museum. I killed a wood-ibis on the wing with the handy little Springfield, and then lost all the credit I had thus gained by a series of inexcusable misses, at long range, before I finally killed a jabiru. Kermit shot a jabiru with the Lüger automatic. The great, splendid birds, standing about as tall as a man, show fight when wounded, and advance against their assailants, clattering their formidable bills. One day we found the nest of a jabiru in a mighty fig-tree, on the edge of a patch of jungle. It was a big platform of sticks, placed on a horizontal branch. There were four half-grown young standing on it. We passed it in the morning, when both parents were also perched alongside; the sky was then overcast, and it was not possible to photograph it with the small camera. In the early afternoon when we again passed it the sun was out, and we tried to get photographs. Only one parent bird was present at this time. It showed no fear. I noticed that, as it stood on a branch near the nest, its bill was slightly open. It was very hot, and I suppose it had opened its bill just as a hen opens her bill in hot weather. As we rode away the old bird and the four young birds were standing motionless, and with gliding flight the other old bird was returning to the nest. It is hard to give an adequate idea of the wealth of bird life in these marshes.

A naturalist could with the utmost advantage spend six months on such a ranch as that we visited. He would have to do some collecting, but only a little. Exhaustive observation in the field is what is now most needed. Most of this wonderful and harmless bird life should be protected by law; and the mammals should receive reasonable protection. The books now most needed are those dealing with the life-histories of wild creatures.

Near the ranch-house, walking familiarly among the cattle, we saw the big, deep-billed Ani blackbirds. They feed on the insects disturbed by the hoofs of the cattle, and often cling to them and pick off the ticks. It was the end of the nesting season, and we did not find their curious communal nests, in which half a dozen females lay their eggs indiscriminately. The common ibises in the ponds near by—which usually went in pairs, instead of in flocks like the wood-ibis—were very tame, and so were the night herons and all the small herons. In flying, the ibises and storks stretch the neck straight in front of them. The jabiru—a splendid bird on the wing—also stretches his neck out in front, but there appears to be a slight downward curve at the base of the neck, which may be due merely to the craw. The big slender herons, on the contrary, bend the long neck back in a beautiful curve, so that the head is nearly between the shoulders. One day I saw what I at first thought was a small yellow-bellied kingfisher hovering over a pond, and finally plunging down to the surface of the water after a school of tiny young fish; but it proved to be a bien-te-ví king-bird. Curved-bill wood-hewers, birds the size and somewhat the coloration of veeries, but with long, slender sickle-bills, were common in the little garden back of the house; their habits were those of creepers, and they scrambled with agility up, along, and under the trunks and branches, and along the posts and rails of the fence, thrusting the bill into crevices for insects. The oven-birds, which had the carriage and somewhat the look of wood-thrushes, I am sure would prove delightful friends on a close acquaintance; they are very individual, not only in the extraordinary domed mud nests they build, but in all their ways, in their bright alertness, their interest in and curiosity about whatever goes on, their rather jerky quickness of movement, and their loud and varied calls. With a little encouragement they become tame and familiar. The parakeets were too noisy, but otherwise were most attractive little birds, as they flew to and fro and scrambled about in the top of the palm behind the house. There was one showy kind of king-bird or tyrant flycatcher, lustrous black with a white head.

One afternoon several score cattle were driven into a big square corral near the house, in order to brand the calves and a number of unbranded yearlings and two-year-olds. A special element of excitement was added by the presence of a dozen big bulls which were to be turned into draught-oxen. The agility, nerve, and prowess of the ranch workmen, the herders or gauchos, were noteworthy. The dark-skinned men were obviously mainly of Indian and negro descent, although some of them also showed a strong strain of white blood. They wore the usual shirt, trousers, and fringed leather apron, with jim-crow hats. Their bare feet must have been literally as tough as horn; for when one of them roped a big bull he would brace himself, bending back until he was almost sitting down and digging his

The entire party on the way back to the ranch

From a photograph by Harper

heels into the ground, and the galloping beast would be stopped short and whirled completely round when the rope tautened. The maddened bulls, and an occasional steer or cow, charged again and again with furious wrath; but two or three ropes would settle on the doomed beast, and down it would go; and when it was released and rose and charged once more, with greater fury than ever, the men, shouting with laughter, would leap up the sides of the heavy stockade.

We stayed at the ranch until a couple of days before Christmas. Hitherto the weather had been lovely. The night before we left there was a torrential tropic downpour. It was not unexpected, for we had been told that the rainy season was overdue. The following forenoon the baggage started, in a couple of two-wheeled ox-carts, for the landing where the steamboat awaited us. Each cart was drawn by eight oxen. The huge wheels were over seven feet high. Early in the afternoon we followed on horseback, and overtook the carts as darkness fell, just before we reached the landing on the river's bank. The last few miles, after the final reaches of higher, tree-clad ground had been passed, were across a level plain of low ground on which the water stood, sometimes only up to the ankles of a man on foot, sometimes as high as his waist. Directly in front of us, many leagues distant, rose the bold mountains that lie west of Corumbá. Behind them the sun was setting and kindled the overcast heavens with lurid splendor. Then the last rose tints faded from the sky; the horses plodded wearily through the water; on every side stretched the marsh, vast, lonely, desolate in the gray of the half-light. We overtook the ox-carts. The cattle strained in the yokes; the drivers wading alongside cracked their whips and uttered strange cries; the carts rocked and swayed as the huge wheels churned through the mud and water. As the last light faded we reached the small patches of dry land at the landing, where the flat-bottomed side-wheel steamboat was moored to the bank. The tired horses and oxen were turned loose to graze. Water stood in the corrals, but the open shed was on dry ground. Under it the half-clad, wild-looking ox-drivers and horse-herders slung their hammocks; and close by they lit a fire and roasted, or scorched, slabs and legs of mutton, spitted on sticks and propped above the smouldering flame.

Next morning, with real regret, we waved good-by to our dusky attendants, as they stood on the bank, grouped around a little fire, beside the big, empty ox-carts. A dozen miles down-stream a rowboat fitted for a spritsail put off from the bank. The owner, a countryman from a small ranch, asked for a tow to Corumbá, which we gave. He had with him in the boat his comely brown wife—who was smoking a very large cigar—their two children, a young man, and a couple of trunks and various other belongings. On Christmas eve we reached Corumbá, and rejoined the other members of the expedition.

CHAPTER IV

THE HEADWATERS OF THE PARAGUAY

At Corumbá our entire party, and all their belongings, came aboard our good little river boat, the *Nyoac*. Christmas Day saw us making our way steadily up-stream against the strong current, and between the green and beautiful banks of the upper Paraguay. The shallow little steamer was jammed with men, dogs, rifles, partially cured skins, boxes of provisions, ammunition, tools, and photographic supplies, bags containing tents, cots, bedding, and clothes, saddles, hammocks, and the other necessaries for a trip through the "great wilderness," the "matto grosso" of western Brazil.

It was a brilliantly clear day, and, although of course in that latitude and at that season the heat was intense later on, it was cool and pleasant in the early morning. We sat on the forward deck, admiring the trees on the brink of the sheer river banks, the lush, rank grass of the marshes, and the many water-birds. The two pilots, one black and one white, stood at the wheel. Colonel Rondon read Thomas à Kempis. Kermit, Cherrie, and Miller squatted outside the railing on the deck over one paddle-wheel and put the final touches on the jaguar-skins. Fiala satisfied himself that the boxes and bags were in place. It was probable that hardship lay in the future; but the day was our own, and the day was pleasant. In the evening the after-deck, open all around, where we dined, was decorated with green boughs and rushes, and we drank the health of the President of the United States and of the President of Brazil.

Now and then we passed little ranches on the river's edge. This is a fertile land, pleasant to live in, and any settler who is willing to work can earn his living. There are mines; there is water-power; there is abundance of rich soil. The country will soon be opened by rail. It offers a fine field for immigration and for agricultural, mining, and business development; and it has a great future.

Cherrie and Miller had secured a little owl a month before in the Chaco, and it was travelling with them in a basket. It was a dear little bird, very tame and affectionate. It liked to be handled and petted; and when Miller, its especial protector, came into the cabin, it would make queer little noises as a signal that it wished to be taken up and perched on his hand. Cherrie and Miller had trapped many mammals. Among them was a tayra weasel, whitish above and black below, as big and bloodthirsty as a fisher-martin; and a tiny opossum no bigger than a mouse. They had taken four species of opossum, but they had not found the curious water-opossum which they had obtained on the rivers flowing into the Caribbean Sea. This opossum, which is black and white, swims in the streams like a muskrat or otter, catching fish and living in burrows which open under water. Miller and Cherrie were puzzled to know why the young throve, leading such an existence of constant immersion; one of them once found a female swimming and diving freely with four quite well-grown young in her pouch.

We saw on the banks screamers—big, crested waders of

archaic type, with spurred wings, rather short bills, and no especial affinities with other modern birds. In one meadow by a pond we saw three marsh-deer, a buck and two does. They stared at us, with their thickly haired tails raised on end. These tails are black underneath, instead of white as in our whitetail deer. One of the vagaries of the ultraconcealing-colorationists has been to uphold the (incidentally quite preposterous) theory that the tail of our deer is colored white beneath so as to harmonize with the sky and thereby mislead the cougar or wolf at the critical moment when it makes its spring; but this marsh-deer shows a black instead of a white flag, and yet has just as much need of protection from its enemies, the jaguar and the cougar. In South America concealing coloration plays no more part in the lives of the adult deer, the tamanduá, the tapir, the peccary, the jaguar, and the puma than it plays in Africa in the lives of such animals as the zebra, the sable antelope, the wildebeeste, the lion, and the hunting hyena.

Next day we spent ascending the São Lourenço. It was narrower than the Paraguay, naturally, and the swirling brown current was, if anything, more rapid. The strange tropical trees, standing densely on the banks, were matted together by long bush ropes—lianas, or vines, some very slender and very long. Sometimes we saw brilliant red or blue flowers, or masses of scarlet berries on a queer palm-like tree, or an array of great white blossoms on a much larger tree. In a lagoon bordered by the taquará bamboo a school of big otters were playing; when they came to the surface, they opened their mouths like seals, and made a loud hissing noise. The crested screamers, dark gray and as large as turkeys, perched on the very topmost branches of the tallest trees. Hyacinth macaws screamed harshly as they flew across the river. Among the trees was the guan, another peculiar bird as big as a big grouse, and with certain habits of the wood-grouse, but not akin to any northern game-bird. The windpipe of the male is very long, extending down to the end of the breast-bone, and the bird utters queer guttural screams. A dead cayman floated down-stream, with a black vulture devouring it. Capybaras stood or squatted on the banks; sometimes they stared stupidly at us; sometimes they plunged into the river at our approach. At long intervals we passed little clearings. In each stood a house of palm-logs, with steeply pitched roof of palm thatch; and near by were patches of corn and mandioc. The dusky owner, and perhaps his family, came out on the bank to watch us as we passed. It was a hot day—the thermometer on the deck in the shade stood at nearly 100 degrees Fahrenheit. Biting flies came aboard even when we were in midstream.

Next day we were ascending the Cuyabá River. It had begun raining in the night, and the heavy downpour continued throughout the forenoon. In the morning we halted at a big cattle-ranch to get fresh milk and beef. There were various houses, sheds, and corrals near the river's edge, and fifty or sixty milch cows were gathered in one corral. Spurred plover, or lapwings, strolled familiarly among the hens. Parakeets and red-headed tanagers lit in the trees over our heads. A kind of primitive house-boat was moored at the bank. A woman was cooking breakfast over a little stove at one end. The crew were ashore. The boat was one of those which are really stores, and which travel up and down these rivers, laden with what the natives most need, and stopping wherever there is a ranch. They are the only stores which many of the country-dwellers see from year's end to year's end. They float down-stream, and up-stream are poled by their crew, or now and then get a tow from a steamer. This one had a house with a tin roof; others bear houses with thatched roofs, or with roofs made of hides. The river wound through vast marshes broken by belts of woodland.

Always the two naturalists had something of interest to tell of their past experience, suggested by some bird or beast we came across. Black and golden orioles, slightly crested, of two different species were found along the river; they nest in colonies, and often we passed such colonies, the long pendulous nests hanging from the boughs of trees directly over the water. Cherrie told us of finding such a colony built round a big wasp-nest, several feet in diameter. These wasps are venomous and irritable, and few foes would dare venture near bird's-nests that were under such formidable shelter; but the birds themselves were entirely unafraid, and obviously were not in any danger of disagreement with their dangerous protectors. We saw a dark ibis flying across the bow of the boat, uttering his deep, two-syllabled note. Miller told how on the Orinoco these ibises plunder the nests of the big river-turtles. They are very skilful in finding where the female turtle has laid her eggs, scratch them out of the sand, break the shells, and suck the contents.

It was astonishing to find so few mosquitoes on these marshes. They did not in any way compare as pests with the mosquitoes on the lower Mississippi, the New Jersey coast, the Red River of the North, or the Kootenay. Back in the forest near Corumbá the naturalists had found them very bad indeed. Cherrie had spent two or three days on a mountain-top which was bare of forest; he had thought there would be few mosquitoes, but the long grass harbored them (they often swarm in long grass and bush, even where there is no water), and at night they were such a torment that as soon as the sun set he had to go to bed under his mosquito-netting. Yet on the vast marshes they were not seriously troublesome in most places. I was informed that they were not in any way a bother on the grassy uplands, the high country north of Cuyabá, which from thence stretches eastward to the coastal region. It is at any rate certain that this inland region of Brazil, including the state of Matto Grosso, which we were traversing, is a healthy region, excellently adapted to settlement; railroads will speedily penetrate it, and then it will witness an astonishing development.

On the morning of the 28th we reached the home buildings of the great São João *fazenda*, the ranch of Senhor João da Costa Marques. Our host himself, and his son, Dom João the younger, who was state secretary of agriculture, and the latter's charming wife, and the president of Matto Grosso, and several other ladies and gentlemen, had come down the river to greet us, from the city of Cuyabá, several hundred miles farther up-stream. As usual, we were treated with whole-hearted and generous hospitality. Some miles below the ranch-house the party met us, on a stern-wheel steamboat and a launch, both decked with many flags. The handsome white ranch-house stood only a few rods back from the river's brink, in a grassy opening dotted with those noble trees, the royal palms. Other trees, buildings of all kinds, flower-gardens, vegetable-gardens, fields, corrals, and enclosures with high white walls stood near the house. A detachment of soldiers or state police, with a band, were in front of the house, and two flagpoles, one with the Brazilian flag already hoisted. The American flag was run up on the other as I stepped ashore, while the band played the national anthems of the two countries. The house held much comfort; and the comfort was all the more appreciated because even indoors the thermometer stood at 97° F. In the late afternoon heavy rain fell, and cooled the air. We were riding at the time. Around the house the birds were tame: the parrots and parakeets crowded and chattered in the tree tops; jacanas played in the wet ground just back of the garden; ibises and screamers called loudly in the swamps a little distance off.

Until we came actually in sight of this great ranch-house we had been passing through a hot, fertile, pleasant wilderness, where the few small palm-roofed houses, each in its little patch of sugar-cane, corn, and mandioc, stood very many miles apart. One of these little houses stood on an old Indian mound, exactly like the mounds which form the only hillocks along the lower Mississippi, and which are also of Indian origin. These occasional Indian mounds, made ages ago, are the highest bits of ground in the immense swamps of the upper Paraguay region. There are still Indian tribes in this neighborhood. We passed an Indian fishing village on the edge of the river, with huts, scaffoldings for drying the fish, hammocks, and rude tables. They cultivated patches of bananas and sugar-cane. Out in a shallow place in the river was a scaffolding on which the Indians stood to spear fish. The Indians were friendly, peaceable souls, for the most part dressed like the poorer classes among the Brazilians.

Next morning there was to have been a great *rodeó*, or round-up, and we determined to have a hunt first, as there were still several kinds of beasts of the chase, notably tapirs and peccaries, of which the naturalists desired specimens. Dom João, our host, and his son accompanied us. Theirs is a noteworthy family. Born in Matto Grosso, in the tropics, our host had the look of a northerner and, although a grandfather, he possessed an abounding vigor and energy such as very few men of any climate or surroundings do possess. All of his sons are doing well. The son who was with us was a stalwart, powerful man, a pleasant companion, an able public servant, a finished horseman, and a skilled hunter. He carried a sharp spear, not a rifle, for in Matto Grosso it is the custom in hunting the jaguar for riflemen and spearmen to go in at him together when he turns at bay, the spearman holding him off if the first shot fails to stop him, so that another shot can be put in. Altogether, our host and his son reminded one of the best type of American ranchmen and planters, of those planters and ranchmen who are adepts in bold and manly field sports, who are capital men of business, and who also often supply to the state skilled and faithful public servants. The hospitality the father and son extended to us was patriarchal: neither, for instance, would sit at table with their guests at the beginning of the formal meals; instead they exercised a close personal supervision over the feast. Our charming hostess, however, sat at the head of the table.

An Indian village

We passed an Indian fishing village on the edge of the river, with huts, scaffoldings for drying the fish, hammocks, and rude tables

From a photograph by Harper

At six in the morning we started, all of us on fine horses. The day was lowering and overcast. A dozen dogs were with us, but only one or two were worth anything. Three or four ordinary countrymen, the ranch hands, or *vaqueiros*, accompanied us; they were mainly of Indian blood, and would have been called peons, or *caboclos*, in other parts of Brazil, but here were always spoken to and of as "camaradas." They were, of course, chosen from among the men who were hunters, and each carried his long, rather heavy and clumsy jaguar-spear. In front rode our vigorous host and his strapping son, the latter also carrying a jaguar-spear. The bridles and saddles of the big ranchmen and of the gentlefolk generally were handsome and were elaborately ornamented with silver. The stirrups, for instance, were not only of silver, but contained so much extra metal in ornamented bars and rings that they would have been awkward for less-practised riders. Indeed, as it was, they were adapted only for the tips of boots with long, pointed toes, and were impossible for our feet; our hosts' stirrups were long, narrow silver slippers. The camaradas, on the other hand, had jim-crow saddles and bridles, and rusty little iron stirrups into which they thrust their naked toes. But all, gentry and commonalty alike, rode equally well and with the same skill and fearlessness. To see our hosts gallop at headlong speed over any kind of country toward the sound of the dogs with their quarry at bay, or to see them handle their horses in a morass, was a pleasure. It was equally a pleasure to see a camarada carrying his heavy spear, leading a hound in a leash, and using his machete to cut his way through the tangled vine-ropes of a jungle, all at the same time and all without the slightest reference to the plunges, and the odd and exceedingly jerky behavior, of his wild, half-broken horse—for on such a ranch most of the horses are apt to come in the categories of half-broken or else of broken-down. One dusky tatterdemalion wore a pair of boots from which he had removed the soles, his bare, spur-clad feet projecting from beneath the uppers. He was on a little devil of a stallion, which he rode blindfold for a couple of miles, and there was a regular circus when he removed the bandage; but evidently it never occurred to him that the animal was hardly a comfortable riding-horse for a man going out hunting and encumbered with a spear, a machete, and other belongings.

The eight hours that we were out we spent chiefly in splashing across the marshes, with excursions now and then into vine-tangled belts and clumps of timber. Some of the bayous we had to cross were uncomfortably boggy. We had to lead the horses through one, wading ahead of them; and even so two of them mired down, and their saddles had to be taken off before they could be gotten out. Among the marsh plants were fields and strips of the great caeté rush. These caeté flags towered above the other and lesser marsh plants. They were higher than the heads of the horsemen. Their two or three huge banana-like leaves stood straight up on end. The large brilliant flowers—orange, red, and yellow—were joined into a singularly shaped and solid string or cluster. Humming-birds buzzed round these flowers; one species, the sickle-billed hummer, has its bill especially adapted for use in these queerly shaped blossoms and gets its food only from them, never appearing around any other plant.

The birds were tame, even those striking and beautiful

birds which under man's persecution are so apt to become scarce and shy. The huge jabiru storks, stalking through the water with stately dignity, sometimes refused to fly until we were only a hundred yards off; one of them flew over our heads at a distance of thirty or forty yards. The screamers, crying *curu-curu*, and the ibises, wailing dolefully, came even closer. The wonderful hyacinth macaws, in twos and threes, accompanied us at times for several hundred yards, hovering over our heads and uttering their rasping screams. In one wood we came on the black howler monkey. The place smelt almost like a menagerie. Not watching with sufficient care I brushed against a sapling on which the venomous fire-ants swarmed. They burnt the skin like red-hot cinders, and left little sores. More than once in the drier parts of the marsh we met small caymans making their way from one pool to another. My horse stepped over one before I saw it. The dead carcasses of others showed that on their wanderings they had encountered jaguars or human foes.

We had been out about three hours when one of the dogs gave tongue in a large belt of woodland and jungle to the left of our line of march through the marsh. The other dogs ran to the sound, and after a while the long barking told that the thing, whatever it was, was at bay or else in some refuge. We made our way toward the place on foot. The dogs were baying excitedly at the mouth of a huge hollow log, and very short examination showed us that there were two peccaries within, doubtless a boar and sow. However, just at this moment the peccaries bolted from an unsuspected opening at the other end of the log, dove into the tangle, and instantly disappeared with the hounds in full cry after them. It was twenty minutes later before we again heard the pack baying. With much difficulty, and by the incessant swinging of the machetes, we opened a trail through the network of vines and branches. This time there was only one peccary, the boar. He was at bay in a half-hollow stump. The dogs were about his head, raving with excitement, and it was not possible to use the rifle; so I borrowed the spear of Dom João the younger, and killed the fierce little boar therewith.

This was an animal akin to our collared peccary, smaller and less fierce than its white-jawed kinsfolk. It is a valiant and truculent little beast, nevertheless, and if given the chance will bite a piece the size of a teacup out of either man or dog. It is found singly or in small parties, feeds on roots, fruits, grass, and delights to make its home in hollow logs. If taken young it makes an affectionate and entertaining pet. When the two were in the hollow log we heard them utter a kind of moaning, or menacing, grunt, long drawn.

An hour or two afterward we unexpectedly struck the fresh tracks of two jaguars and at once loosed the dogs, who tore off yelling, on the line of the scent. Unfortunately, just at this moment the clouds burst and a deluge of rain drove in our faces. So heavy was the downpour that the dogs lost the trail and we lost the dogs. We found them again only owing to one of our *caboclos;* an Indian with a queer Mongolian face, and no brain at all that I could discover, apart from his special dealings with wild creatures, cattle, and horses. He rode in a huddle of rags; but nothing escaped his eyes, and he rode anything anywhere. The downpour continued so heavily that we

Wood ibis

From a photograph by Elwin R. Sanborn

South American jabiru

From a photograph by Elwin R. Sanborn

Sariema

From a photograph by Miller

knew the *rodeó* had been abandoned, and we turned our faces for the long, dripping, splashing ride homeward. Through the gusts of driving rain we could hardly see the way. Once the rain lightened, and half a mile away the sunshine gleamed through a rift in the leaden cloud-mass. Suddenly in this rift of shimmering brightness there appeared a flock of beautiful white egrets. With strong, graceful wing-beats the birds urged their flight, their plumage flashing in the sun. They then crossed the rift and were swallowed in the gray gloom of the day.

On the marsh the dogs several times roused capybaras. Where there were no ponds of sufficient size the capybaras sought refuge in flight through the tangled marsh. They ran well. Kermit and Fiala went after one on foot, full-speed, for a mile and a half, with two hounds which then bayed it—literally bayed it, for the capybara fought with the courage of a gigantic woodchuck. If the pack overtook a capybara, they of course speedily finished it; but a single dog of our not very valorous outfit was not able to overmatch its shrill-squeaking opponent.

Near the ranch-house, about forty feet up in a big tree, was a jabiru's nest containing young jabirus. The young birds exercised themselves by walking solemnly round the edge of the nest and opening and shutting their wings. Their heads and necks were down-covered, instead of being naked like those of their parents. Fiala wished to take a moving-picture of them while thus engaged, and so, after arranging his machine, he asked Harper to rouse the young birds by throwing a stick up to the nest. He did so, whereupon one young jabiru hastily opened its wings in the desired fashion, at the same time seizing the stick in its bill!

It dropped it at once, with an air of comic disappointment, when it found that the stick was not edible.

There were many strange birds round about. Toucans were not uncommon. I have never seen any other bird take such grotesque and comic attitudes as the toucan. This day I saw one standing in the top of a tree with the big bill pointing straight into the air and the tail also cocked perpendicularly. The toucan is a born comedian. On the river and in the ponds we saw the finfoot, a bird with feet like a grebe and bill and tail like those of a darter, but, like so many South American birds, with no close affiliations among other species. The exceedingly rich bird fauna of South America contains many species which seem to be survivals from a very remote geologic past, whose kinsfolk have perished under the changed conditions of recent ages; and in the case of many, like the hoatzin and screamer, their like is not known elsewhere. Herons of many species swarmed in this neighborhood. The handsomest was the richly colored tiger bittern. Two other species were so unlike ordinary herons that I did not recognize them as herons at all until Cherrie told me what they were. One had a dark body, a white-speckled or ocellated neck, and a bill almost like that of an ibis. The other looked white, but was really mauve-colored, with black on the head. When perched on a tree it stood like an ibis; and instead of the measured wing-beats characteristic of a heron's flight, it flew with a quick, vigorous flapping of the wings. There were queer mammals, too, as well as birds. In the fields Miller trapped mice of a kind entirely new.

Next morning the sky was leaden, and a drenching

rain fell as we began our descent of the river. The rainy season had fairly begun. For our good fortune we were still where we had the cabins aboard the boat, and the ranch-house, in which to dry our clothes and soggy shoes; but in the intensely humid atmosphere, hot and steaming, they stayed wet a long time, and were still moist when we put them on again. Before we left the house where we had been treated with such courteous hospitality—the finest ranch-house in Matto Grosso, on a huge ranch where there are some sixty thousand head of horned cattle—the son of our host, Dom João the younger, the jaguar-hunter, presented me with two magnificent volumes on the palms of Brazil, the work of Doctor Barboso Rodriguez, onetime director of the Botanical Gardens at Rio Janeiro. The two folios were in a box of native cedar. No gift more appropriate, none that I would in the future value more as a reminder of my stay in Matto Grosso, could have been given me.

All that afternoon the rain continued. It was still pouring in torrents when we left the Cuyabá for the São Lourenço and steamed up the latter a few miles before anchoring; Dom João the younger had accompanied us in his launch. The little river steamer was of very open build, as is necessary in such a hot climate; and to keep things dry necessitated also keeping the atmosphere stifling. The German taxidermist who was with Colonel Rondon's party, Reinisch, a very good fellow from Vienna, sat on a stool, alternately drenched with rain and sweltering with heat, and muttered to himself: "Ach, Schweinerei!"

Two small caymans, of the common species, with prominent eyes, were at the bank where we moored, and betrayed an astonishing and stupid tameness. Neither the size of the boat nor the commotion caused by the paddles in any way affected them. They lay inshore, not twenty feet from us, half out of water; they paid not the slightest heed to our presence, and only reluctantly left when repeatedly poked at, and after having been repeatedly hit with clods of mud and sticks; and even then one first crawled up on shore, to find out if thereby he could not rid himself of the annoyance we caused him.

Next morning it was still raining, but we set off on a hunt, anyway, going afoot. A couple of brown camaradas led the way, and Colonel Rondon, Dom João, Kermit, and I followed. The incessant downpour speedily wet us to the skin. We made our way slowly through the forest, the machetes playing right and left, up and down, at every step, for the trees were tangled in a network of vines and creepers. Some of the vines were as thick as a man's leg. Mosquitoes hummed about us, the venomous fire-ants stung us, the sharp spines of a small palm tore our hands—afterward some of the wounds festered. Hour after hour we thus walked on through the Brazilian forest. We saw monkeys, the common yellowish kind, a species of cebus; a couple were shot for the museum and the others raced off among the upper branches of the trees. Then we came on a party of coatis, which look like reddish, long-snouted, long-tailed, lanky raccoons. They were in the top of a big tree. One, when shot at and missed, bounced down to the ground, and ran off through the bushes; Kermit ran after it and secured it. He came back, to find us peering hopelessly up into the tree top, trying to place where the other coatis were. Kermit solved the difficulty by going up along some huge twisted lianas for forty or fifty feet and exploring the upper branches; whereupon down came three other coatis through the branches, one being caught by the dogs and the other two escaping. Coatis fight savagely with both teeth and claws. Miller told us that he once saw one of them kill a dog. They feed on all small mammals, birds, and reptiles, and even on some large ones; they kill iguanas; Cherrie saw a rattling chase through the trees, a coati following an iguana at full speed. We heard the rush of a couple of tapirs, as they broke away in the jungle in front of the dogs, and headed, according to their custom, for the river; but we never saw them. One of the party shot a bush deer—a very pretty, graceful creature, smaller than our whitetail deer, but kin to it and doubtless the southernmost representative of the whitetail group.

The whitetail deer—using the word to designate a group of deer which can either be called a subgenus with many species, or a widely spread species diverging into many varieties—is the only North American species which has spread down into and has outlying representatives in South America. It has been contended that the species has spread from South America northward. I do not think so; and the specimen thus obtained furnished a probable refutation of the theory. It was a buck, and had just shed its small antlers. The antlers are, therefore, shed at the same time as in the north, and it appears that they are grown at the same time as in the north. Yet this variety now dwells in the tropics south of the equator, where the spring, and the breeding season for most birds, comes at the time of the northern fall in September, October, and November. That the deer is an intrusive immigrant, and that it has not yet been in South America long enough to change its mating season in accordance with the climate, as the birds—geologically doubtless very old residents—have changed their breeding season, is rendered probable by the fact that it conforms so exactly in the time of its antler growth to the universal rule which obtains in the great arctogeal realm, where deer of many species abound and where the fossil forms show that they have long existed. The marsh-deer, which has diverged much further from the northern type than this bush deer (its horns show a likeness to those of a blacktail), often keeps its antlers until June or July, although it begins to grow them again in August; however, too much stress must not be laid on this fact, inasmuch as the wapiti and the cow caribou both keep their antlers until spring. The specialization of the marsh-deer, by the way, is further shown in its hoofs, which, thanks to its semiaquatic mode of life, have grown long, like those of such African swamp antelopes as the lechwe and situtunga.

Miller, when we presented the monkeys to him, told us that the females both of these monkeys and of the howlers themselves took care of the young, the males not assisting them, and moreover that when the young one was a male he had always found the mother keeping by herself, away from the old males. On the other hand, among the marmosets he found the fathers taking as much care of the young as the mothers; if the mother had twins, the father would usually carry one, and sometimes both, around with him.

After we had been out four hours our camaradas got

lost; three several times they travelled round in a complete circle; and we had to set them right with the compass. About noon the rain, which had been falling almost without interruption for forty-eight hours, let up, and in an hour or two the sun came out. We went back to the river, and found our rowboat. In it the hounds—a motley and rather worthless lot—and the rest of the party were ferried across to the opposite bank, while Colonel Rondon and I stayed in the boat, on the chance that a tapir might be roused and take to the river. However, no tapir was found; Kermit killed a collared peccary, and I shot a capybara representing a color-phase the naturalists wished.

Next morning, January 1, 1914, we were up at five and had a good New Year's Day breakfast of hardtack, ham, sardines, and coffee before setting out on an all-day's hunt on foot. I much feared that the pack was almost or quite worthless for jaguars, but there were two or three of the great spotted cats in the neighborhood and it seemed worth while to make a try for them, anyhow. After an hour or two we found the fresh tracks of two, and after them we went. Our party consisted of Colonel Rondon, Lieutenant Rogaciano—an excellent man, himself a native of Matto Grosso, of old Matto Grosso stock—two others of the party from the São João ranch, Kermit, and myself, together with four dark-skinned camaradas, cowhands from the same ranch. We soon found that the dogs would not by themselves follow the jaguar trail; nor would the camaradas, although they carried spears. Kermit was the one of our party who possessed the requisite speed, endurance, and eyesight, and accordingly he led. Two of the dogs would follow the track half a dozen yards ahead of him, but no farther; and two of the camaradas could just about keep up with him. For an hour we went through thick jungle, where the machetes were constantly at work. Then the trail struck off straight across the marshes, for jaguars swim and wade as freely as marsh-deer. It was a hard walk. The sun was out. We were drenched with sweat. We were torn by the spines of the innumerable clusters of small palms with thorns like needles. We were bitten by the hosts of fire-ants, and by the mosquitoes, which we scarcely noticed where the fire-ants were found, exactly as all dread of the latter vanished when we were menaced by the big red wasps, of which a dozen stings will disable a man, and if he is weak or in bad health will seriously menace his life. In the marsh we were continually wading, now up to our knees, now up to our hips. Twice we came to long bayous so deep that we had to swim them, holding our rifles above water in our right hands. The floating masses of marsh grass, and the slimy stems of the water-plants, doubled our work as we swam, cumbered by our clothing and boots and holding our rifles aloft. One result of the swim, by the way, was that my watch, a veteran of Cuba and Africa, came to an indignant halt. Then on we went, hampered by the weight of our drenched clothes while our soggy boots squelched as we walked. There was no breeze. In the undimmed sky the sun stood almost overhead. The heat beat on us in waves. By noon I could only go forward at a slow walk, and two of the party were worse off than I was. Kermit, with the dogs and two camaradas close behind him, disappeared across the marshes at a trot. At last, when he was out of sight, and it was obviously useless to follow him, the rest of us turned back toward the boat. The two exhausted members of the party gave out, and we left them under a tree. Colonel Rondon and Lieutenant Rogaciano were not much tired; I was somewhat tired, but was perfectly able to go for several hours more if I did not try to go too fast; and we three walked on to the river, reaching it about half past four, after eleven hours' stiff walking with nothing to eat. We were soon on the boat. A relief party went back for the two men under the tree, and soon after it reached them Kermit also turned up with his hounds and his camaradas trailing wearily behind him. He had followed the jaguar trail until the dogs were so tired that even after he had bathed them, and then held their noses in the fresh footprints, they would pay no heed to the scent. A hunter of scientific tastes, a hunter-naturalist, or even an outdoors naturalist, or faunal naturalist interested in big mammals, with a pack of hounds such as those with which Paul Rainey hunted lion and leopard in Africa, or such a pack as the packs of Johnny Goff and Jake Borah with which I hunted cougar, lynx, and bear in the Rockies, or such packs as those of the Mississippi and Louisiana planters with whom I have hunted bear, wildcat, and deer in the cane-brakes of the lower Mississippi, would not only enjoy fine hunting in these vast marshes of the upper Paraguay, but would also do work of real scientific value as regards all the big cats.

Only a limited number of the naturalists who have worked in the tropics have had any experience with the big beasts whose life-histories possess such peculiar interest. Of all the biologists who have seriously studied the South American fauna on the ground, Bates probably rendered most service; but he hardly seems even to have seen the animals with which the hunter is fairly familiar. His interests, and those of the other biologists of his kind, lay in other directions. In consequence, in treating of the life-histories of the very interesting big game, we have been largely forced to rely either on native report, in which acutely accurate observation is invariably mixed with wild fable, or else on the chance remarks of travellers or mere sportsmen, who had not the training to make them understand even what it was desirable to observe. Nowadays there is a growing proportion of big-game hunters, of sportsmen, who are of the Schilling, Selous, and Shiras type. These men do work of capital value for science. The mere big-game butcher is tending to disappear as a type. On the other hand, the big-game hunter who is a good observer, a good field naturalist, occupies at present a more important position than ever before, and it is now recognized that he can do work which the closet naturalist cannot do. The big-game hunter of this type and the outdoors, faunal naturalist, the student of the life-histories of big mammals, have open to them in South America a wonderful field in which to work.

The fire-ants, of which I have above spoken, are generally found on a species of small tree or sapling, with a greenish trunk. They bend the whole body as they bite, the tail and head being thrust downward. A few seconds after the bite the poison causes considerable pain; later it may make a tiny festering sore. There is certainly the most extraordinary diversity in the traits by which nature achieves the perpetuation of species. Among the warrior and predaceous insects the prowess is in some cases of such type as to render the possessor practically immune from danger. In other cases the condition of its exercise may normally be the sacrifice of the life of the possessor. There are wasps that prey on formidable fighting spiders, which yet instinctively so handle themselves that the prey practically never succeeds in either defending itself or retaliating, being captured and paralyzed with unerring efficiency and with entire security to the wasp. The wasp's safety is absolute. On the other hand, these fighting ants, including the soldiers even among the termites, are frantically eager for a success which generally means their annihilation; the condition of their efficiency is absolute indifference to their own security. Probably the majority of the ants that actually lay hold on a foe suffer death in consequence; certainly they not merely run the risk of but eagerly invite death.

The following day we descended the São Lourenço to its junction with the Paraguay, and once more began the ascent of the latter. At one cattle-ranch where we stopped, the troupials, or big black and yellow orioles, had built a large colony of their nests on a dead tree near the primitive little ranch-house. The birds were breeding; the old ones were feeding the young. In this neighborhood the naturalists found many birds that were new to them, including a tiny woodpecker no bigger than a ruby-crowned kinglet. They had collected two night monkeys—nocturnal monkeys, not as agile as the ordinary monkey; these two were found at dawn, having stayed out too late.

The early morning was always lovely on these rivers, and at that hour many birds and beasts were to be seen. One morning we saw a fine marsh buck, holding his head aloft as he stared at us, his red coat vivid against the green marsh. Another of these marsh-deer swam the river ahead of us; I shot at it as it landed, and ought to have got it, but did not. As always with these marsh-deer—and as with so many other deer—I was struck by the revealing or advertising quality of its red coloration; there was nothing in its normal surroundings with which this coloration harmonized; so far as it had any effect whatever it was always a revealing and not a concealing effect. When the animal fled the black of the erect tail was an additional revealing mark, although not of such startlingly advertising quality as the flag of the whitetail. The whitetail, in one of its forms, and with the ordinary whitetail custom of displaying the white flag as it runs, is found in the immediate neighborhood of the swamp-deer. It has the same foes. Evidently it is of no survival consequence whether the running deer displays a white or a black flag. Any competent observer of big game must be struck by the fact that in the great majority of the species the coloration is not concealing, and that in many it has a highly revealing quality. Moreover, if the spotted or striped young represent the ancestral coloration, and if, as seems probable, the spots and stripes have, on the whole, some slight concealing value, it is evident that in the life history of most of these large mammals, both among those that prey and those that are preyed on, concealing coloration has not been a survival factor; throughout the ages during which they have survived they have gradually lost whatever of concealing coloration they may once have had—if any—and have developed a coloration which under present conditions has no concealing and perhaps even has a revealing quality,

A jabiru's nest

The young birds exercised themselves by walking sedately round the edge of the nest

From a photograph by Harper

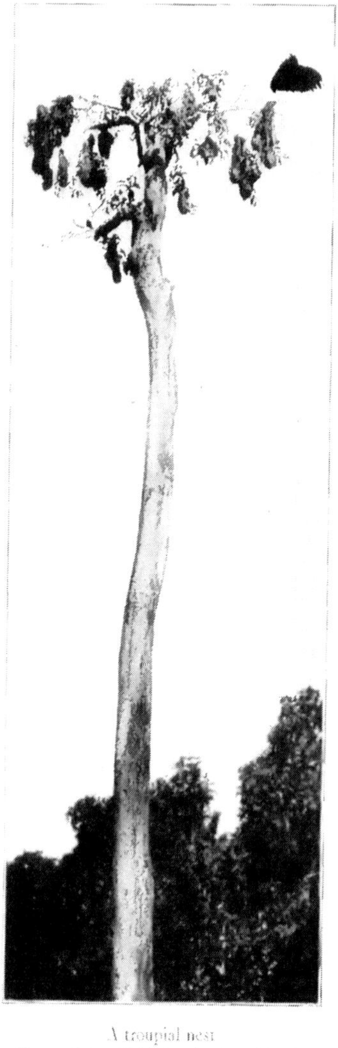

A troupial nest

The troupials, or big black and yellow orioles, had built a large colony of their nests on a dead tree

From a photograph by Kermit Roosevelt

and which in all probability never would have had a concealing value in any "environmental complex" in which the species as a whole lived during its ancestral development. Indeed, it seems astonishing, when one observes these big beasts—and big waders and other water-birds—in their native surroundings, to find how utterly nonharmful their often strikingly revealing coloration is. Evidently the various other survival factors, such as habit, and in many cases cover, etc., are of such overmastering importance that the coloration is generally of no consequence whatever, one way or the other, and is only very rarely a factor of any serious weight.

The junction of the São Lourenço and the Paraguay is a day's journey above Corumbá. From Corumbá there is a regular service by shallow steamers to Cuyabá, at the head of one fork, and to São Luis de Cáceres, at the head of the other. The steamers are not powerful and the voyage to each little city takes a week. There are other forks that are navigable. Above Cuyabá and Cáceres launches go up-stream for several days' journey, except during the dryest parts of the season. North of this marshy plain lies the highland, the Plan Alto, where the nights are cool and the climate healthy. But I wish emphatically to record my view that these marshy plains, although hot, are also healthy; and, moreover, the mosquitoes, in most places, are not in sufficient numbers to be a serious pest, although of course there must be nets for protection against them at night. The country is excellently suited for settlement, and offers a remarkable field for cattle-growing. Moreover, it is a paradise for water-birds and for many other kinds of birds, and for many mammals. It is literally an ideal place in which a field naturalist could spend six months or a year. It is readily accessible, it offers an almost virgin field for work, and the life would be healthy as well as delightfully attractive. The man should have a steam-launch. In it he could with comfort cover all parts of the country from south of Coimbra to north of Cuyabá and Cáceres. There would have to be a good deal of collecting (although nothing in the nature of butchery should be tolerated), for the region has only been superficially worked, especially as regards mammals. But if the man were only a collector he would leave undone the part of the work best worth doing. The region offers extraordinary opportunities for the study of the life-histories of birds which, because of their size, their beauty, or their habits, are of exceptional interest. All kinds of problems would be worked out. For example, on the morning of the 3d, as we were ascending the Paraguay, we again and again saw in the trees on the bank big nests of sticks, into and out of which parakeets were flying by the dozen. Some of them had straws or twigs in their bills. In some of the big globular nests we could make out several holes of exit or entrance. Apparently these parakeets were building or remodelling communal nests; but whether they had themselves built these nests, or had taken old nests and added to or modified them, we could not tell. There was so much of interest all along the banks that we were continually longing to stop and spend days where we were. Mixed flocks of scores of cormorants and darters covered certain trees, both at sunset and after sunrise. Although there was no deep forest, merely belts or fringes of trees along the river, or in patches back of it, we frequently saw mon-

Snake-birds and cormorants

Mixed flocks of scores of cormorants and darters covered certain trees, both at sunset and after sunrise

From photographs by Harper

keys in this riverine tree-fringe—active common monkeys and black howlers of more leisurely gait. We saw caymans and capybaras sitting socially near one another on the sand-banks. At night we heard the calling of large flights of tree-ducks. These were now the most common of all the ducks, although there were many muscovy ducks also. The evenings were pleasant and not hot, as we sat on the forward deck; there was a waxing moon. The screamers were among the most noticeable birds. They were noisy; they perched on the very tops of the trees, not down among the branches; and they were not shy. They should be carefully protected by law, for they readily become tame, and then come familiarly round the houses. From the steamer we now and then saw beautiful orchids in the trees on the river bank.

One afternoon we stopped at the home buildings or headquarters of one of the great outlying ranches of the Brazil Land and Cattle Company, the Farquahar syndicate, under the management of Murdo Mackenzie—than whom we have had in the United States no better citizen or more competent cattleman. On this ranch there are some seventy thousand head of stock. We were warmly greeted by McLean, the head of the ranch, and his assistant Ramsey, an old Texan friend. Among the other assistants, all equally cordial, were several Belgians and Frenchmen. The hands were Paraguayans and Brazilians, and a few Indians—a hard-bit set, each of whom always goes armed and knows how to use his arms, for there are constant collisions with cattle thieves from across the Bolivian border, and the ranch has to protect itself. These cowhands, *vaqueiros*, were of the type with which we were now familiar: dark-skinned, lean, hard-faced men, in slouch-hats, worn shirts and trousers, and fringed leather aprons, with heavy spurs on their bare feet. They are wonderful riders and ropers, and fear neither man nor beast. I noticed one Indian *vaqueiro* standing in exactly the attitude of a Shilluk of the White Nile, with the sole of one foot against the other leg, above the knee. This is a region with extraordinary possibilities of cattle-raising.

At this ranch there was a tannery; a slaughter-house; a cannery; a church; buildings of various kinds and all degrees of comfort for the thirty or forty families who made the place their headquarters; and the handsome, white, two-story big house, standing among lemon-trees and flamboyants on the river-brink. There were all kinds of pets around the house. The most fascinating was a wee, spotted fawn which loved being petted. Half a dozen curassows of different species strolled through the rooms; there were also parrots of several different species, and immediately outside the house four or five herons, with unclipped wings, which would let us come within a few feet and then fly gracefully off, shortly afterward returning to the same spot. They included big and little white egrets and also the mauve and pearl-colored heron, with a partially black head and many-colored bill, which flies with quick, repeated wing-flappings, instead of the usual slow heron wing-beats.

In the warehouse were scores of skins of jaguar, puma, ocelot, and jaguarundi, and one skin of the big, small-toothed red wolf. These were all brought in by the cow-hands and by friendly Indians, a price being put on each, as they destroyed the stock. The jaguars occasionally killed horses and full-grown cows, but not bulls. The pumas killed the calves. The others killed an occasional very young calf, but ordinarily only sheep, little pigs, and chickens. There was one black jaguar-skin; melanism is much more common among jaguars than pumas, although once Miller saw a black puma that had been killed by Indians. The patterns of the jaguar-skins, and even more of the ocelot-skins, showed wide variation, no two being alike. The pumas were for the most part bright red, but some were reddish gray, there being much the same dichromatism that I found among their Colorado kinsfolk. The jaguarundis were dark brownish gray. All these animals, the spotted jaguars and ocelots, the monochrome black jaguars, red pumas, and dark-gray jaguarundis, were killed in the same locality, with the same environment. A glance at the skins and a moment's serious thought would have been enough to show any sincere thinker that in these cats the coloration pattern, whether concealing or revealing, is of no consequence one way or the other as a survival factor. The spotted patterns conferred no benefit as compared with the nearly or quite monochrome blacks, reds, and dark grays. The bodily condition of the various beasts was equally good, showing that their success in life, that is, their ability to catch their prey, was unaffected by their several color schemes. Except white, there is no color so conspicuously advertising as black; yet the black jaguar had been a fine, well-fed, powerful beast. The spotted patterns in the forests, and perhaps even in the marshes which the jaguars so frequently traversed, are *probably* a shade less conspicuous than the monochrome red and gray, but the puma and jaguarundi are just as hard to see, and evidently find it just as easy to catch prey, as the jaguar and ocelot. The little fawn which we saw was spotted; the grown deer had lost the spots; if the spots do really help to conceal the wearer, it is evident that the deer has found the original concealing coloration of so little value that it has actually been lost in the course of the development of the species. When these big cats and the deer are considered, together with the dogs, tapirs, peccaries, capybaras, and big ant-eaters which live in the same environment, and when we also consider the difference between the young and the adult deer and tapirs (both of which when adult have substituted a complete or partial monochrome for the ancestral spots and streaks), it is evident that in the present life and in the ancestral development of the big mammals of South America coloration is not and has not been a survival factor; any pattern and any color may accompany the persistence and development of the qualities and attributes which are survival factors. Indeed, it seems hard to believe that in their ordinary environments such color schemes as the bright red of the marsh-deer, the black of the black jaguar, and the black with white stripes of the great tamanduá, are not positive detriments to the wearers. Yet such is evidently not the case. Evidently the other factors in species-survival are of such overwhelming importance that the coloration becomes negligible from this standpoint, whether it be concealing or revealing. The cats mould themselves to the ground as they crouch or crawl. They take advantage of the tiniest scrap of cover. They move with extraordinary stealth and patience. The other animals which try to sneak off in such manner as to escape observation approach more or less closely to the ideal which the cats most nearly realize. Wariness, sharp senses, the habit of being rigidly motionless when there is the least suspicion of danger, and ability to take advantage of cover, all count. On the bare, open, treeless plain, whether marsh, meadow, or upland, anything above the level of the grass is seen at once. A marsh-deer out in the open makes no effort to avoid observation; its concern is purely to see its foes in time to leave a dangerous neighborhood. The deer of the neighboring forest skulk and hide and lie still in dense cover to avoid being seen. The white-lipped peccaries make no effort to escape observation by being either noiseless or motionless; they trust for defence to their gregariousness and truculence. The collared peccary also trusts to its truculence, but seeks refuge in a hole where it can face any opponent with its formidable biting apparatus. As for the giant tamanduá, in spite of its fighting prowess I am wholly unable to understand how such a slow and clumsy beast has been able through the ages to exist and thrive surrounded by jaguars and pumas. Speaking generally, the animals that seek to escape observation trust primarily to smell to discover their foes or their prey, and see whatever moves and do not see whatever is motionless.

By the morning of January 5 we had left the marsh region. There were low hills here and there, and the land was covered with dense forest. From time to time we passed little clearings with palm-thatched houses. We were approaching Cáceres, where the easiest part of our trip would end. We had lived in much comfort on the little steamer. The food was plentiful and the cooking good. At night we slept on deck in cots or hammocks.

The mosquitoes were rarely troublesome, although in the daytime we were sometimes bothered by numbers of biting horse-flies. The bird life was wonderful. One of the characteristic sights we were always seeing was that of a number of heads and necks of cormorants and snake-birds, without any bodies, projecting above water, and disappearing as the steamer approached. Skimmers and thick-billed tern were plentiful here right in the heart of the continent. In addition to the spurred lapwing, characteristic and most interesting resident of most of South America, we found tiny red-legged plover which also breed and are at home in the tropics. The contrasts in habits between closely allied species are wonderful. Among the plovers and bay snipe there are species that live all the year round in almost the same places, in tropical and subtropical lands; and other related forms which wander over the whole earth, and spend nearly all their time, now in the arctic and cold temperate regions of the far north, now in the cold temperate regions of the south. These latter wide-wandering birds of the seashore and the river bank pass most of their lives in regions of almost perpetual sunlight. They spend the breeding season, the northern summer, in the land of the midnight sun, during the long arctic day. They then fly for endless distances down across the north temperate zone, across the equator, through the lands where the days and nights are always of equal length, into another hemisphere, and spend another summer of long days and long twilights in the far south, where the antarctic winds cool them, while their nesting home, at the other end of the world, is shrouded beneath the iron desolation of the polar night.

In the late afternoon of the 5th we reached the quaint old-fashioned little town of São Luis de Cáceres, on the outermost fringe of the settled region of the state of Matto Grosso, the last town we should see before reaching the villages of the Amazon. As we approached we passed half-clad black washerwomen on the river's edge. The men, with the local band, were gathered at the steeply sloping foot of the main street, where the steamer came to her moorings. Groups of women and girls, white and brown, watched us from the low bluff; their skirts and bodices were red, blue, green, of all colors. Sigg had gone ahead with much of the baggage; he met us in an improvised motor-boat, consisting of a dugout to the side of which he had clamped our Evinrude motor; he was giving several of the local citizens of prominence a ride, to their huge enjoyment. The streets of the little town were unpaved, with narrow brick sidewalks. The one-story houses were white or blue, with roofs of red tiles and window-shutters of latticed woodwork, come down from colonial days and tracing back through Christian and Moorish Portugal to a remote Arab ancestry. Pretty faces, some dark, some light, looked out from these windows; their mothers' mothers, for generations past, must thus have looked out of similar windows in the vanished colonial days. But now even here in Cáceres the spirit of the new Brazil is moving; a fine new government school has been started, and we met its principal, an earnest man doing excellent work, one of the many teachers who, during the last few years, have been brought to Matto Grosso from São Paulo, a centre of the new educational movement which will do so much for Brazil.

Father Zahm went to spend the night with some French Franciscan friars, capital fellows. I spent the night at the comfortable house of Lieutenant Lyra; a hot-weather house with thick walls, big doors, and an open patio bordered by a gallery. Lieutenant Lyra was to accompany us; he was an old companion of Colonel Rondon's explorations. We visited one or two of the stores to make some final purchases, and in the evening strolled through the dusky streets and under the trees of the plaza; the women and girls sat in groups in the doorways or at the windows, and here and there a stringed instrument tinkled in the darkness.

From Cáceres onward we were entering the scene of Colonel Rondon's explorations. For some eighteen years he was occupied in exploring and in opening telegraph-lines through the eastern or north-middle part of the great forest state, the wilderness state of the "matto grosso"—the "great wilderness," or, as Australians would call it, "the bush." Then, in 1907, he began to penetrate the unknown region lying to the north and west. He was the head of the exploring expeditions sent out by the Brazilian Government to traverse for the first time this unknown land; to map for the first time the courses of the rivers which from the same divide run into the upper portions of the Tapajos and the Madeira, two of the mighty affluents of the Amazon, and to build telegraph-lines across to the Madeira, where a line of Brazilian settlements, connected by steamboat lines and a railroad, again occurs. Three times he penetrated into this absolutely unknown, Indian-haunted wilderness, being absent for a year or two at a time and suffering every imaginable hardship, before he made his way through to the Madeira and completed the telegraph-line across. The officers and men of the Brazilian Army and the civilian scientists who followed him shared the toil and the credit of the task. Some of his men died of beriberi; some were killed or wounded by the Indians; he himself almost died of fever; again and again his whole party was reduced almost to the last extremity by starvation, disease, hardship, and the over-exhaustion due to wearing fatigues. In dealing with the wild, naked savages he showed a combination of fearlessness, wariness, good judgment, and resolute patience and kindliness. The result was that they ultimately became his firm friends, guarded the telegraph-lines, and helped the few soldiers left at the isolated, widely separated little posts. He and his assistants explored, and mapped for the first time, the Juruena and the Gy-Paraná, two important affluents of the Tapajos and the Madeira respectively. The Tapajos and the Madeira, like the Orinoco and Rio Negro, have been highways of travel for a couple of centuries. The Madeira (as later the Tapajos) was the chief means of ingress, a century and a half ago, to the little Portuguese settlements of this far interior region of Brazil; one of these little towns, named Matto Grosso, being the original capital of the province. It has long been abandoned by the government, and practically so by its inhabitants, the ruins of palace, fortress, and church now rising amid the rank tropical luxuriance of the wild forest. The mouths of the main affluents of these highway rivers were as a rule well known. But in many cases nothing but the mouth was known. The river itself was not known, and it was placed on the map by guesswork. Colonel Rondon found, for example, that the course of the Gy-Paraná was put down on the map two degrees out of its proper place. He, with his party, was the first to find out its sources, the first to traverse its upper course, the first to map its length. He and his assistants performed a similar service for the Juruena, discovering the sources, discovering and descending some of the branches, and for the first time making a trustworthy map of the main river itself, until its junction with the Tapajos. Near the watershed between the Juruena and the Gy-Paraná he established his farthest station to the westward, named José Bonofacio, after one of the chief republican patriots of Brazil. A couple of days' march northwestward from this station, he in 1909 came across a part of the stream of a river running northward between the Gy-Paraná and the Juruena; he could only guess where it debouched, believing it to be into the Madeira, although it was possible that it entered the Gy-Paraná or Tapajos. The region through which it flows was unknown, no civilized man having ever penetrated it; and as all conjecture as to what the river was, as to its length, and as to its place of entering into some highway river, was mere guesswork, he had entered it on his sketch maps as the Rio da Dúvida, the River of Doubt. Among the officers of the Brazilian Army and the scientific civilians who have accompanied him there have been not only expert cartographers, photographers, and telegraphists, but astronomers, geologists, botanists, and zoologists. Their reports, published in excellent shape by the Brazilian Government, make an invaluable series of volumes, reflecting the highest credit on the explorers, and on the government itself. Colonel Rondon's own accounts of his explorations, of the Indian tribes he has visited, and of the beautiful and wonderful things he has seen, possess a peculiar interest.

CHAPTER V

UP THE RIVER OF TAPIRS

After leaving Cáceres we went up the Sepotuba, which in the local Indian dialect means River of Tapirs. This river is only navigable for boats of size when the water is high. It is a swift, fairly clear stream, rushing down from the Plan Alto, the high uplands, through the tropical lowland forest. On the right hand, or western bank, and here and there on the left bank, the forest is broken by natural pastures and meadows, and at one of these places, known as Porto Campo, sixty or seventy miles above the mouth, there is a good-sized cattle-ranch. Here we halted, because the launch, and the two pranchas—native trading-boats with houses on their decks—which it towed, could not carry our entire party and outfit. Accordingly most of the baggage and some of the party were sent ahead to where we were to meet our pack-train, at Tapirapoan. Meanwhile the rest of us made our first camp under tents at Porto Campo, to wait the return of the boats. The tents were placed in a line, with the tent of Colonel Rondon and the tent in which Kermit and I slept, in the middle, beside one another. In front of these two, on tall poles, stood the Brazilian and American flags; and at sunrise and sunset the flags were hoisted and hauled down while the trumpet sounded and all of us stood at attention. Camp was pitched beside the ranch buildings. In the trees near the tents grew wonderful violet orchids.

Many birds were around us; I saw some of them, and Cherrie and Miller many, many more. They ranged from party-colored macaws, green parrots, and big gregarious cuckoos down to a brilliant green-and-chestnut kingfisher, five and a quarter inches long, and a tiny orange-and-green manakin, smaller than any bird I have ever seen except a hummer. We also saw a bird that really was protectively colored; a kind of whippoorwill which even the sharp-eyed naturalists could only make out because it moved its head. We saw orange-bellied squirrels with showy orange tails. Lizards were common. We killed our first poisonous snake (the second we had seen), an evil lance-headed jararaca that was swimming the river. We also saw a black-and-orange harmless snake, nearly eight feet long, which we were told was akin to the mussurama; and various other snakes. One day while paddling in a canoe on the river, hoping that the dogs might drive a tapir to us, they drove into the water a couple of small bush deer instead. There was no point in shooting them; we caught them with ropes thrown over their heads; for the naturalists needed them as specimens, and all of us needed the meat. One of the men was stung by a single big red maribundi wasp. For twenty-four hours he was in great pain and incapacitated for work. In a lagoon two of the dogs had the tips of their tails bitten off by piranhas as they swam, and the ranch hands told us that in this lagoon one of their hounds had been torn to pieces and completely devoured by the ravenous fish. It was a further illustration of the uncertainty of temper and behavior of these ferocious little monsters. In other lagoons they had again and again left us and our dogs unmolested. They vary locally in aggressiveness just as sharks and crocodiles in different seas and rivers vary.

On the morning of January 9th we started out for a tapir-hunt. Tapirs are hunted with canoes, as they dwell in thick jungle and take to the water when hounds follow them. In this region there were extensive papyrus-swamps and big lagoons, back from the river, and often the tapirs fled to these for refuge, throwing off the hounds. In these places it was exceedingly difficult to get them; our best chance was to keep to the river in canoes, and paddle toward the spot in the direction of which the hounds, by the noise, seemed to be heading. We started in four canoes. Three of them were Indian dugouts, very low in the water. The fourth was our Canadian canoe, a beauty; light, safe, roomy, made of thin slats of wood and cement-covered canvas. Colonel Rondon, Fiala with his camera, and I went in this canoe, together with two paddlers. The paddlers were natives of the poorer class. They were good men. The bowsman was of nearly pure white blood; the steersman was of nearly pure negro blood, and was evidently the stronger character and better man of the two. The other canoes carried a couple of fazendeiros, ranchmen, who had come up from Cáceres with their dogs. These dugouts were manned by Indian and half-caste paddlers, and the fazendeiros, who were of nearly pure white blood, also at times paddled vigorously. All were dressed in substantially similar clothes, the difference being that those of the camaradas, the poorer men or laborers, were in tatters. In the canoes no man wore anything save a shirt, trousers, and hat, the feet being bare. On horseback they wore long leather leggings which were really

The great ant-eater

South American tapir

From photographs by Elwin R. Sanborn

simply high, rather flexible boots with the soles off; their spurs were on their tough bare feet. There was every gradation between and among the nearly pure whites, negroes, and Indians. On the whole, there was most white blood in the upper ranks, and most Indian and negro blood among the camaradas; but there were exceptions in both classes, and there was no discrimination on account of color. All alike were courteous and friendly.

The hounds were at first carried in two of the dugouts, and then let loose on the banks. We went up-stream for a couple of hours against the swift current, the paddlers making good headway with their pointed paddles—the broad blade of each paddle was tipped with a long point, so that it could be thrust into the mud to keep the low dugout against the bank. The tropical forest came down almost like a wall, the tall trees laced together with vines, and the spaces between their trunks filled with a low, dense jungle. In most places it could only be penetrated by a man with a machete. With few exceptions the trees were unknown to me, and their native names told me nothing. On most of them the foliage was thick; among the exceptions were the cecropias, growing by preference on new-formed alluvial soil bare of other trees, whose rather scanty leaf bunches were, as I was informed, the favorite food of sloths. We saw one or two squirrels among the trees, and a family of monkeys. There were few sand-banks in the river, and no water-fowl save an occasional cormorant. But as we pushed along near the shore, where the branches overhung and dipped in the swirling water, we continually roused little flocks of bats. They were hanging from the boughs right over the river, and when our approach roused them they zigzagged rapidly in front of us for a few rods, and then again dove in among the branches.

At last we landed at a point of ground where there was little jungle, and where the forest was composed of palms and was fairly open. It was a lovely bit of forest. The colonel strolled off in one direction, returning an hour later with a squirrel for the naturalists. Meanwhile Fiala and I went through the palm wood to a papyrus-swamp. Many trails led through the woods, and especially along the borders of the swamp; and, although their principal makers had evidently been cattle, yet there were in them footprints of both tapir and deer. The tapir makes a footprint much like that of a small rhinoceros, being one of the odd-toed ungulates. We could hear the dogs now and then, evidently scattered and running on various trails. They were a worthless lot of cur-hounds. They would chase tapir or deer or anything else that ran away from them as long as the trail was easy to follow; but they were not stanch, even after animals that fled, and they would have nothing whatever to do with animals that were formidable.

While standing by the marsh we heard something coming along one of the game paths. In a moment a buck of the bigger species of bush deer appeared, a very pretty and graceful creature. It stopped and darted back as soon as it saw us, giving us no chance for a shot; but in another moment we caught glimpses of it running by at full speed, back among the palms. I covered an opening between two tree-trunks. By good luck the buck appeared in the right place, giving me just time to hold well ahead of him and fire. At the report he went down in a heap, the "umbrella-pointed" bullet going in at one shoulder, and ranging forward, breaking the neck. The leaden portion of the bullet, in the proper mushroom or umbrella shape, stopped under the neck skin on the farther side. It is a very effective bullet.

Miller particularly wished specimens of these various species of bush deer, because their mutual relationships have not yet been satisfactorily worked out. This was an old buck. The antlers were single spikes, five or six inches long; they were old and white and would soon have been shed. In the stomach were the remains of both leaves and grasses, but especially the former; the buck was both a browser and grazer. There were also seeds, but no berries or nuts such as I have sometimes found in deers' stomachs. This species, which is abundant in this neighborhood, is solitary in its habits, not going in herds. At this time the rut was past, the bucks no longer sought the does, the fawns had not been born, and the yearlings had left their mothers; so that each animal usually went by itself. When chased they were very apt to take to the water. This instinct of taking to the water, by the way, is quite explicable as regards both deer and tapir, for it affords them refuge against their present-day natural foes, but it is a little puzzling to see the jaguar readily climbing trees to escape dogs; for ages have passed since there were in its habitat any natural foes from which it needed to seek safety in trees. But it is possible that the habit has been kept alive by its seeking refuge in them on occasion from the big peccaries, which are among the beasts on which it ordinarily preys.

We hung the buck in a tree. The colonel returned, and

not long afterward one of the paddlers who had been watching the river called out to us that there was a tapir in the water, a good distance up-stream, and that two of the other boats were after it. We jumped into the canoe and the two paddlers dug their blades in the water as they drove her against the strong current, edging over for the opposite bank. The tapir was coming down-stream at a great rate, only its queer head above water, while the dugouts were closing rapidly on it, the paddlers uttering loud cries. As the tapir turned slightly to one side or the other the long, slightly upturned snout and the strongly pronounced arch of the crest along the head and upper neck gave it a marked and unusual aspect. I could not shoot, for it was directly in line with one of the pursuing dugouts. Suddenly it dived, the snout being slightly curved downward as it did so. There was no trace of it; we gazed eagerly in all directions; the dugout in front came alongside our canoe and the paddlers rested, their paddles ready. Then we made out the tapir clambering up the bank. It had dived at right angles to the course it was following and swum under water to the very edge of the shore, rising under the overhanging tree-branches at a point where a drinking-trail for game led down a break in the bank. The branches partially hid it, and it was in deep shadow, so that it did not offer a very good shot. My bullet went into its body too far back, and the tapir disappeared in the forest at a gallop as if unhurt, although the bullet really secured it, by making it unwilling to trust to its speed and leave the neighborhood of the water. Three or four of the hounds were by this time swimming the river, leaving the others yelling on the opposite side; and

Colonel Roosevelt and Colonel Rondon with bush deer

We hung the buck in a tree

From a photograph by Fiala

as soon as the swimmers reached the shore they were put on the tapir's trail and galloped after it, giving tongue. In a couple of minutes we saw the tapir take to the water far up-stream, and after it we went as fast as the paddles could urge us through the water. We were not in time to head it, but fortunately some of the dogs had come down to the river's edge at the very point where the tapir was about to land, and turned it back. Two or three of the dogs were swimming. We were more than half the breadth of the river away from the tapir, and somewhat down-stream, when it dived. It made an astonishingly long swim beneath the water this time, almost as if it had been a hippopotamus, for it passed completely under our canoe and rose between us and the hither bank. I shot it, the bullet going into its brain, while it was thirty or forty yards from shore. It sank at once.

There was now nothing to do but wait until the body floated. I feared that the strong current would roll it down-stream over the river bed, but my companions assured me that this was not so, and that the body would remain where it was until it rose, which would be in an hour or two. They were right, except as to the time. For over a couple of hours we paddled, or anchored ourselves by clutching branches close to the spot, or else drifted down a mile and paddled up again near the shore, to see if the body had caught anywhere. Then we crossed the river and had lunch at the lovely natural picnic-ground where the buck was hung up. We had very nearly given up the tapir when it suddenly floated only a few rods from where it had sunk. With no little difficulty the big, round black body was hoisted into the canoe, and we all turned our prows down-stream. The skies had been lowering for some time, and now—too late to interfere with the hunt or cause us any annoyance—a heavy downpour of rain came on and beat upon us. Little we cared, as the canoe raced forward, with the tapir and the buck lying in the bottom, and a dry, comfortable camp ahead of us.

When we reached camp, and Father Zahm saw the tapir, he reminded me of something I had completely forgotten. When, some six years previously, he had spoken to me in the White House about taking this South American trip, I had answered that I could not, as I intended to go to Africa, but added that I hoped some day to go to South America and that if I did so I should try to shoot both a jaguar and a tapir, as they were the characteristic big-game animals of the country. "Well," said Father Zahm, "now you've shot them both!" The storm continued heavy until after sunset. Then the rain stopped and the full moon broke through the cloud-rack. Father Zahm and I walked up and down in the moonlight, talking of many things, from Dante, and our own plans for the future, to the deeds and the wanderings of the old-time Spanish conquistadores in their search for the Gilded King, and of the Portuguese adventurers who then divided with them the mastery of the oceans and of the unknown continents beyond.

This was an attractive and interesting camp in more ways than one. The *vaqueiros* with their wives and families were housed on the two sides of the field in which our tents were pitched. On one side was a big, whitewashed, tile-roofed house in which the foreman dwelt—an olive-skinned, slightly built, wiry man, with an olive-skinned wife and eight as pretty, fair-haired children as one could wish to see. He usually went barefoot, and his manners were not merely good but distinguished. Corrals and outbuildings were near this big house. On the opposite side of the field stood the row of steep-roofed, palm-thatched huts in which the ordinary cowhands lived with their dusky helpmeets and children. Each night from these palm-thatched quarters we heard the faint sounds of a music that went far back of civilization to a savage ancestry near by in point of time and otherwise immeasurably remote; for through the still, hot air, under the brilliant moonlight, we heard the monotonous throbbing of a tom-tom drum, and the twanging of some odd stringed instrument. The small black turkey-buzzards, here always called crows, were as tame as chickens near the big house, walking on the ground or perched in the trees beside the corral, waiting for the offal of the slaughtered cattle. Two palm-trees near our tent were crowded with the long, hanging nests of one of the cacique orioles. We lived well, with plenty of tapir beef, which was good, and venison of the bush deer, which was excellent; and as much ordinary beef as we wished, and fresh milk, too—a rarity in this country. There were very few mosquitoes, and everything was as comfortable as possible.

The tapir I killed was a big one. I did not wish to kill another, unless, of course, it became advisable to do so for food; whereas I did wish to get some specimens of the big, white-lipped peccary, the "queixa" (pronounced "cashada") of the Brazilians, which would make our collection of the big mammals of the Brazilian forests almost complete. The remaining members of the party killed two or three more tapirs. One was a bull, full grown but very much smaller than the animal I had killed. The hunters said that this was a distinct kind. The skull and skin were sent back with the other specimens to the American Museum, where after due examination and comparison its specific identity will be established. Tapirs are solitary beasts. Two are rarely found together, except in the case of a cow and its spotted and streaked calf. They live in dense cover, usually lying down in the daytime and at night coming out to feed, and going to the river or to some lagoon to bathe and swim. From this camp Sigg took Lieutenant Lyra back to Cáceres to get something that had been overlooked. They went in a rowboat to which the motor had been attached, and at night on the way back almost ran over a tapir that was swimming. But in unfrequented places tapirs both feed and bathe during the day. The stomach of the one I shot contained big palm-nuts; they had been swallowed without enough mastication to break the kernel, the outer pulp being what the tapir prized. Tapirs gallop well, and their tough hide and wedge shape enable them to go at speed through very dense cover. They try to stamp on, and even to bite, a foe, but are only clumsy fighters.

The tapir is a very archaic type of ungulate, not unlike the non-specialized beasts of the oligocene. From some such ancestral type the highly specialized one-toed modern horse has evolved, while during the uncounted ages that saw the horse thus develop the tapir has continued substantially unchanged. Originally the tapirs dwelt in the northern hemisphere, but there they gradually died out, the more specialized horse, and even for long ages the

The return from a day's hunt
Tapir, white-lipped peccary, and bush deer
From a photograph by Miller

rhinoceros, persisting after they had vanished; and nowadays the surviving tapirs are found in Malaysia and South America, far from their original home. The relations of the horse and tapir in the paleontological history of South America are very curious. Both were, geologically speaking, comparatively recent immigrants, and if they came at different dates it is almost certain that the horse came later. The horse for an age or two, certainly for many hundreds of thousands of years, throve greatly and developed not only several different species but even different genera. It was much the most highly specialized of the two, and in the other continental regions where both were found the horse outlasted the tapir. But in South America the tapir outlasted the horse. From unknown causes the various genera and species of horses died out, while the tapir has persisted. The highly specialized, highly developed beasts, which represented such a full evolutionary development, died out, while their less specialized remote kinsfolk, which had not developed, clung to life and throve; and this although the direct reverse was occurring in North America and in the Old World. It is one of the innumerable and at present insoluble problems in the history of life on our planet.

I spent a couple of days of hard work in getting the big white-lipped peccaries—white-lipped being rather a misnomer, as the entire under jaw and lower cheek are white. They were said to be found on the other side of, and some distance back from, the river. Colonel Rondon had sent out one of our attendants, an old follower of his, a full-blood Parecís Indian, to look for tracks. This was an excellent man, who dressed and behaved just like the other good men we had, and was called Antonio Parecís. He found the tracks of a herd of thirty or forty cashadas, and the following morning we started after them.

On the first day we killed nothing. We were rather too large a party, for one or two of the visiting fazendeiros came along with their dogs. I doubt whether these men very much wished to overtake our game, for the big peccary is a murderous foe of dogs (and is sometimes dangerous to men). One of their number frankly refused to come or to let his dogs come, explaining that the fierce wild swine were "very badly brought up" (a literal translation of his words) and that respectable dogs and men ought not to go near them. The other fazendeiros merely feared for their dogs; a groundless fear, I believe, as I do not think that the dogs could by any exertion have been dragged into dangerous proximity with such foes. The ranch foreman, Benedetto, came with us, and two or three other camaradas, including Antonio, the Parecís Indian. The horses were swum across the river, each being led beside a dugout. Then we crossed with the dogs; our horses were saddled, and we started.

It was a picturesque cavalcade. The native hunters, of every shade from white to dark copper, all wore leather leggings that left the soles of their feet bare, and on their bare heels wore spurs with wheels four inches across. They went in single file, for no other mode of travel was possible; and the two or three leading men kept their machetes out, and had to cut every yard of our way while we were in the forest. The hunters rode little stallions, and their hounds were gelded.

Most of the time we were in forest or swampy jungle.

Part of the time we crossed or skirted marshy plains. In one of them a herd of half-wild cattle was feeding. Herons, storks, ducks, and ibises were in these marshes, and we saw one flock of lovely roseate spoonbills.

In one grove the fig-trees were killing the palms, just as in Africa they kill the sandalwood-trees. In the gloom of this grove there were no flowers, no bushes; the air was heavy; the ground was brown with mouldering leaves. Almost every palm was serving as a prop for a fig-tree. The fig-trees were in every stage of growth. The youngest ones merely ran up the palms as vines. In the next stage the vine had thickened and was sending out shoots, wrapping the palm stem in a deadly hold. Some of the shoots were thrown round the stem like the tentacles of an immense cuttlefish. Others looked like claws, that were hooked into every crevice, and round every projection. In the stage beyond this the palm had been killed, and its dead carcass appeared between the big, winding vine-trunks; and later the palm had disappeared and the vines had united into a great fig-tree. Water stood in black pools at the foot of the murdered trees, and of the trees that had murdered them. There was something sinister and evil in the dark stillness of the grove; it seemed as if sentient beings had writhed themselves round and were strangling other sentient beings.

We passed through wonderfully beautiful woods of tall palms, the ouaouaça palm—wawasa palm, as it should be spelled in English. The trunks rose tall and strong and slender, and the fronds were branches twenty or thirty feet long, with the many long, narrow green blades starting from the midrib at right angles in pairs. Round the ponds stood stately burity palms, rising like huge columns, with great branches that looked like fans, as the long, stiff blades radiated from the end of the midrib. One tree was gorgeous with the brilliant hues of a flock of party-colored macaws. Green parrots flew shrieking overhead.

Now and then we were bitten and stung by the venomous fire-ants, and ticks crawled upon us. Once we were assailed by more serious foes, in the shape of a nest of maribundi wasps, not the biggest kind, but about the size of our hornets. We were at the time passing through dense jungle, under tall trees, in a spot where the down timber, holes, tangled creepers, and thorns made the going difficult. The leading men were not assailed, although they were now and then cutting the trail. Colonel Rondon and I were in the middle of the column, and the swarm attacked us; both of us were badly stung on the face, neck, and hands, the colonel even more severely than I was. He wheeled and rode to the rear and I to the front; our horses were stung too; and we went at a rate that a moment previously I would have deemed impossible over such ground.

At the close of the day, when we were almost back at the river, the dogs killed a jaguar kitten. There was no trace of the mother. Some accident must have befallen her, and the kitten was trying to shift for herself. She was very emaciated. In her stomach were the remains of a pigeon and some tendons from the skeleton or dried carcass of some big animal. The loathsome berni flies, which deposit eggs in living beings—cattle, dogs, monkeys, rodents, men—had been at it. There were seven huge, white grubs making big abscess-like swellings over its eyes. These flies deposit their grubs in men. In 1909, on Colonel

Rondon's hardest trip, every man of the party had from one to five grubs deposited in him, the fly acting with great speed, and driving its ovipositor through clothing. The grubs cause torture; but a couple of cross cuts with a lancet permit the loathsome creatures to be squeezed out.

In these forests the multitude of insects that bite, sting, devour, and prey upon other creatures, often with accompaniments of atrocious suffering, passes belief. The very pathetic myth of "beneficent nature" could not deceive even the least wise being if he once saw for himself the iron cruelty of life in the tropics. Of course "nature"—in common parlance a wholly inaccurate term, by the way, especially when used as if to express a single entity—is entirely ruthless, no less so as regards types than as regards individuals, and entirely indifferent to good or evil, and works out her ends or no ends with utter disregard of pain and woe.

The following morning at sunrise we started again. This time only Colonel Rondon and I went with Benedetto and Antonio the Indian. We brought along four dogs which it was fondly hoped might chase the cashadas. Two of them disappeared on the track of a tapir and we saw them no more; one of the others promptly fled when we came across the tracks of our game, and would not even venture after them in our company; the remaining one did not actually run away and occasionally gave tongue, but could not be persuaded to advance unless there was a man ahead of him. However, Colonel Rondon, Benedetto, and Antonio formed a trio of hunters who could do fairly well without dogs.

After four hours of riding, Benedetto, who was in the

lead, suddenly stopped and pointed downward. We were riding along a grassy intervale between masses of forest, and he had found the fresh track of a herd of big peccaries crossing from left to right. There were apparently thirty or forty in the herd. The small peccaries go singly or in small parties, and when chased take refuge in holes or hollow logs, where they show valiant fight; but the big peccaries go in herds of considerable size, and are so truculent that they are reluctant to run, and prefer either to move slowly off chattering their tusks and grunting, or else actually to charge. Where much persecuted the survivors gradually grow more willing to run, but their instinct is not to run but to trust to their truculence and their mass-action for safety. They inflict a fearful bite and frequently kill dogs. They often charge the hunters and I have heard of men being badly wounded by them, while almost every man who hunts them often is occasionally forced to scramble up a tree to avoid a charge. But I have never heard of a man being killed by them. They sometimes surround the tree in which the man has taken refuge and keep him up it. Cherrie, on one occasion in Costa Rica, was thus kept up a tree for several hours by a great herd of three or four hundred of these peccaries; and this although he killed several of them. Ordinarily, however, after making their charge they do not turn, but pass on out of sight. Their great foe is the jaguar, but unless he exercises much caution they will turn the tables on him. Cherrie, also in Costa Rica, came on the body of a jaguar which had evidently been killed by a herd of peccaries some twenty-four hours previously. The ground was trampled up by their hoofs, and the carcass was rent and slit into pieces.

Benedetto, as soon as we discovered the tracks, slipped off his horse, changed his leggings for sandals, threw his rifle over his arm, and took the trail of the herd, followed by the only dog which would accompany him. The peccaries had gone into a broad belt of forest, with a marsh on the farther side. At first Antonio led the colonel and me, all of us on horseback, at a canter round this belt to the marsh side, thinking the peccaries had gone almost through it. But we could hear nothing. The dog only occasionally barked, and then not loudly. Finally we heard a shot. Benedetto had found the herd, which showed no fear of him; he had backed out and fired a signal shot. We all three went into the forest on foot toward where the shot had been fired. It was dense jungle and stiflingly hot. We could not see clearly for more than a few feet, or move easily without free use of the machetes. Soon we heard the ominous groaning of the herd, in front of us, and almost on each side. Then Benedetto joined us, and the dog appeared in the rear. We moved slowly forward, toward the sound of the fierce moaning grunts which were varied at times by a castanet chattering of the tusks. Then we dimly made out the dark forms of the peccaries moving very slowly to the left. My companions each chose a tree to climb at need and pointed out one for me. I fired at the half-seen form of a hog, through the vines, leaves, and branches; the colonel fired; I fired three more shots at other hogs; and the Indian also fired. The peccaries did not charge; walking and trotting, with bristles erect, groaning and clacking their tusks, they disappeared into the jungle. We could not see one of them clearly; and not one was left dead. But a few paces on we came across one of my wounded ones, standing at bay by a palm trunk; and I killed it forthwith. The dog would not even trail the wounded ones; but here Antonio came to the front. With eyes almost as quick and sure as those of a wild beast he had watched after every shot, and was able to tell the results in each case. He said that in addition to the one I had just killed I had wounded two others so seriously that he did not think they would go far, and that Colonel Rondon and he himself had each badly wounded one; and, moreover, he showed the trails each wounded animal had taken. The event justified him. In a few minutes we found my second one dead. Then we found Antonio's. Then we found my third one alive and at bay, and I killed it with another bullet. Finally we found the colonel's. I told him I should ask the authorities of the American museum to mount his and one or two of mine in a group, to commemorate our hunting together.

If we had not used crippling rifles the peccaries might have gotten away, for in the dark jungle, with the masses of intervening leaves and branches, it was impossible to be sure of placing each bullet properly in the half-seen moving beast. We found where the herd had wallowed in the mud. The stomachs of the peccaries we killed contained wild figs, palm nuts, and bundles of root fibres. The dead beasts were covered with ticks. They were at least twice the weight of the smaller peccaries.

On the ride home we saw a buck of the small species of bush deer, not half the size of the kind I had already shot. It was only a patch of red in the bush, a good distance off, but I was lucky enough to hit it. In spite of its small size it was a full-grown male, of a species we had not yet obtained. The antlers had recently been shed, and the new antler growth had just begun. A great jabiru stork let us ride by him a hundred and fifty yards off without thinking it worth while to take flight. This day we saw many of the beautiful violet orchids; and in the swamps were multitudes of flowers, red, yellow, lilac, of which I did not know the names.

I alluded above to the queer custom these people in the interior of Brazil have of gelding their hunting-dogs. This absurd habit is doubtless the chief reason why there are so few hounds worth their salt in the more serious kinds of hunting, where the quarry is the jaguar or big peccary. Thus far we had seen but one dog as good as the ordinary cougar hound or bear hound in such packs as those with which I had hunted in the Rockies and in the cane-brakes of the lower Mississippi. It can hardly be otherwise when every dog that shows himself worth anything is promptly put out of the category of breeders—the theory apparently being that the dog will then last longer. All the breeding is from worthless dogs, and no dog of proved worth leaves descendants.

The country along this river is a fine natural cattle country, and some day it will surely see a great development. It was opened to development by Colonel Rondon only five or six years ago. Already an occasional cattle-ranch is to be found along the banks. When railroads are built into these interior portions of Matto Grosso the whole region will grow and thrive amazingly—and so will the railroads. The growth will not be merely material. An immense amount will be done in education; using the word *education* in its broadest and most accurate sense, as applying to both mind and spirit, to both the child and the man. Colonel Rondon is not merely an explorer. He has been and is now a leader in the movement for the vital betterment of his people, the people of Matto Grosso. The poorer people of the back country everywhere suffer because of the harsh and improper laws of debt. In practice these laws have resulted in establishing a system of peonage, such as has grown up here and there in our own nation. A radical change is needed in this matter; and the colonel is fighting for the change. In school matters the colonel has precisely the ideas of our wisest and most advanced men and women in the United States. Cherrie—who is not only an exceedingly efficient naturalist and explorer in the tropics, but is also a thoroughly good citizen at home—is the chairman of the school board of the town of Newfane, in Vermont. He and the colonel, and Kermit and I, talked over school matters at length, and were in hearty accord as to the vital educational needs of both Brazil and the United States: the need of combining industrial with purely mental training, and the need of having the wide-spread popular education, which is and must be supported and paid for by the government, made a purely governmental and absolutely non-sectarian function, administered by the state alone, without interference with, nor furtherance of, the beliefs of any reputable church. The colonel is also head of the Indian service of Brazil, being what corresponds roughly with our commissioner of Indian affairs. Here also he is taking the exact view that is taken in the United States by the stanchest and wisest friends of the Indians. The Indians must be treated with intelligent and sympathetic under-

Kermit Roosevelt

From a photograph by Fiala

standing, no less than with justice and firmness; and until they become citizens, absorbed into the general body politic, they must be the wards of the nation, and not of any private association, lay or clerical, no matter how well-meaning.

The Sepotuba River was scientifically explored and mapped for the first time by Colonel Rondon in 1908, as head of the Brazilian Telegraphic Commission. This was during the second year of his exploration and opening of the unknown northwestern wilderness of Matto Grosso. Most of this wilderness had never previously been trodden by the foot of a civilized man. Not only were careful maps made and much other scientific work accomplished, but posts were established and telegraph-lines constructed. When Colonel Rondon began the work he was a major. He was given two promotions, to lieutenant-colonel and colonel, while absent in the wilderness. His longest and most important exploring trip, and the one fraught with most danger and hardship, was begun by him in 1909, on May 3d, the anniversary of the discovery of Brazil. He left Tapirapoan on that day, and he reached the Madeira River on Christmas, December 25, of the same year, having descended the Gy-Paraná. The mouth of this river had long been known, but its upper course for half its length was absolutely unknown when Rondon descended it. Among those who took part under him in this piece of exploration were the present Captain Amilcar and Lieutenant Lyra; and two better or more efficient men for such wilderness work it would be impossible to find. They acted as his two chief assistants on our trip. In 1909 the party exhausted all their food, including even the salt, by

August. For the last four months they lived exclusively on the game they killed, on fruits, and on wild honey. Their equipage was what the men could carry on their backs. By the time the party reached the Madeira they were worn out by fatigue, exposure, and semi-starvation, and their enfeebled bodies were racked by fever.

The work of exploration accomplished by Colonel Rondon and his associates during these years was as remarkable as, and in its results even more important than, any similar work undertaken elsewhere on the globe at or about the same time. Its value was recognized in Brazil. It received no recognition by the geographical societies of Europe or the United States.

The work done by the original explorers of such a wilderness necessitates the undergoing of untold hardship and danger. Their successors, even their immediate successors, have a relatively easy time. Soon the road becomes so well beaten that it can be traversed without hardship by any man who does not venture from it—although if he goes off into the wilderness for even a day, hunting or collecting, he will have a slight taste of what his predecessors endured. The wilderness explored by Colonel Rondon is not yet wholly subdued, and still holds menace to human life. At Cáceres he received notice of the death of one of his gallant subordinates, Captain Cardozo. He died from beriberi, far out in the wilderness along our proposed line of march. Colonel Rondon also received news that a boat ascending the Gy-Paraná, to carry provisions to meet those of our party who were to descend that stream, had been upset, the provisions lost, and three men drowned. The risk and hardship are such that the ordinary men, the camaradas, do not like to go into the wilderness. The men who go with the Telegraphic Commission on the rougher and wilder work are paid seven times as much as they earn in civilization. On this trip of ours Colonel Rondon met with much difficulty in securing some one who could cook. He asked the cook on the little steamer *Nyoac* to go with us; but the cook with unaffected horror responded: "Senhor, *I* have never done anything to deserve punishment!"

Five days after leaving us, the launch, with one of the native trading-boats lashed alongside, returned. On the 13th we broke camp, loaded ourselves and all our belongings on the launch and the house-boat, and started up-stream for Tapirapoan. All told there were about thirty men, with five dogs and tents, bedding and provisions; fresh beef, growing rapidly less fresh; skins—all and everything jammed together.

It rained most of the first day and part of the first night. After that the weather was generally overcast and pleasant for travelling; but sometimes rain and torrid sunshine alternated. The cooking—and it was good cooking—was done at a funny little open-air fireplace, with two or three cooking-pots placed at the stern of the house-boat.

The fireplace was a platform of earth, taken from ant-hills, and heaped and spread on the boards of the boat. Around it the dusky cook worked with philosophic solemnity in rain and shine. Our attendants, friendly souls with skins of every shade and hue, slept most of the time, curled up among boxes, bundles, and slabs of beef. An enormous land turtle was tethered toward the bow of the house-boat. When the men slept too near it, it made futile efforts to scramble over them; and in return now and then one of them gravely used it for a seat.

Slowly the throbbing engine drove the launch and its unwieldy side-partner against the swift current. The river had risen. We made about a mile and a half an hour. Ahead of us the brown water street stretched in curves between endless walls of dense tropical forest. It was like passing through a gigantic greenhouse. Wawasa and burity palms, cecropias, huge figs, feathery bamboos, strange yellow-stemmed trees, low trees with enormous leaves, tall trees with foliage as delicate as lace, trees with buttressed trunks, trees with boles rising smooth and straight to lofty heights, all woven together by a tangle of vines, crowded down to the edge of the river. Their drooping branches hung down to the water, forming a screen through which it was impossible to see the bank, and exceedingly difficult to penetrate to the bank. Rarely one of them showed flowers—large white blossoms, or small red or yellow blossoms. More often the lilac flowers of the begonia-vine made large patches of color. Innumerable epiphytes covered the limbs, and even grew on the roughened trunks. We saw little bird life—a darter now and then, and kingfishers flitting from perch to perch. At long intervals we passed a ranch. At one the large, red-tiled, whitewashed house stood on a grassy slope behind mango-trees. The wooden shutters were thrown back from the unglazed windows, and the big rooms were utterly bare—not a book, not an ornament. A palm, loaded with scores of the pendulous nests of the troupials, stood near the door. Behind were orange-trees and coffee-plants, and near by fields of bananas, rice, and tobacco. The sallow foreman was courteous and hospitable. His dark-skinned women-folk kept in the furtive background. Like most of the ranches, it was owned by a company with headquarters at Cáceres.

The trip was pleasant and interesting, although there was not much to do on the boat. It was too crowded to move around save with a definite purpose. We enjoyed the scenery; we talked—in English, Portuguese, bad French, and broken German. Some of us wrote. Fiala made sketches of improved tents, hammocks, and other field equipment, suggested by what he had already seen. Some of us read books. Colonel Rondon, neat, trim, alert, and soldierly, studied a standard work on applied geographical astronomy. Father Zahm read a novel by Fogazzaro. Kermit read Camoens and a couple of Brazilian novels, "O Guarani" and "Innocencia." My own reading varied from "Quentin Durward" and Gibbon to the "Chanson de Roland." Miller took out his little pet owl Moses, from the basket in which Moses dwelt, and gave him food and water. Moses crooned and chuckled gratefully when he was stroked and tickled.

Late the first evening we moored to the bank by a little fazenda of the poorer type. The houses were of palm-leaves. Even the walls were made of the huge fronds or leafy branches of the wawasa palm, stuck upright in the ground and the blades plaited together. Some of us went ashore. Some stayed on the boats. There were no mosquitoes, the weather was not oppressively hot, and we slept well. By five o'clock next morning we had each drunk a cup of delicious Brazilian coffee, and the boats were under way.

All day we steamed slowly up-stream. We passed two

or three fazendas. At one, where we halted to get milk, the trees were overgrown with pretty little yellow orchids. At dark we moored at a spot where there were no branches to prevent our placing the boats directly alongside the bank. There were hardly any mosquitoes. Most of the party took their hammocks ashore, and the camp was pitched amid singularly beautiful surroundings. The trees were wawasa palms, some with the fronds cresting very tall trunks, some with the fronds—seemingly longer—rising almost from the ground. The fronds were of great length; some could not have been less than fifty feet long. Bushes and tall grass, dew-drenched and glittering with the green of emeralds, grew in the open spaces between. We left at sunrise the following morning. One of the sailors had strayed inland. He got turned round and could not find the river; and we started before discovering his absence. We stopped at once, and with much difficulty he forced his way through the vine-laced and thorn-guarded jungle toward the sound of the launch's engines and of the bugle which was blown. In this dense jungle, when the sun is behind clouds, a man without a compass who strays a hundred yards from the river may readily become hopelessly lost.

As we ascended the river the wawasa palms became constantly more numerous. At this point, for many miles, they gave their own character to the forest on the river banks. Everywhere their long, curving fronds rose among the other trees, and in places their lofty trunks made them hold their heads higher than the other trees. But they were never as tall as the giants among the ordinary trees. On one towering palm we noticed a mass of beautiful violet orchids growing from the side of the trunk, half-way to the top. On another big tree, not a palm, which stood in a little opening, there hung well over a hundred troupials' nests. Besides two or three small ranches we this day passed a large ranch. The various houses and sheds, all palm-thatched, stood by the river in a big space of cleared ground, dotted with wawasa palms. A native house-boat was moored by the bank. Women and children looked from the unglazed windows of the houses; men stood in front of them. The biggest house was enclosed by a stockade of palm-logs, thrust end-on into the ground. Cows and oxen grazed round about; and carts with solid wheels, each wheel made of a single disk of wood, were tilted on their poles.

We made our noonday halt on an island where very tall trees grew, bearing fruits that were pleasant to the taste. Other trees on the island were covered with rich red and yellow blossoms; and masses of delicate blue flowers and of star-shaped white flowers grew underfoot. Hither and thither across the surface of the river flew swallows, with so much white in their plumage that as they flashed in the sun they seemed to have snow-white bodies, borne by dark wings. The current of the river grew swifter; there were stretches of broken water that were almost rapids; the laboring engine strained and sobbed as with increasing difficulty it urged forward the launch and her clumsy consort. At nightfall we moored beside the bank, where the forest was open enough to permit a comfortable camp. That night the ants ate large holes in Miller's mosquito-netting, and almost devoured his socks and shoe-laces.

At sunrise we again started. There were occasional stretches of swift, broken water, almost rapids, in the river; everywhere the current was swift, and our progress was slow. The prancha was towed at the end of a hawser, and her crew poled. Even thus we only just made the riffle in more than one case. Two or three times cormorants and snake-birds, perched on snags in the river or on trees alongside it, permitted the boat to come within a few yards. In one piece of high forest we saw a party of toucans, conspicuous even among the tree tops because of their huge bills and the leisurely expertness with which they crawled, climbed, and hopped among the branches. We went by several fazendas.

Shortly before noon—January 16—we reached Tapirapoan, the headquarters of the Telegraphic Commission. It was an attractive place, on the river-front, and it was gayly bedecked with flags, not only those of Brazil and the United States, but of all the other American republics, in our honor. There was a large, green square, with trees standing in the middle of it. On one side of this square were the buildings of the Telegraphic Commission, on the other those of a big ranch, of which this is the headquarters. In addition, there were stables, sheds, outhouses, and corrals; and there were cultivated fields near by. Milch cows, beef-cattle, oxen, and mules wandered almost at will. There were two or three wagons and carts, and a traction automobile, used in the construction of the telegraph-line, but not available in the rainy season, at the time of our trip.

Here we were to begin our trip overland, on pack-mules and pack-oxen, scores of which had been gathered to meet

Two pranchas being pulled by launch with our baggage and provisions

The prancha was towed at the end of a hawser and her crew poled

From a photograph by Harper

us. Several days were needed to apportion the loads and arrange for the several divisions in which it was necessary that so large a party should attempt the long wilderness march, through a country where there was not much food for man or beast, and where it was always possible to run into a district in which fatal cattle or horse diseases were prevalent. Fiala, with his usual efficiency, took charge of handling the outfit of the American portion of the expedition, with Sigg as an active and useful assistant. Harper, who like the others worked with whole-hearted zeal and cheerfulness, also helped him, except when he was engaged in helping the naturalists. The two latter, Cherrie and Miller, had so far done the hardest and the best work of the expedition. They had collected about a thousand birds and two hundred and fifty mammals. It was not probable that they would do as well during the remainder of our trip, for we intended thenceforth to halt as little, and march as steadily, as the country, the weather, and the condition of our means of transportation permitted. I kept continually wishing that they had more time in which to study the absorbingly interesting life-histories of the beautiful and wonderful beasts and birds we were all the time seeing. Every first-rate museum must still employ competent collectors; but I think that a museum could now confer most lasting benefit, and could do work of most permanent good, by sending out into the immense wildernesses, where wild nature is at her best, trained observers with the gift of recording what they have observed. Such men should be collectors, for collecting is still necessary; but they should also, and indeed primarily, be able themselves to see, and to set vividly before the eyes of others, the full life-histories of the creatures that dwell in the waste spaces of the world.

At this point both Cherrie and Miller collected a number of mammals and birds which they had not previously obtained; whether any were new to science could only be determined after the specimens reached the American Museum. While making the round of his small mammal traps one morning, Miller encountered an army of the formidable foraging ants. The species was a large black one, moving with a well-extended front. These ants, sometimes called army-ants, like the driver-ants of Africa, move in big bodies and destroy or make prey of every living thing that is unable or unwilling to get out of their path in time. They run fast, and everything runs away from their advance. Insects form their chief prey; and the most dangerous and aggressive lower-life creatures make astonishingly little resistance to them. Miller's attention was first attracted to this army of ants by noticing a big centiped, nine or ten inches long, trying to flee before them. A number of ants were biting it, and it writhed at each bite, but did not try to use its long curved jaws against its assailants. On other occasions he saw big scorpions and big hairy spiders trying to escape in the same way, and showing the same helpless inability to injure their ravenous foes, or to defend themselves. The ants climb trees to a great height, much higher than most birds' nests, and at once kill and tear to pieces any fledglings in the nests they reach. But they are not as common as some writers seem to imagine; days may elapse before their armies are encountered, and doubtless most nests are never visited or threatened by them. In some instances it seems likely that the birds save themselves and their young in other ways. Some nests are inaccessible. From others it is probable that the parents remove the young. Miller once, in Guiana, had been watching for some days a nest of ant-wrens which contained young. Going thither one morning, he found the tree, and the nest itself, swarming with foraging ants. He at first thought that the fledglings had been devoured, but he soon saw the parents, only about thirty yards off, with food in their beaks. They were engaged in entering a dense part of the jungle, coming out again without food in their beaks, and soon reappearing once more with food. Miller never found their new nests, but their actions left him certain that they were feeding their young, which they must have themselves removed from the old nest. These ant-wrens hover in front of and over the columns of foraging ants, feeding not only on the other insects aroused by the ants, but on the ants themselves. This fact has been doubted; but Miller has shot them with the ants in their bills and in their stomachs. Dragon-flies, in numbers, often hover over the columns, darting down at them; Miller could not be certain he had seen them actually seizing the ants, but this was his belief. I have myself seen these ants plunder a nest of the dangerous and highly aggressive wasps, while the wasps buzzed about in great excitement, but seemed unable effectively to retaliate. I have also seen them clear a sapling tenanted by their kinsmen, the poisonous red ants, or fire-ants; the fire-ants fought and I have no doubt injured or killed some of their swarming and active black foes; but the latter quickly did away with them. I have only come across black foraging ants; but there are red species. They attack human beings precisely as they attack all animals, and precipitate flight is the only resort.

Around our camp here butterflies of gorgeous coloring swarmed, and there were many fungi as delicately shaped and tinted as flowers. The scents in the woods were wonderful. There were many whippoorwills, or rather Brazilian birds related to them; they uttered at intervals through the night a succession of notes suggesting both those of our whippoorwill and those of our big chuck-will's-widow of the Gulf States, but not identical with either. There were other birds which were nearly akin to familiar birds of the United States: a dull-colored catbird, a dull-colored robin, and a sparrow belonging to the same genus as our common song-sparrow and sweetheart sparrow; Miller had heard this sparrow singing by day and night, fourteen thousand feet up on the Andes, and its song suggested the songs of both of our sparrows. There were doves and wood-peckers of various species. Other birds bore no resemblance to any of ours. One honey-creeper was a perfect little gem, with plumage that was black, purple, and turquoise, and brilliant scarlet feet. Two of the birds which Cherrie and Miller procured were of extraordinary nesting habits. One, a nunlet, in shape resembles a short-tailed bluebird. It is plumbeous, with a fulvous belly and white tail coverts. It is a stupid little bird, and does not like to fly away even when shot at. It catches its prey and ordinarily acts like a rather dull flycatcher, perching on some dead tree, swooping on insects and then returning to its perch, and never going on the ground to feed or run about. But it nests in burrows which it digs itself, one bird usually digging, while the other bird perches in a bush near by. Sometimes these burrows are in the side of a sand-bank, the sand being so loose that it is a marvel that it does not cave in. Sometimes the burrows are in the level plain, running down about three feet, and then rising at an angle. The nest consists of a few leaves and grasses, and the eggs are white. The other bird, called a nun or waxbill, is about the size of a thrush, grayish in color, with a waxy red bill. It also burrows in the level soil, the burrow being five feet long; and over the mouth of the burrow it heaps a pile of sticks and leaves.

At this camp the heat was great—from 91° to 104° Fahrenheit—and the air very heavy, being saturated with moisture; and there were many rain-storms. But there were no mosquitoes, and we were very comfortable. Thanks to the neighborhood of the ranch, we fared sumptuously, with plenty of beef, chickens, and fresh milk. Two of the Brazilian dishes were delicious: canja, a thick soup of chicken and rice, the best soup a hungry man ever tasted; and beef chopped in rather small pieces and served with a well-flavored but simple gravy. The mule allotted me as a riding-beast was a powerful animal, with easy gaits. The Brazilian Government had waiting for me a very handsome silver-mounted saddle and bridle; I was much pleased with both. However, my exceedingly rough and shabby clothing made an incongruous contrast.

At Tapirapoan we broke up our baggage—as well as our party. We sent forward the Canadian canoe—which, with the motor-engine and some kerosene, went in a cart drawn by six oxen—and a hundred sealed tin cases of provisions, each containing rations for a day for six men. They had been put up in New York under the special direction of Fiala, for use when we got where we wished to take good and varied food in small compass. All the skins, skulls, and alcoholic specimens, and all the baggage not absolutely necessary, were sent back down the Paraguay and to New York, in charge of Harper. The separate baggage-trains, under the charge of Captain Amilcar, were organized to go in one detachment. The main body of the expedition, consisting of the American members, and of Colonel Rondon, Lieutenant Lyra, and Doctor Cajazeira, with their baggage and provisions, formed another detachment.

CHAPTER VI

THROUGH THE HIGHLAND WILDERNESS OF WESTERN BRAZIL

WE were now in the land of the bloodsucking bats, the vampire bats that suck the blood of living creatures, clinging to or hovering against the shoulder of a horse or cow, or the hand or foot of a sleeping man, and making a wound from which the blood continues to flow long after the bat's thirst has been satiated. At Tapirapoan there were milch cattle; and one of the calves turned up one morning weak from loss of blood, which was still trickling from a wound, forward of the shoulder, made by a bat. But the bats do little damage in this neighborhood compared to what they do in some other places, where not only the mules and cattle but the chickens have to be housed behind bat-proof protection at night or their lives may pay the penalty. The chief and habitual offenders are various species of rather small bats; but it is said that other kinds of Brazilian bats seem to have become, at least sporadically and locally, affected by the evil example and occasionally vary their customary diet by draughts of living blood. One of the Brazilian members of our party, Hoehne, the botanist, was a zoologist also. He informed me that he had known even the big fruit-eating bats to take to bloodsucking. They did not, according to his observations, themselves make the original wound; but after it had been made by one of the true vampires they would lap the flowing blood and enlarge the wound. South America makes up for its lack, relatively to Africa and India, of large man-eating carnivores by the extraordinary ferocity or bloodthirstiness of certain small creatures of which the kinsfolk elsewhere are harmless. It is only here that fish no bigger than trout kill swimmers, and bats the size of the ordinary "flittermice" of the northern hemisphere drain the life-blood of big beasts and of man himself.

There was not much large mammalian life in the neighborhood. Kermit hunted industriously and brought in an occasional armadillo, coati, or agouti for the naturalists. Miller trapped rats and a queer opossum new to the collection. Cherrie got many birds. Cherrie and Miller skinned their specimens in a little open hut or shed. Moses the small pet owl, sat on a cross-bar overhead, an interested spectator, and chuckled whenever he was petted. Two wrens, who bred just outside the hut, were much excited by the presence of Moses, and paid him visits of noisy unfriendliness. The little white-throated sparrows came familiarly about the palm cabins and whitewashed houses and trilled on the rooftrees. It was a simple song, with just a hint of our northern whitethroat's sweet and plaintive melody, and of the opening bars of our song-sparrow's pleasant, homely lay. It brought back dear memories of glorious April mornings on Long Island, when through the singing of robin and song-sparrow comes the piercing cadence of the meadow-lark; and of the far northland woods in June, fragrant with the breath of pine and balsam-fir, where sweetheart sparrows sing from wet spruce thickets and rapid brooks rush under the drenched and swaying alder-boughs.

From Tapirapoan our course lay northward up to and across the Plan Alto, the highland wilderness of Brazil. From the edges of this highland country, which is geologically very ancient, the affluents of the Amazon to the north, and of the Plate to the south, flow, with immense and devious loops and windings.

Two days before we ourselves started with our mule-train, a train of pack-oxen left, loaded with provisions, tools, and other things, which we would not need until, after a month or six weeks, we began our descent into the valley of the Amazon. There were about seventy oxen. Most of them were well broken, but there were about a score which were either not broken at all or else very badly broken. These were loaded with much difficulty, and bucked like wild broncos. Again and again they scattered their loads over the corral and over the first part of the road. The pack-men, however—copper-colored, black, and dusky-white—were not only masters of their art, but possessed tempers that could not be ruffled; when they showed severity it was because severity was needed, and not because they were angry. They finally got all their longhorned beasts loaded and started on the trail with them.

On January 21 we ourselves started, with the mule-train. Of course, as always in such a journey, there was some confusion before the men and the animals of the train settled down to the routine performance of duty. In addition to the pack-animals we all had riding-mules. The first day we journeyed about twelve miles, then crossing the Sepotuba and camping beside it, below a series of falls, or rather rapids. The country was level. It was a great natural pasture, covered with a very open forest of low, twisted trees, bearing a superficial likeness to the cross-timbers of Texas and Oklahoma. It is as well fitted for stock-raising as Oklahoma; and there is also much fine agricultural land, while the river will ultimately yield electric power. It is a fine country for settlement. The heat is great at noon; but the nights are not uncomfortable. We were supposed to be in the middle of the rainy season, but hitherto most of the days had been fine, varied with showers. The astonishing thing was the absence of mosquitoes. Insect pests that work by day can be stood, and especially by settlers, because they are far less serious foes in the clearings than in the woods. The mosquitoes and other night foes offer the really serious and unpleasant problem, because they break one's rest. Hitherto, during our travels up the Paraguay and its tributaries, in this level, marshy tropical region of western Brazil, we had practically not been bothered by mosquitoes at all, in our home camps. Out in the woods they were at times a serious nuisance, and Cherrie and Miller had been subjected to real torment by them during some of their special expeditions; but there were practically none on the ranches and in our camps in the open fields by the river, even when marshes were close by. I was puzzled—and delighted—by their absence. Settlers need not be deterred from coming to this region by the fear of insect foes.

This does not mean that there are not such foes. Outside of the clearings, and of the beaten tracks of travel, they teem. There are ticks, poisonous ants, wasps—of which some species are really serious menaces—biting flies and gnats. I merely mean that, unlike so many other tropical regions, this particular region is, from the standpoint of the settler and the ordinary traveller, relatively free from insect pests, and a pleasant place of residence. The original explorer, and to an only less degree the hard-working field naturalist or big-game hunter, have to face these pests, just as they have to face countless risks, hardships, and difficulties. This is inherent in their several professions or avocations. Many regions in the United States where life is now absolutely comfortable and easy-going offered most formidable problems to the first explorers a century or two ago. We must not fall into the foolish error of thinking that the first explorers need not suffer terrible hardships, merely because the ordinary travellers, and even the settlers who come after them, do not have to endure such danger, privation, and wearing fatigue—although the first among the genuine settlers also have to undergo exceedingly trying experiences. The early explorers and adventurers make fairly well-beaten trails at heavy cost to themselves. Ordinary travellers, with little discomfort and no danger, can then traverse these trails; but it is incumbent on them neither to boast of their own experiences nor to misjudge the efforts of the pioneers because, thanks to these very efforts, their own lines fall in pleasant places. The ordinary traveller, who never goes off the beaten route and who on this beaten route is carried by others, without himself doing anything or risking anything, does not need to show much more initiative and intelligence than an express package. He does nothing; others do all the work, show all the forethought, take all the risk—and are entitled to all the credit. He and his valise are carried in practically the same fashion; and for each the achievement stands about on the same plane. If this kind of traveller is a writer, he can of course do admirable work, work of the highest value; but the value comes because he is a writer and observer, not because of any particular credit that attaches to him as a traveller. We all recognize this truth as far as highly civilized regions are concerned: when Bryce writes of the American commonwealth, or Lowell of European legislative assemblies, our admiration is for the insight and thought of the observer, and we are not concerned with his travels. When a man travels across Arizona in a Pullman car, we do not think of him as having performed a feat bearing even the most remote resemblance to the feats of the first explorers of those waterless wastes; whatever admiration we feel in connection with his trip is reserved for the traffic-superintendent, engineer, fireman, and brakeman. But as regards the less-known continents, such as South America, we sometimes fail to remember these obvious truths. There yet remains plenty of exploring work to be done in South America, as hard, as dangerous, and almost as important as any that has already been done; work such as has recently been done, or is now being done, by men and women such as Haseman, Farrabee, and Miss Snethlage. The collecting naturalists who go into the wilds and do first-class work encounter every kind of risk and undergo every kind of hardship and exertion. Explorers and naturalists of the right type have open to them in South America a field of extraordinary attraction and difficulty. But to excavate ruins that have already long been known, to visit out-of-the-way towns that date from colonial days, to traverse old, even if uncomfortable, routes of travel, or to ascend or descend highway rivers like the Amazon, the Paraguay, and the lower Orinoco—all of these exploits are well worth performing, but they in no sense represent exploration or adventure, and they do not entitle the performer, no matter how well he writes and no matter how much of real value he contributes to human knowledge, to compare himself in any way with the real wilderness wanderer, or to criticise the latter. Such a performance entails no hardship or difficulty worth heeding. Its value depends purely on observation, not on action. The man *does* little; he merely records what he sees. He is only the man of the beaten routes. The true wilderness wanderer, on the contrary, must be a man of action as well as of observation. He must have the heart and the body to do and to endure, no less than the eye to see and the brain to note and record.

Let me make it clear that I am not depreciating the excellent work of so many of the men who have not gone off the beaten trails. I merely wish to make it plain that this excellent work must not be put in the class with that of the wilderness explorer. It is excellent work, nevertheless, and has its place, just as the work of the true explorer has its place. Both stand in sharpest contrast with the actions of those alleged explorers, among whom Mr. Savage Landor stands in unpleasant prominence.

From the Sepotuba rapids our course at the outset lay westward. The first day's march away from the river lay through dense tropical forest. Away from the broad, beaten route every step of a man's progress represented slashing a trail with the machete through the tangle of bushes, low trees, thorny scrub, and interlaced creepers. There were palms of new kinds, very tall, slender, straight, and graceful, with rather short and few fronds. The wild plantains, or pacovas, thronged the spaces among the trunks of the tall trees; their boles were short, and their broad, erect leaves gigantic; they bore brilliant red-and-orange flowers. There were trees whose trunks bellied into huge swellings. There were towering trees with buttressed trunks, whose leaves made a fretwork against the sky far overhead. Gorgeous red-and-green trogons, with long tails, perched motionless on the lower branches and uttered a loud, thrice-repeated whistle. We heard the calling of the false bell-bird, which is gray instead of white like the true bell-birds; it keeps among the very topmost branches. Heavy rain fell shortly after we reached our camping-place.

Next morning at sunrise we climbed a steep slope to the edge of the Parecís plateau, at a level of about two thousand feet above the sea. We were on the Plan Alto, the high central plain of Brazil, the healthy land of dry air, of cool nights, of clear, running brooks. The sun was directly behind us when we topped the rise. Reining in, we looked back over the vast Paraguayan marshes, shimmering in the long morning lights. Then, turning again, we rode forward, casting shadows far before us. It was twenty miles to the next water, and in hot weather the journey across this waterless, shadeless, sandy stretch of country is hard on the mules and oxen. But on this day the sky speedily grew overcast and a cool wind blew in our faces as we travelled at a quick, running walk over the immense rolling plain. The ground was sandy; it was

Colonel Roosevelt and Colonel Rondon looking over the vast landscape

The ground was sandy, covered with grass and with a sparse growth of stunted, twisted trees, never more than a few feet high

From a photograph by Kermit Roosevelt

covered with grass and with a sparse growth of stunted, twisted trees, never more than a few feet high. There were rheas—ostriches—and small pampas-deer on this plain; the coloration of the rheas made it difficult to see them at a distance, whereas the bright red coats of the little deer, and their uplifted flags as they ran, advertised them afar off. We also saw the footprints of cougars and of the small-toothed, big, red wolf. Cougars are the most inveterate enemies of these small South American deer, both those of the open grassy plain and those of the forest.

It is not nearly as easy to get lost on these open plains as in the dense forest; and where there is a long, reasonably straight road or river to come back to, a man even without a compass is safe. But in these thick South American forests, especially on cloudy days, a compass is an absolute necessity. We were struck by the fact that the native hunters and ranchmen on such days continually lost themselves and, if permitted, travelled for miles through the forest either in circles or in exactly the wrong direction. They had no such sense of direction as the forest-dwelling 'Ndorobo hunters in Africa had, or as the true forest-dwelling Indians of South America are said to have. On certainly half a dozen occasions our guides went completely astray, and we had to take command, to disregard their assertions, and to lead the way aright by sole reliance on our compasses.

On this cool day we travelled well. The air was wonderful; the vast open spaces gave a sense of abounding vigor and freedom. Early in the afternoon we reached a station made by Colonel Rondon in the course of his first explorations. There were several houses with whitewashed walls, stone floors, and tiled or thatched roofs. They stood in a wide, gently sloping valley. Through it ran a rapid brook of cool water, in which we enjoyed delightful baths. The heavy, intensely humid atmosphere of the low, marshy plains had gone; the air was clear and fresh; the sky was brilliant; far and wide we looked over a landscape that seemed limitless; the breeze that blew in our faces might have come from our own northern plains. The midday sun was very hot; but it was hard to realize that we were in the torrid zone. There were no mosquitoes, so that we never put up our nets when we went to bed; but wrapped ourselves in our blankets and slept soundly through the cool, pleasant nights. Surely in the future this region will be the home of a healthy, highly civilized population. It is good for cattle-raising, and the valleys are fitted for agriculture. From June to September the nights are often really cold. Any sound northern race could live here; and in such a land, with such a climate, there would be much joy of living.

On these plains the Telegraphic Commission uses motor-trucks; and these now served to relieve the mules and oxen; for some of them, especially among the oxen, already showed the effects of the strain. Travelling in a wild country with a pack-train is not easy on the pack-animals. It was strange to see these big motor-vans out in the wilderness where there was not a settler, not a civilized man except the employees of the Telegraphic Commission. They were handled by Lieutenant Lauriadó, who, with Lieutenant Mello, had taken special charge of our transport service; both were exceptionally good and competent men.

The following day we again rode on across the Plan Alto. In the early afternoon, in the midst of a downpour of rain, we crossed the divide between the basins of the Paraguay and the Amazon. That evening we camped on a brook whose waters ultimately ran into the Tapajos. The rain fell throughout the afternoon, now lightly, now heavily, and the mule-train did not get up until dark. But enough tents and flies were pitched to shelter all of us. Fires were lit, and—after a fourteen hours' fast—we feasted royally on beans and rice and pork and beef, seated around oxskins spread upon the ground. The sky cleared; the stars blazed down through the cool night; and wrapped in our blankets we slept soundly, warm and comfortable.

Next morning the trail had turned, and our course led northward and at times east of north. We traversed the same high, rolling plains of coarse grass and stunted trees. Kermit, riding a big, iron-mouthed, bull-headed white mule, rode off to one side on a hunt, and rejoined the line of march carrying two bucks of the little pampas-deer, or field deer, behind his saddle. These deer are very pretty and graceful, with a tail like that of the Columbian black-tail. Standing motionless facing one, in the sparse scrub, they are hard to make out; if seen sideways the reddish of their coats, contrasted with the greens and grays of the landscape, betrays them; and when they bound off the upraised white tail is very conspicuous. They carefully avoid the woods in which their cousins the little bush deer are found, and go singly or in couples. Their odor can be made out at quite a distance, but it is not rank. They still carried their antlers. Their venison was delicious.

We came across many queer insects. One red grasshopper when it flew seemed as big as a small sparrow; and we passed in some places such multitudes of active little green grasshoppers that they frightened the mules. At our camping-place we saw an extraordinary colony of spiders. It was among some dwarf trees, standing a few yards apart from one another by the water. When we reached the camping-place, early in the afternoon—the pack-train did not get in until nearly sunset, just ahead of the rain—no spiders were out. They were under the leaves of the trees. Their webs were tenantless, and indeed for the most part were broken down. But at dusk they came out from their hiding-places, two or three hundred of them in all, and at once began to repair the old and spin new webs. Each spun its own circular web, and sat in the middle; and each web was connected on several sides with other webs, while those nearest the trees were hung to them by spun ropes, so to speak. The result was a kind of sheet of web consisting of scores of wheels, in each of which the owner and proprietor sat; and there were half a dozen such sheets, each extending between two trees. The webs could hardly be seen, and the effect was of scores of big, formidable-looking spiders poised in midair, equidistant from one another, between each pair of trees. When darkness and rain fell they were still out, fixing their webs, and pouncing on the occasional insects that blundered into the webs. I have no question that they are nocturnal; they certainly hide in the daytime, and it seems impossible that they can come out only for a few minutes at dusk.

In the evenings, after supper or dinner—it is hard to

tell by what title the exceedingly movable evening meal should be called—the members of the party sometimes told stories of incidents in their past lives. Most of them were men of varied experiences. Rondon and Lyra told of the hardship and suffering of the first trips through the wilderness across which we were going with such comfort. On this very plateau they had once lived for weeks on the fruits of the various fruit-bearing trees. Naturally they became emaciated and feeble. In the forests of the Amazonian basin they did better because they often shot birds and plundered the hives of the wild honey-bees. In cutting the trail for the telegraph-line through the Juruena basin they lost every single one of the hundred and sixty mules with which they had started. Those men pay dear who build the first foundations of empire! Fiala told of the long polar nights and of white bears that came round the snow huts of the explorers, greedy to eat them, and themselves destined to be eaten by them. Of all the party Cherrie's experiences had covered the widest range. This was partly owing to the fact that the latter-day naturalist of the most vigorous type who goes into the untrodden wastes of the world must see and do many strange things; and still more owing to the character of the man himself. The things he had seen and done and undergone often enabled him to cast the light of his own past experience on unexpected subjects. Once we were talking about the proper weapons for cavalry, and some one mentioned the theory that the lance is especially formidable because of the moral effect it produces on the enemy. Cherrie nodded emphatically; and a little cross-examination elicited the fact that he was speaking from lively personal recollection of his own feelings when charged by lancers. It was while he was fighting with the Venezuelan insurgents in an unsuccessful uprising against the tyranny of Castro. He was on foot, with five Venezuelans, all cool men and good shots. In an open plain they were charged by twenty of Castro's lancers, who galloped out from behind cover two or three hundred yards off. It was a war in which neither side gave quarter and in which the wounded and the prisoners were butchered—just as President Madero was butchered in Mexico. Cherrie knew that it meant death for him and his companions if the charge came home; and the sight of the horsemen running in at full speed, with their long lances in rest and the blades glittering, left an indelible impression on his mind. But he and his companions shot deliberately and accurately; ten of the lancers were killed, the nearest falling within fifty yards; and the others rode off in headlong haste. A cool man with a rifle, if he has mastered his weapon, need fear no foe.

At this camp the auto-vans again joined us. They were to go direct to the first telegraph station, at the great falls of the Utiarity, on the Rio Papagaio. Of course they travelled faster than the mule-train. Father Zahm, attended by Sigg, started for the falls in them. Cherrie and Miller also went in them, because they had found that it was very difficult to collect birds, and especially mammals, when we were moving every day, packing up early each morning and the mule-train arriving late in the afternoon or not until nightfall. Moreover, there was much rain, which made it difficult to work except under the tents. Accordingly, the two naturalists desired to get to a place where they could spend several days and collect steadily, thereby doing more effective work. The rest of us continued with the mule-train, as was necessary.

It was always a picturesque sight when camp was broken, and again at nightfall when the laden mules came stringing in and their burdens were thrown down, while the tents were pitched and the fires lit. We breakfasted before leaving camp, the aluminum cups and plates being placed on ox-hides, round which we sat, on the ground or on camp-stools. We fared well, on rice, beans, and crackers, with canned corned beef, and salmon or any game that had been shot, and coffee, tea, and matté. I then usually sat down somewhere to write, and when the mules were nearly ready I popped my writing-materials into my duffel-bag—war-sack, as we would have called it in the old days on the plains. I found that the mules usually arrived so late in the afternoon or evening that I could not depend upon being able to write at that time. Of course, if we made a very early start I could not write at all. At night there were no mosquitoes. In the daytime gnats and sand-flies and horse-flies sometimes bothered us a little, but not much. Small stingless bees lit on us in numbers and crawled over the skin, making a slight tickling; but we did not mind them until they became very numerous. There was a good deal of rain, but not enough to cause any serious annoyance.

Colonel Rondon and Lieutenant Lyra held many discussions as to whither the Rio da Dúvida flowed, and where its mouth might be. Its provisional name—"River of Doubt"—was given it precisely because of this ignorance concerning it; an ignorance which it was one of the purposes of our trip to dispel. It might go into the Gy-

Paraná, in which case its course must be very short; it might flow into the Madeira low down, in which case its course would be very long; or, which was unlikely, it might flow into the Tapajos. There was another river, of which Colonel Rondon had come across the headwaters, whose course was equally doubtful, although in its case there was rather more probability of its flowing into the Juruena, by which name the Tapajos is known for its upper half. To this unknown river Colonel Rondon had given the name Ananás, because when he came across it he found a deserted Indian field with pineapples, which the hungry explorers ate greedily. Among the things the colonel and I hoped to accomplish on the trip was to do a little work in clearing up one or the other of these two doubtful geographical points, and thereby to push a little forward the knowledge of this region. Originally, as described in the first chapter, my trip was undertaken primarily in the interest of the American Museum of Natural History of New York, to add to our knowledge of the birds and mammals of the far interior of the western Brazilian wilderness; and the labels of our baggage and scientific equipment, printed by the museum, were entitled "Colonel Roosevelt's South American Expedition for the American Museum of Natural History." But, as I have already mentioned, at Rio the Brazilian Government, through the secretary of foreign affairs, Doctor Lauro Müller, suggested that I should combine the expedition with one by Colonel Rondon, which they contemplated making, and thereby make both expeditions of broader scientific interest. I accepted the proposal with much pleasure; and we found, when we joined Colonel Rondon and his associates, that their baggage and equipment had been labelled by the Brazilian Government "Expedição Scientifica Roosevelt-Rondon." This thenceforth became the proper and official title of the expedition. Cherrie and Miller did the chief zoological work. The geological work was done by a Brazilian member of the expedition, Euzebio Oliveira. The astronomical work necessary for obtaining the exact geographical location of the rivers and points of note was to be done by Lieutenant Lyra, under the supervision of Colonel Rondon; and at the telegraph stations this astronomical work would be checked by wire communications with one of Colonel Rondon's assistants at Cuyabá, Lieutenant Caetano, thereby securing a minutely accurate comparison of time. The sketch-maps and surveying and cartographical work generally were to be made under the supervision of Colonel Rondon by Lyra, with assistance from Fiala and Kermit. Captain Amilcar handled the worst problem—transportation; the medical member was Doctor Cajazeira.

At night around the camp-fire my Brazilian companions often spoke of the first explorers of this vast wilderness of western Brazil—men whose very names are now hardly known, but who did each his part in opening the country which will some day see such growth and development. Among the most notable of them was a Portuguese, Ricardo Franco, who spent forty years at the work, during the last quarter of the eighteenth and the opening years of the nineteenth centuries. He ascended for long distances the Xingu and the Tapajos, and went up the Madeira and Guaporé, crossing to the headwaters of the Paraguay and partially exploring there also. He worked among and with the Indians, much as Mungo Park worked with the natives of West Africa, having none of the aids, instruments, and comforts with which even the hardiest of modern explorers are provided. He was one of the men who established the beginnings of the province of Matto Grosso. For many years the sole method of communication between this remote interior province and civilization was by the long, difficult, and perilous route which led up the Amazon and Madeira; and its then capital, the town of Matto Grosso, the seat of the captain-general, with its palace, cathedral, and fortress, was accordingly placed far to the west, near the Guaporé. When less circuitous lines of communication were established farther eastward the old capital was abandoned, and the tropic wilderness surged over the lonely little town. The tomb of the old colonial explorer still stands in the ruined cathedral, where the forest has once more come to its own. But civilization is again advancing to reclaim the lost town and to revive the memory of the wilderness wanderer who helped to found it. Colonel Rondon has named a river after Franco; a range of mountains has also been named after him; and the colonel, acting for the Brazilian Government, has established a telegraph station in what was once the palace of the captain-general.

Our northward trail led along the high ground a league or two to the east of the northward-flowing Rio Sacre. Each night we camped on one of the small tributary brooks that fed it. Fiala, Kermit, and I occupied one tent. In the daytime the "pium" flies, vicious little sand-flies, became bad enough to make us finally use gloves and head-nets. There were many heavy rains, which made the travelling hard for the mules. The soil was more often clay than sand, and it was slippery when wet. The weather was overcast, and there was usually no oppressive heat even at noon. At intervals along the trail we came on the staring skull and bleached skeleton of a mule or ox. Day after day we rode forward across endless flats of grass and of low open scrubby forest, the trees standing far apart and in most places being but little higher than the head of a horseman. Some of them carried blossoms, white, orange, yellow, pink; and there were many flowers, the most beautiful being the morning-glories. Among the trees were bastard rubber-trees, and dwarf palmetto; if the latter grew more than a few feet high their tops were torn and dishevelled by the wind. There was very little bird or mammal life; there were few long vistas, for in most places it was not possible to see far among the gray, gnarled trunks of the wind-beaten little trees. Yet the desolate landscape had a certain charm of its own, although not a charm that would be felt by any man who does not take pleasure in mere space, and freedom and wildness, and in plains standing empty to the sun, the wind, and the rain. The country bore some resemblance to the country west of Redjaf on the White Nile, the home of the giant eland; only here there was no big game, no chance of seeing the towering form of the giraffe, the black bulk of elephant or buffalo, the herds of straw-colored hartebeests, or the ghostly shimmer of the sun glinting on the coats of roan and eland as they vanished silently in the gray sea of withered scrub.

One feature in common with the African landscape was the abundance of ant-hills, some as high as a man.

They were red in the clay country, gray where it was sandy; and the dirt houses were also in trees, while their raised tunnels traversed trees and ground alike. At some of the camping-places we had to be on our watch against the swarms of leaf-carrying ants. These are so called in the books—the Brazilians call them "carregadores," or porters—because they are always carrying bits of leaves and blades of grass to their underground homes. They are inveterate burden-bearers, and they industriously cut into pieces and carry off any garment they can get at; and we had to guard our shoes and clothes from them, just as we had often had to guard all our belongings against the termites. These ants did not bite us; but we encountered huge black ants, an inch and a quarter long, which were very vicious, and their bite was not only painful but quite poisonous. Praying-mantes were common, and one evening at supper one had a comical encounter with a young dog, a jovial near-puppy, of Colonel Rondon's, named Cartucho. He had been christened the jolly-cum-pup, from a character in one of Frank Stockton's stories, which I suppose are now remembered only by elderly people, and by them only if they are natives of the United States. Cartucho was lying with his head on the ox-hide that served as table, waiting with poorly dissembled impatience for his share of the banquet. The mantis flew down on the ox-hide and proceeded to crawl over it, taking little flights from one corner to another; and whenever it thought itself menaced it assumed an attitude of seeming devotion and real defiance. Soon it lit in front of Cartucho's nose. Cartucho cocked his big ears forward, stretched his neck, and cautiously sniffed at the new arrival, not with any hostile design, but merely to find out whether it would prove to be a playmate. The mantis promptly assumed an attitude of prayer. This struck Cartucho as both novel and interesting, and he thrust his sniffing black nose still nearer. The mantis dexterously thrust forward first one and then the other armed fore leg, touching the intrusive nose, which was instantly jerked back and again slowly and inquiringly brought forward. Then the mantis suddenly flew in Cartucho's face, whereupon Cartucho, with a smothered yelp of dismay, almost turned a back somersault; and the triumphant mantis flew back to the middle of the ox-hide, among the plates, where it reared erect and defied the laughing and applauding company.

On the morning of the 29th we were rather late in starting, because the rain had continued through the night into the morning, drenching everything. After nightfall there had been some mosquitoes, and the piums were a pest during daylight; where one bites it leaves a tiny black spot on the skin which lasts for several weeks. In the slippery mud one of the pack-mules fell and injured itself so that it had to be abandoned. Soon after starting we came on the telegraph-line, which runs from Cayubá; this was the first time we had seen it. Two Parecís Indians joined us, leading a pack-bullock. They were dressed in hat, shirt, trousers, and sandals, precisely like the ordinary Brazilian *caboclos*, as the poor backwoods peasants, usually with little white blood in them, are colloquially and half-derisively styled—*caboclo* being originally a Guaraný word meaning "naked savage." These two Indians were in the employ of the Telegraphic Commission, and had been patrolling the telegraph-line. The bullock carried their personal belongings and the tools with which they could repair a break. The commission pays the ordinary Indian worker 66 cents a day; a very good worker gets $1, and the chief $1.66. No man gets anything unless he works. Colonel Rondon, by just, kindly, and understanding treatment of these Indians, who previously had often been exploited and maltreated by rubber-gatherers, has made them the loyal friends of the government. He has gathered them at the telegraph stations, where they cultivate fields of mandioc, beans, potatoes, maize, and other vegetables, and where he is introducing them to stock-raising; and the entire work of guarding and patrolling the line is theirs.

After six hours' march we came to the crossing of the Rio Sacre at the beautiful waterfall appropriately called the Salto Bello. This is the end of the automobile road. Here there is a small Parecís village. The men of the village work the ferry by which everything is taken across the deep and rapid river. The ferry-boat is made of planking placed on three dugout canoes, and runs on a trolley. Before crossing we enjoyed a good swim in the swift, clear, cool water. The Indian village, where we camped, is placed on a jutting tongue of land round which the river sweeps just before it leaps from the overhanging precipice. The falls themselves are very lovely. Just above them is a wooded island, but the river joins again before it races forward for the final plunge. There is a sheer drop of forty or fifty yards, with a breadth two or three times as great; and the volume of water is large. On the left or hither bank a cliff extends for several hundred yards below the falls. Green vines have flung themselves down over

The Salto Bello Falls

There is a sheer drop of forty or fifty yards, and a breadth perhaps three times as great

From a photograph by Miller

its face, and they are met by other vines thrusting upward from the mass of vegetation at its foot, glistening in the perpetual mist from the cataract, and clothing even the rock surfaces in vivid green. The river, after throwing itself over the rock wall, rushes off in long curves at the bottom of a thickly wooded ravine, the white water churning among the black bowlders. There is a perpetual rainbow at the foot of the falls. The masses of green water that are hurling themselves over the brink dissolve into shifting, foaming columns of snowy lace.

On the edge of the cliff below the falls Colonel Rondon had placed benches, giving a curious touch of rather conventional tourist-civilization to this cataract far out in the lonely wilderness. It is well worth visiting for its beauty. It is also of extreme interest because of the promise it holds for the future. Lieutenant Lyra informed me that they had calculated that this fall would furnish thirty-six thousand horse-power. Eight miles off we were to see another fall of much greater height and power. There are many rivers in this region which would furnish almost unlimited motive force to populous manufacturing communities. The country round about is healthy. It is an upland region of good climate; we were visiting it in the rainy season, the season when the nights are far less cool than in the dry season, and yet we found it delightful. There is much fertile soil in the neighborhood of the streams, and the teeming lowlands of the Amazon and the Paraguay could readily—and with immense advantage to both sides—be made tributary to an industrial civilization seated on these highlands. A telegraph-line has been built to and across them. A railroad should follow. Such a line could be easily built, for there are no serious natural obstacles. In advance of its construction a trolley-line could be run from Cuyabá to the falls, using the power furnished by the latter. Once this is done the land will offer extraordinary opportunities to settlers of the right kind: to home-makers and to enterprising business men of foresight, coolness, and sagacity who are willing to work with the settlers, the immigrants, the home-makers, for an advantage which shall be mutual.

The Parecís Indians, whom we met here, were exceedingly interesting. They were to all appearance an unusually cheerful, good-humored, pleasant-natured people. Their teeth were bad; otherwise they appeared strong and vigorous, and there were plenty of children. The colonel was received as a valued friend and as a leader who was to be followed and obeyed. He is raising them by degrees—the only way by which to make the rise permanent. In this village he has got them to substitute for the flimsy Indian cabins houses of the type usual among the poorer field laborers and back-country dwellers in Brazil. These houses have roofs of palm thatch, steeply pitched. They are usually open at the sides, consisting merely of a framework of timbers, with a wall at the back; but some have the ordinary four walls, of erect palm-logs. The hammocks are slung in the houses, and the cooking is also done in them, with pots placed on small open fires, or occasionally in a kind of clay oven. The big gourds for water, and the wicker baskets, are placed on the ground, or hung on the poles.

The men had adopted, and were wearing, shirts and trousers, but the women had made little change in their clothing. A few wore print dresses, but obviously only for ornament. Most of them, especially the girls and young married women, wore nothing but a loin-cloth in addition to bead necklaces and bracelets. The nursing mothers—and almost all the mothers were nursing—sometimes carried the child slung against their side or hip, seated in a cloth belt, or sling, which went over the opposite shoulder of the mother. The women seemed to be well treated, although polygamy is practised. The children were loved by every one; they were petted by both men and women, and they behaved well to one another, the boys not seeming to bully the girls or the smaller boys. Most of the children were naked, but the girls early wore the loin-cloth; and some, both of the little boys and the little girls, wore colored print garments, to the evident pride of themselves and their parents. In each house there were several families, and life went on with no privacy but with good humor, consideration, and fundamentally good manners. The man or woman who had nothing to do lay in a hammock or squatted on the ground leaning against a post or wall. The children played together, or lay in little hammocks, or tagged round after their mothers; and when called they came trustfully up to us to be petted or given some small trinket; they were friendly little souls, and accustomed to good treatment. One woman was weaving a cloth, another was making a hammock; others made ready melons and other vegetables and cooked them over tiny fires. The men, who had come in from work at the ferry or along the telegraph-lines, did some work themselves, or played with the children; one cut a small boy's hair, and then had his own hair cut by a friend. But the absorbing amusement of the men was an extraordinary game of ball.

In our family we have always relished Oliver Herford's nonsense rhymes, including the account of Willie's displeasure with his goat:

> "I do not like my billy goat,
> I wish that he was dead;
> Because he kicked me, so he did,
> He kicked me with his head."

Well, these Parecís Indians enthusiastically play football with their heads. The game is not only native to them, but I have never heard or read of its being played by any other tribe or people. They use a light hollow rubber ball, of their own manufacture. It is circular and about eight inches in diameter. The players are divided into two sides, and stationed much as in association football, and the ball is placed on the ground to be put in play as in football. Then a player runs forward, throws himself flat on the ground, and butts the ball toward the opposite side. This first butt, when the ball is on the ground, never lifts it much and it rolls and bounds toward the opponents. One or two of the latter run toward it; one throws himself flat on his face and butts the ball back. Usually this butt lifts it, and it flies back in a curve well up in the air; and an opposite player, rushing toward it, catches it on his head with such a swing of his brawny neck, and such precision and address that the ball bounds back through the air as a football soars after a drop-kick. If the ball flies off to one side or the other it is brought back, and again put in play. Often it will be sent to and

One woman was making a hammock

From a photograph by Kermit Roosevelt

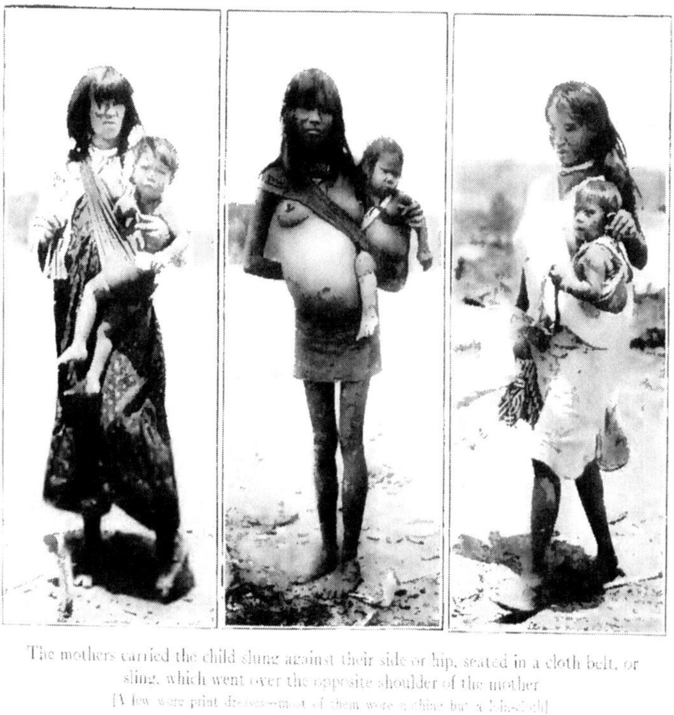

The mothers carried the child slung against their side or hip, seated in a cloth belt, or sling, which went over the opposite shoulder of the mother

[A few wore print dresses—most of them wore nothing but a loin-cloth]

From photographs by Cherrie and Miller

fro a dozen times, from head to head, until finally it rises with such a sweep that it passes far over the heads of the opposite players and descends behind them. Then shrill, rolling cries of good-humored triumph arise from the victors; and the game instantly begins again with fresh zest. There are, of course, no such rules as in a specialized ball-game of civilization; and I saw no disputes. There may be eight or ten, or many more, players on each side. The ball is never touched with the hands or feet, or with anything except the top of the head. It is hard to decide whether to wonder most at the dexterity and strength with which it is hit or butted with the head, as it comes down through the air, or at the reckless speed and skill with which the players throw themselves headlong on the ground to return the ball if it comes low down. Why they do not grind off their noses I cannot imagine. Some of the players hardly ever failed to catch and return the ball if it came in their neighborhood, and with such a vigorous toss of the head that it often flew in a great curve for a really astonishing distance.

That night a pack-ox got into the tent in which Kermit and I were sleeping, entering first at one end and then at the other. It is extraordinary that he did not waken us; but we slept undisturbed while the ox deliberately ate our shirts, socks, and underclothes! It chewed them into rags. One of my socks escaped, and my undershirt, although chewed full of holes, was still good for some weeks' wear; but the other things were in fragments.

In the morning Colonel Rondon arranged for us to have breakfast over on the benches under the trees by the waterfall, whose roar, lulled to a thunderous murmur, had been in our ears before we slept and when we waked. There could have been no more picturesque place for the breakfast of such a party as ours. All travellers who really care to see what is most beautiful and most characteristic of the far interior of South America should in their journey visit this region, and see the two great waterfalls. They are even now easy of access; and as soon as the traffic warrants it they will be made still more so; then, from São Luis de Cáceres, they will be speedily reached by light steamboat up the Sepotuba and by a day or two's automobile ride, with a couple of days on horseback in between.

The colonel held a very serious council with the Parecís Indians over an incident which caused him grave concern. One of the commission's employees, a negro, had killed a wild Nhambiquara Indian; but it appeared that he had really been urged on and aided by the Parecís, as the members of the tribe to which the dead Indian belonged were much given to carrying off the Parecís women and in other ways making themselves bad neighbors. The colonel tried hard to get at the truth of the matter; he went to the biggest Indian house, where he sat in a hammock—an Indian child cuddling solemnly up to him, by the way—while the Indians sat in other hammocks, and stood round about; but it was impossible to get an absolutely frank statement.

It appeared, however, that the Nhambiquaras had made a descent on the Parecís village in the momentary absence of the men of the village; but the latter, notified by the screaming of the women, had returned in time to rescue them. The negro was with them and, having a good rifle, he killed one of the aggressors. The Parecís were, of

The kick-off: a player runs forward, throws himself flat on the ground, and butts the ball toward the opposite side

From a photograph by Kermit Roosevelt

Often it will be sent to and fro a dozen times from head to head until finally it rises

From a photograph [illegible] Fiala

The game of headball played by Parecis Indians at Utiarity Falls

course, in the right, but the colonel could not afford to have his men take sides in a tribal quarrel.

It was only a two hours' march across to the Papagaio at the Falls of Utiarity, so named by their discoverer, Colonel Rondon, after the sacred falcon of the Parecís. On the way we passed our Indian friends, themselves bound thither; both the men and the women bore burdens—the burdens of some of the women, poor things, were heavy—and even the small naked children carried the live hens. At Utiarity there is a big Parecís settlement and a telegraph station kept by one of the employees of the commission. His pretty brown wife is acting as schoolmistress to a group of little Parecís girls. The Parecís chief has been made a major and wears a uniform accordingly. The commission has erected good buildings for its own employees and has superintended the erection of good houses for the Indians. Most of the latter still prefer the simplicity of the loin-cloth, in their ordinary lives, but they proudly wore their civilized clothes in our honor. When in the late afternoon the men began to play a regular match game of headball, with a scorer or umpire to keep count, they soon discarded most of their clothes, coming down to nothing but trousers or a loin-cloth. Two or three of them had their faces stained with red ochre. Among the women and children looking on were a couple of little girls who paraded about on stilts.

The great waterfall was half a mile below us. Lovely though we had found Salto Bello, these falls were far superior in beauty and majesty. They are twice as high and twice as broad; and the lay of the land is such that the various landscapes in which the waterfall is a feature are more striking. A few hundred yards above the falls the river turns at an angle and widens. The broad, rapid shallows are crested with whitecaps. Beyond this wide expanse of flecked and hurrying water rise the mist columns of the cataract; and as these columns are swayed and broken by the wind the forest appears through and between them. From below the view is one of singular grandeur. The fall is over a shelving ledge of rock which goes in a nearly straight line across the river's course. But at the left there is a salient in the cliff-line, and here accordingly a great cataract of foaming water comes down almost as a separate body, in advance of the line of the main fall. I doubt whether, excepting, of course, Niagara, there is a waterfall in North America which outranks this if both volume and beauty are considered. Above the fall the river flows through a wide valley with gently sloping sides. Below, it slips along, a torrent of whity-green water, at the bottom of a deep gorge; and the sides of the gorge are clothed with a towering growth of tropical forest.

Next morning the cacique of these Indians, in his major's uniform, came to breakfast, and bore himself with entire propriety. It was raining heavily—it rained most of the time—and a few minutes previously I had noticed the cacique's two wives, with three or four other young women, going out to the mandioc fields. It was a picturesque group. The women were all mothers, and each carried a nursing child. They wore loin-cloths or short skirts. Each carried on her back a wickerwork basket supported by a head-strap which went around her forehead. Each carried a belt slung diagonally across her body, over her right shoulder; in this the child was car-

The Falls of Utiarity

I doubt whether, excepting, of course, Niagara, there is a waterfall in North America which outranks this if both volume and beauty are considered

From a photograph by Cherrie

ried, against and perhaps astride of her left hip. They were comely women, who did not look jaded or cowed; and they laughed cheerfully and nodded to us as they passed through the rain, on their way to the fields. But the contrast between them and the chief in his soldier's uniform seated at breakfast was rather too striking; and incidentally it etched in bold lines the folly of those who idealize the life of even exceptionally good and pleasant-natured savages.

Although it was the rainy season, the trip up to this point had not been difficult, and from May to October, when the climate is dry and at its best, there would be practically no hardship at all for travellers and visitors. This is a healthy plateau. But, of course, the men who do the first pioneering, even in country like this, encounter dangers and run risks; and they make payment with their bodies. At more than one halting-place we had come across the forlorn grave of some soldier or laborer of the commission. The grave-mound lay within a rude stockade; and an uninscribed wooden cross, gray and weather-beaten, marked the last resting-place of the unknown and forgotten man beneath, the man who had paid with his humble life the cost of pushing the frontier of civilization into the wild savagery of the wilderness. Farther west the conditions become less healthy. At this station Colonel Rondon received news of sickness and of some deaths among the employees of the commission in the country to the westward, which we were soon to enter. Beriberi and malignant malarial fever were the diseases which claimed the major number of the victims.

Surely these are "the men who do the work for which

they draw the wage." Kermit had with him the same copy of Kipling's poems which he had carried through Africa. At these falls there was one sunset of angry splendor; and we contrasted this going down of the sun, through broken rain-clouds and over leagues of wet tropical forest, with the desert sunsets we had seen in Arizona and Sonora, and along the Guaso Nyiro north and west of Mount Kenia, when the barren mountains were changed into flaming "ramparts of slaughter and peril" standing above "the wine-dark flats below."

It rained during most of the day after our arrival at Utiarity. Whenever there was any let-up the men promptly came forth from their houses and played headball with the utmost vigor; and we would listen to their shrill undulating cries of applause and triumph until we also grew interested and strolled over to look on. They are more infatuated with the game than an American boy is with baseball or football. It is an extraordinary thing that this strange and exciting game should be played by, and only by, one little tribe of Indians in what is almost the very centre of South America. If any traveller or ethnologist knows of a tribe elsewhere that plays a similar game, I wish he would let me know. To play it demands great activity, vigor, skill, and endurance. Looking at the strong, supple bodies of the players, and at the number of children roundabout, it seemed as if the tribe must be in vigorous health; yet the Parecís have decreased in numbers, for measles and smallpox have been fatal to them.

By the evening the rain was coming down more heavily than ever. It was not possible to keep the moisture out of our belongings; everything became mouldy except

A lonely grave by the wayside

At more than one halting-place we had come across the forlorn grave of some soldier or laborer of the commission

From a photograph by Cherrie

The Parecís dance

Most of them wore on one leg anklets which rattled

From a photograph by Miller

what became rusty. It rained all that night; and daylight saw the downpour continuing with no prospect of cessation. The pack-mules could not have gone on with the march; they were already rather done up by their previous ten days' labor through rain and mud, and it seemed advisable to wait until the weather became better before attempting to go forward. Moreover, there had been no chance to take the desired astronomical observations. There was very little grass for the mules; but there was abundance of a small-leaved plant eight or ten inches high—unfortunately, not very nourishing—on which they fed greedily. In such weather and over such muddy trails oxen travel better than mules.

In spite of the weather Cherrie and Miller, whom, together with Father Zahm and Sigg, we had found awaiting us, made good collections of birds and mammals. Among the latter were opossums and mice that were new to them. The birds included various forms so unlike our home birds that the enumeration of their names would mean nothing. One of the most interesting was a large black-and-white woodpecker, the white predominating in the plumage. Several of these woodpeckers were usually found together. They were showy, noisy, and restless, and perched on twigs, in ordinary bird fashion, at least as often as they clung to the trunks in orthodox woodpecker style. The prettiest bird was a tiny manakin, coal-black, with a red-and-orange head.

On February 2 the rain let up, although the sky remained overcast and there were occasional showers. I walked off with my rifle for a couple of leagues; at that distance, from a slight hillock, the mist columns of the falls were conspicuous in the landscape. The only mammal I saw on the walk was a rather hairy armadillo, with a flexible tail, which I picked up and brought back to Miller—it showed none of the speed of the nine-banded armadillos we met on our jaguar-hunt. Judging by its actions, as it trotted about before it saw me, it must be diurnal in habits. It was new to the collection.

I spent much of the afternoon by the waterfall. Under the overcast sky the great cataract lost the deep green and fleecy-white of the sunlit falling waters. Instead it showed opaline hues and tints of topaz and amethyst. At all times, and under all lights, it was majestic and beautiful.

Colonel Rondon had given the Indians various presents, those for the women including calico prints, and, what they especially prized, bottles of scented oil, from Paris, for their hair. The men held a dance in the late afternoon. For this occasion most, but not all, of them cast aside their civilized clothing, and appeared as doubtless they would all have appeared had none but themselves been present. They were absolutely naked except for a beaded string round the waist. Most of them were spotted and dashed with red paint, and on one leg wore anklets which rattled. A number carried pipes through which they blew a kind of deep stifled whistle in time to the dancing. One of them had his pipe leading into a huge gourd, which gave out a hollow, moaning boom. Many wore two red or green or yellow macaw feathers in their hair, and one had a macaw feather stuck transversely through the septum of his nose. They circled slowly round and round, chanting and stamping their feet, while the anklet rattles

The dance of the Parecis Indians

A number carried pipes through which they blew a kind of deep stifled whistle in time to the dancing

From a photograph by Kermit Roosevelt

clattered and the pipes droned. They advanced to the wall of one of the houses, again and again chanting and bowing before it; I was told this was a demand for drink. They entered one house and danced in a ring around the cooking-fire in the middle of the earth floor; I was told that they were then reciting the deeds of mighty hunters and describing how they brought in the game. They drank freely from gourds and pannikins of a fermented drink made from mandioc which were brought out to them. During the first part of the dance the women remained in the houses, and all the doors and windows were shut and blankets hung to prevent the possibility of seeing out. But during the second part all the women and girls came out and looked on. They were themselves to have danced when the men had finished, but were overcome with shyness at the thought of dancing with so many strangers looking on. The children played about with unconcern throughout the ceremony, one of them throwing high in the air, and again catching in his hands, a loaded feather, a kind of shuttlecock.

In the evening the growing moon shone through the cloud-rack. Anything approaching fair weather always put our men in good spirits; and the muleteers squatted in a circle, by a fire near a pile of packs, and listened to a long monotonously and rather mournfully chanted song about a dance and a love-affair. We ourselves worked busily with our photographs and our writing. There was so much humidity in the air that everything grew damp and stayed damp, and mould gathered quickly. At this season it is a country in which writing, taking photographs, and preparing specimens are all works of difficulty, at least so far as concerns preserving and sending home the results of the labor; and a man's clothing is never really dry.

From here Father Zahm returned to Tapirapoan, accompanied by Sigg.

CHAPTER VII

WITH A MULE-TRAIN ACROSS NHAMBIQUARA LAND

FROM this point we were to enter a still wilder region, the land of the naked Nhambiquaras. On February 3 the weather cleared and we started with the mule-train and two ox-carts. Fiala and Lieutenant Lauriadó stayed at Utiarity to take canoes and go down the Papagaio, which had not been descended by any scientific party, and perhaps by no one. They were then to descend the Juruena and Tapajos, thereby performing a necessary part of the work of the expedition. Our remaining party consisted of Colonel Rondon, Lieutenant Lyra, the doctor, Oliveira, Cherrie, Miller, Kermit, and myself. On the Juruena we expected to meet the pack ox-train with Captain Amilcar and Lieutenant Mello; the other Brazilian members of the party had returned. We had now begun the difficult part of the expedition. The pium flies were becoming a pest. There was much fever and beriberi in the country we were entering. The feed for the animals was poor; the rains had made the trails slippery and difficult; and many, both of the mules and the oxen, were already weak, and some had to be abandoned. We left the canoe, the motor, and the gasolene; we had hoped to try them on the Amazonian rivers, but we were obliged to cut down everything that was not absolutely indispensable.

Before leaving we prepared for shipment back to the

museum some of the bigger skins, and also some of the weapons and utensils of the Indians, which Kermit had collected. These included woven fillets, and fillets made of macaw feathers, for use in the dances; woven belts; a gourd in which the sacred drink is offered to the god Enoerey; wickerwork baskets; flutes or pipes; anklet rattles; hammocks; a belt of the kind used by the women in carrying the babies, with the weaving-frame. All these were Parecís articles. He also secured from the Nhambiquaras wickerwork baskets of a different type and bows and arrows. The bows were seven feet long and the arrows five feet. There were blunt-headed arrows for birds, arrows with long, sharp wooden blades for tapir, deer, and other mammals; and the poisoned war-arrows, with sharp barbs, poison-coated and bound on by fine thongs, and with a long, hollow wooden guard to slip over the entire point and protect it until the time came to use it. When people talk glibly of "idle" savages they ignore the immense labor entailed by many of their industries, and the really extraordinary amount of work they accomplish by the skilful use of their primitive and ineffective tools.

It was not until early in the afternoon that we started into the "sertão," * as Brazilians call the wilderness. We drove with us a herd of oxen for food. After going about fifteen miles we camped beside the swampy headwaters of a little brook. It was at the spot where nearly seven years previously Rondon and Lyra had camped on the trip when they discovered Utiarity Falls and penetrated to the Juruena. When they reached this place they had

* Pronounced "sairtown," as nearly as, with our preposterous methods of spelling and pronunciation, I can render it.

been thirty-six hours without food. They killed a bush deer—a small deer—and ate literally every particle. The dogs devoured the entire skin. For much of the time on this trip they lived on wild fruit, and the two dogs that remained alive would wait eagerly under the trees and eat the fruit that was shaken down.

In the late afternoon the piums were rather bad at this camp, but we had gloves and head-nets, and were not bothered; and although there were some mosquitoes we slept well under our mosquito-nets. The frogs in the swamp uttered a peculiar, loud shout. Miller told of a little tree-frog in Colombia which swelled itself out with air until it looked like the frog in Æsop's fables, and then brayed like a mule; and Cherrie told of a huge frog in Guiana that uttered a short, loud roar.

Next day the weather was still fair. Our march lay through country like that which we had been traversing for ten days. Skeletons of mules and oxen were more frequent; and once or twice by the wayside we passed the graves of officers or men who had died on the road. Barbed wire encircled the desolate little mounds. We camped on the west bank of the Burity River. Here there is a balsa, or ferry, run by two Parecís Indians, as employees of the Telegraphic Commission, under the colonel. Each had a thatched house, and each had two wives—all these Indians are pagans. All were dressed much like the poorer peasants of the Brazilian back country, and all were pleasant and well-behaved. The women ran the ferry about as well as the men. They had no cultivated fields, and for weeks they had been living only on game and honey; and they hailed with joy our advent and the quantities of beans and rice which, together with some beef, the colonel left with them. They feasted most of the night. Their houses contained their hammocks, baskets, and other belongings, and they owned some poultry. In one house was a tiny parakeet, very much at home, and familiar, but by no means friendly, with strangers. There are wild Nhambiquaras in the neighborhood, and recently several of these had menaced the two ferrymen with an attack, even shooting arrows at them. The ferrymen had driven them off by firing their rifles in the air; and they expected and received the colonel's praise for their self-restraint; for the colonel is doing all he can to persuade the Indians to stop their blood feuds. The rifles were short and light Winchester carbines, of the kind so universally used by the rubber-gatherers and other adventurous wanderers in the forest wilderness of Brazil. There were a number of rubber-trees in the neighborhood, by the way.

We enjoyed a good bath in the Burity, although it was impossible to make headway by swimming against the racing current. There were few mosquitoes. On the other hand, various kinds of piums were a little too abundant; they vary from things like small gnats to things like black flies. The small stingless bees have no fear and can hardly be frightened away when they light on the hands or face; but they never bite, and merely cause a slight tickling as they crawl over the skin. There were some big bees, however, which, although they crawled about harmlessly after lighting if they were undisturbed, yet stung fiercely if they were molested. The insects were not ordinarily a serious bother, but there were occasional hours when they were too numerous for comfort, and now and then I had to do my writing in a head-net and gauntlets.

The night we reached the Burity it rained heavily, and next day the rain continued. In the morning the mules were ferried over, while the oxen were swum across. Half a dozen of our men—whites, Indians, and negroes, all stark naked and uttering wild cries—drove the oxen into the river and then, with powerful overhand strokes, swam behind and alongside them as they crossed, half-breasting the swift current. It was a fine sight to see the big, long-horned, staring beasts swimming strongly, while the sinewy naked men urged them forward, utterly at ease in the rushing water. We made only a short day's journey, for, owing to the lack of grass, the mules had to be driven off nearly three miles from our line of march, in order to get them feed. We camped at the headwaters of a little brook called Huatsui, which is Parecís for "monkey."

Accompanying us on this march was a soldier bound for one of the remoter posts. With him trudged his wife. They made the whole journey on foot. There were two children. One was so young that it had to be carried alternately by the father and mother. The other, a small boy of eight, and much the best of the party, was already a competent wilderness worker. He bore his share of the belongings on the march, and when camp was reached sometimes himself put up the family shelter. They were mainly of negro blood. Struck by the woman's uncomplaining endurance of fatigue, we offered to take her and the baby in the automobile, while it accompanied us. But, alas! this proved to be one of those melancholy cases where the effort to relieve hardship well endured results only in showing that those who endure the adversity cannot stand even a slight prosperity. The woman proved a querulous traveller in the auto, complaining that she was not made as comfortable as, apparently, she had expected; and after one day the husband declared he was not willing to have her go unless he went too; and the family resumed their walk.

In this neighborhood there were multitudes of the big, gregarious, crepuscular or nocturnal spiders which I have before mentioned. On arriving in camp, at about four in the afternoon, I ran into a number of remains of their webs, and saw a very few of the spiders themselves sitting in the webs midway between trees. I then strolled a couple of miles up the road ahead of us under the line of telegraph-poles. It was still bright sunlight and no spiders were out; in fact, I did not suspect their presence along the line of telegraph-poles, although I ought to have done so, for I continually ran into long strings of tough, fine web, which got across my face or hands or rifle barrel. I returned just at sunset and the spiders were out in force. I saw dozens of colonies, each of scores or hundreds of individuals. Many were among the small trees alongside the broad, cleared trail. But most were dependent from the wire itself. Their webs had all been made or repaired since I had passed. Each was sitting in the middle of his own wheel, and all the wheels were joined to one another; and the whole pendent fabric hung by fine ropes from the wire above, and was in some cases steadied by guy-ropes, thrown thirty feet off to little trees alongside. I watched them until nightfall, and evidently, to them, after their day's rest, their day's work had just begun. Next morn-

Tres Burity

From a photograph by Kermit Roosevelt

The kitchen under the ox hide at Campos Novos

From a photograph by Theodore Roosevelt

ing—owing to a desire to find out what the facts were as regards the ox-carts, which were in difficulties—Cherrie, Miller, Kermit, and I walked back to the Burity River, where Colonel Rondon had spent the night. It was a misty, overcast morning, and the spiders in the webs that hung from the telegraph-wire were just going to their day homes. These were in and under the big white china insulators on the telegraph-poles. Hundreds of spiders were already climbing up into these. When, two or three hours later, we returned, the sun was out, and not a spider was to be seen.

Here we had to cut down our baggage and rearrange the loads for the mule-train. Cherrie and Miller had a most workmanlike equipment, including a very light tent and two light flies. One fly they gave for the kitchen use, one fly was allotted to Kermit and me, and they kept only the tent for themselves. Colonel Rondon and Lyra went in one tent, the doctor and Oliveira in another. Each of us got rid of everything above the sheer necessities. This was necessary because of the condition of the baggage-animals. The oxen were so weak that the effort to bring on the carts had to be abandoned. Nine of the pack-mules had already been left on the road during the three days' march from Utiarity. In the first expeditions into this country all the baggage-animals had died; and even in our case the loss was becoming very heavy. This state of affairs is due to the scarcity of forage and the type of country. Good grass is scanty, and the endless leagues of sparse, scrubby forest render it exceedingly difficult to find the animals when they wander. They must be turned absolutely loose to roam about and pick up their scanty subsistence, and must be given as long a time as possible to feed and rest; even under these conditions most of them grow weak when, as in our case, it is impossible to carry corn. They cannot be found again until after daylight, and then hours must be spent in gathering them; and this means that the march must be made chiefly during the heat of the day, the most trying time. Often some of the animals would not be brought in until so late that it was well on in the forenoon, perhaps midday, before the bulk of the pack-train started; and they reached the camping-place as often after nightfall as before it. Under such conditions many of the mules and oxen grew constantly weaker, and ultimately gave out; and it was imperative to load them as lightly as possible, and discard all luxuries, especially heavy or bulky luxuries. Travelling through a wild country where there is little food for man or beast is beset with difficulties almost inconceivable to the man who does not himself know this kind of wilderness, and especially to the man who only knows the ease of civilization. A scientific party of some size, with the equipment necessary in order to do scientific work, can only go at all if the men who actually handle the problems of food and transportation do their work thoroughly.

Our march continued through the same type of high, nearly level upland, covered with scanty, scrubby forest. It is the kind of country known to the Brazilians as chapadão—pronounced almost as if it were a French word and spelled *shapadón*. Our camp on the fourth night was in a beautiful spot, an open grassy space, beside a clear, cool, rushing little river. We ourselves reached this, and waded our beasts across the deep, narrow stream, in the late afternoon; and we then enjoyed a bath and swim. The loose bullocks arrived at sunset, and with shrill cries the mounted herdsmen urged them into and across the swift water. The mule-train arrived long after nightfall, and it was not deemed wise to try to cross the laden animals. Accordingly the loads were taken off and brought over on the heads of the men; it was fine to see the sinewy, naked figures bearing their burdens through the broken moonlit water to the hither bank. The night was cool and pleasant. We kindled a fire and sat beside the blaze. Then, healthily hungry, we gathered around the ox-hides to a delicious dinner of soup, beef, beans, rice, and coffee.

Next day we made a short march, crossed a brook, and camped by another clear, deep, rapid little river, swollen by the rains. All these rivers that we were crossing run actually into the Juruena, and therefore form part of the headwaters of the Tapajos; for the Tapajos is a mighty river, and the basin which holds its headwaters covers an immense extent of country. This country and the adjacent regions, forming the high interior of western Brazil, will surely some day support a large industrial population; of which the advent would be hastened, although not necessarily in permanently better fashion, if Colonel Rondon's anticipations about the development of mining, especially gold-mining, are realized. In any event the region will be a healthy home for a considerable agricultural and pastoral population. Above all, the many swift streams, with their numerous waterfalls, some of great height and volume, offer the chance for the upgrowth of a number of big manufacturing communities, knit by railroads to one another and to the Atlantic coast and the valleys of the Paraguay, Madeira, and Amazon, and feeding and being fed by the dwellers in the rich, hot, alluvial lowlands that surround this elevated territory. The work of Colonel Rondon and his associates of the Telegraphic Commission has been to open this great and virgin land to the knowledge of the world and to the service of their nation. In doing so they have incidentally founded the Brazilian school of exploration. Before their day almost all the scientific and regular exploration of Brazil was done by foreigners. But, of course, there was much exploration and settlement by nameless Brazilians, who were merely endeavoring to make new homes or advance their private fortunes: in recent years by rubber-gatherers, for instance, and a century ago by those bold and restless adventurers, partly of Portuguese and partly of Indian blood, the Paolistas, from one of whom Colonel Rondon is himself descended on his father's side.

The camp by this river was in some old and grown-up fields, once the seat of a rather extensive maize and mandioc cultivation by the Nhambiquaras. On this day Cherrie got a number of birds new to the collection, and two or three of them probably new to science. We had found the birds for the most part in worn plumage, for the breeding season, the southern spring and northern fall, was over. But some birds were still breeding. In the tropics the breeding season is more irregular than in the north. Some birds breed at very different times from that chosen by the majority of their fellows; some can hardly be said to have any regular season; Cherrie had found one species of honey-creeper breeding in every month of the year. Just before sunset and just after sunrise big, noisy, blue-and-yellow macaws flew over this camp. They were plentiful enough to form a loose flock, but each pair kept to itself, the two individuals always close together and always separated from the rest. Although not an abundant, it was an interesting, fauna which the two naturalists found in this upland country, where hitherto no collections of birds and mammals had been made. Miller trapped several species of opossums, mice, and rats which were new to him. Cherrie got many birds which he did not recognize. At this camp, among totally strange forms, he found an old and familiar acquaintance. Before breakfast he brought in several birds: a dark-colored flycatcher, with white forehead and rump and two very long tail-feathers; a black and slate-blue tanager; a black ant-thrush with a concealed white spot on its back, at the base of the neck, and its dull-colored mate; and other birds which he believed to be new to science, but whose relationships with any of our birds are so remote that it is hard to describe them save in technical language. Finally, among these unfamiliar forms was a veery, and the sight of the rufous-olive back and faintly spotted throat of this singer of our northern Junes made us almost homesick.

Next day was brilliantly clear. The mules could not be brought in until quite late in the morning, and we had to march twenty miles under the burning tropical sun, right in the hottest part of the day. From a rise of ground we looked back over the vast, sunlit landscape, the endless rolling stretches of low forest. Midway on our journey we crossed a brook. The dogs minded the heat much. They continually ran off to one side, lay down in a shady place, waited until we were several hundred yards ahead, and then raced after us, overtook us, and repeated the performance. The pack-train came in about sunset; but we ourselves reached the Juruena in the middle of the afternoon.

The Juruena is the name by which the Tapajos goes along its upper course. Where we crossed, it was a deep, rapid stream, flowing in a heavily wooded valley with rather steep sides. We were ferried across on the usual balsa, a platform on three dugouts, running by the force of the current on a wire trolley. There was a clearing on each side, with a few palms, and on the farther bank were the buildings of the telegraph station. This is a wild country, and the station was guarded by a few soldiers under the command of Lieutenant Marino, a native of Rio Grande do Sul, a blond man who looked like an Englishman—an agreeable companion, and a good and resolute officer, as all must be who do their work in this wilderness. The Juruena was first followed at the end of the eighteenth century by the Portuguese explorer Franco, and not again until over a hundred years had elapsed, when the Telegraphic Commission not only descended, but for the first time accurately placed and mapped its course.

There were several houses on the rise of the farther bank, all with thatched roofs, some of them with walls of upright tree-trunks, some of them daub and wattle. Into one of the latter, with two rooms, we took our belongings. The sand-flies were bothersome at night, coming through the interstices in the ordinary mosquito-nets. The first night they did this I got no sleep until morning, when it was cool enough for me to roll myself in my blanket and put on a head-net. Afterward we used fine nets of a kind of cheese-cloth. They were hot, but they kept out all, or almost all, of the sand-flies and other small tormentors.

Here we overtook the rearmost division of Captain Amilcar's bullock-train. Our own route had diverged, in order to pass the great falls. Captain Amilcar had come direct, overtaking the pack-oxen, which had left Tapirapoan before we did, laden with material for the Dúvida trip. He had brought the oxen through in fine shape, losing only three beasts with their loads, and had himself left the Juruena the morning of the day we reached there. His weakest animals left that evening, to make the march by moonlight; and as it was desirable to give them thirty-six hours' start, we halted for a day on the banks of the river. It was not a wasted day. In addition to bathing and washing our clothes, the naturalists made some valuable additions to the collection—including a boldly marked black, blue, and white jay—and our photographs were developed and our writing brought abreast of the date. Travelling through a tropical wilderness in the rainy season, when the amount of baggage that can be taken is strictly limited, entails not only a good deal of work, but also the exercise of considerable ingenuity if the writing and photographing, and especially the preservation, of the specimens are to be done in satisfactory shape.

At the telegraph office we received news that the voyage of Lauriadó and Fiala down the Papagaio had opened with a misadventure. In some bad rapids, not many miles below the falls, two of the canoes had been upset, half of their provisions and all of Fiala's baggage lost, and Fiala himself nearly drowned. The Papagaio is known both at the source and the mouth; to descend it did not represent a plunge into the unknown, as in the case of the Dúvida or the Ananás; but the actual water work, over the part that was unexplored, offered the same possibilities of mischance and disaster. It is a hazardous thing to descend a swift, unknown river rushing through an uninhabited wilderness. To descend or ascend the ordinary great highway rivers of South America, such as the Amazon, Paraguay, Tapajos, and, in its lower course, the Orinoco, is now so safe and easy, whether by steamboat or big, native cargo-boat, that people are apt to forget the very serious difficulties offered by the streams, often themselves great rivers, which run into or form the upper courses of these same water highways. Few things are easier than the former feat, and few more difficult than the latter; and experience in ordinary travelling on the lower courses of the rivers is of no benefit whatever in enabling a man to form a judgment as to what can be done, and how to do it, on the upper courses. Failure to remember this fact is one of the obstacles in the way of securing a proper appreciation of the needs, and the results, of South American exploration.

At the Juruena we met a party of Nhambiquaras, very friendly and sociable, and very glad to see Colonel Rondon. They were originally exceedingly hostile and suspicious, but the colonel's unwearied thoughtfulness and good temper, joined with his indomitable resolution, enabled him to avoid war and to secure their friendship and even their aid. He never killed one. Many of them are known to him personally. He is on remarkably good terms with them, and they are very fond of him—although this does not prevent them from now and then yielding to tempta-

At the Juruena we met a party of Nhambiquaras, very friendly and sociable, and very glad to see Colonel Rondon

From a photograph by Kermit Roosevelt

tion, even at his expense, and stealing a dog or something else which strikes them as offering an irresistible attraction. They cannot be employed at steady work; but they do occasional odd jobs, and are excellent at hunting up strayed mules or oxen; and a few of the men have begun to wear clothes, purely for ornament. Their confidence and bold friendliness showed how well they had been treated. Probably half of our visitors were men; several were small boys; one was a woman with a baby; the others were young married women and girls.

Nowhere in Africa did we come across wilder or more absolutely primitive savages, although these Indians were pleasanter and better-featured than any of the African tribes at the same stage of culture. Both sexes were well-made and rather good-looking, with fairly good teeth, although some of them seemed to have skin diseases. They were a laughing, easy-tempered crew, and the women were as well-fed as the men, and were obviously well-treated, from the savage standpoint; there was no male brutality like that which forms such a revolting feature in the life of the Australian black fellows and, although to a somewhat less degree, in the life of so many negro and Indian tribes. They were practically absolutely naked. In many savage tribes the men go absolutely naked, but the women wear a breech-clout or loin-cloth. In certain tribes we saw near Lake Victoria Nyanza, and on the upper White Nile, both men and women were practically naked. Among these Nhambiquaras the women were more completely naked than the men, although the difference was not essential. The men wore a string around the waist. Most of them wore nothing else, but a few had loosely hanging from this string in front a scanty tuft of dried grass, or a small piece of cloth, which, however, was of purely symbolic use so far as either protection or modesty was concerned. The women did not wear a stitch of any kind anywhere on their bodies. They did not have on so much as a string, or a bead, or even an ornament in their hair. They were all, men and women, boys and well-grown young girls, as entirely at ease and unconscious as so many friendly animals. All of them—men, women, and children, laughing and talking—crowded around us, whether we were on horseback or on foot. They flocked into the house, and when I sat down to write surrounded me so closely that I had to push them gently away. The women and girls often stood holding one another's hands, or with their arms over one another's shoulders or around one another's waists, offering an attractive picture. The men had holes pierced through the septum of the nose and through the upper lip, and wore a straw through each hole. The women were not marked or mutilated. It seems like a contradiction in terms, but it is nevertheless a fact that the behavior of these completely naked women and men was entirely modest. There was never an indecent look or a consciously indecent gesture. They had no blankets or hammocks, and when night came simply lay down in the sand. Colonel Rondon stated that they never wore a covering by night or by day, and if it was cool slept one on each side of a small fire. Their huts were merely slight shelters against the rain.

The moon was nearly full, and after nightfall a few of the Indians suddenly held an improvised dance for us in front of our house. There were four men, a small boy,

Nhambiquara child with a pet monkey

The men had holes pierced through the septum of the nose and through the upper lip, and wore a straw through each hole

From photographs by Miller and Cherrie

and two young women or grown girls. Two of the men had been doing some work for the commission, and were dressed, one completely and one partially, in ordinary clothes. Two of the men and the boy were practically naked, and the two young women were absolutely so. All of them danced in a circle, without a touch of embarrassment or impropriety. The two girls kept hold of each other's hands throughout, dancing among the men as modestly as possible, and with the occasional interchange of a laugh or jest, in as good taste and temper as in any dance in civilization. The dance consisted in slowly going round in a circle, first one way then the other, rhythmically beating time with the feet to the music of the song they were chanting. The chants—there were three of them, all told—were measured and rather slowly uttered melodies, varied with an occasional half-subdued shrill cry. The women continually uttered a kind of long-drawn wailing or droning; I am not enough of a musician to say whether it was an overtone or the sustaining of the burden of the ballad. The young boy sang better than any of the others. It was a strange and interesting sight to see these utterly wild, friendly savages, circling in their slow dance, and chanting their immemorial melodies, in the brilliant tropical moonlight, with the river rushing by in the background, through the lonely heart of the wilderness.

The Indians stayed with us, feasting, dancing, and singing, until the early hours of the morning. They then suddenly and silently disappeared in the darkness, and did not return. In the morning we discovered that they had gone off with one of Colonel Rondon's dogs. Probably the temptation had proved irresistible to one of their number, and the others had been afraid to interfere, and also afraid to stay in or return to our neighborhood. We had not time to go after them; but Rondon remarked that as soon as he again came to the neighborhood he would take some soldiers, hunt up the Indians, and reclaim the dog. It has been his mixture of firmness, good nature, and good judgment that has enabled him to control these bold, warlike savages, and even to reduce the warfare between them and the Parecís. In spite of their good nature and laughter, their fearlessness and familiarity showed how necessary it was not to let them get the upper hand. They are always required to leave all their arms a mile or two away before they come into the encampment. They are much wilder and more savage, and at a much lower cultural level, than the Parecís.

In the afternoon of the day following our arrival there was a heavy rain-storm which drove into the unglazed windows, and here and there came through the roof and walls of our daub-and-wattle house. The heat was intense and there was much moisture in this valley. During the downpour I looked out at the dreary little houses, showing through the driving rain, while the sheets of muddy water slid past their door-sills; and I felt a sincere respect for the lieutenant and his soldiers who were holding this desolate outpost of civilization. It is an unhealthy spot; there has been much malarial fever and beriberi—an obscure and deadly disease.

Next morning we resumed our march. It soon began to rain and we were drenched when, some fifteen miles on, we reached the river where we were to camp. After the

Maloca or beehive hut of the Nhambiquaras

From a photograph by Kermit Roosevelt

A Nhambiquara shelter hut and utensils

Their huts were merely flimsy shelters against the rain

From a photograph by Kermit Roosevelt

great heat we felt quite cold in our wet clothes, and gladly crowded round a fire which was kindled under a thatched shed, beside the cabin of the ferrymen. This ferry-boat was so small that it could only take one mule, or at most two, at a time. The mules and a span of six oxen dragging an ox-cart, which we had overtaken, were ferried slowly to the farther side that afternoon, as there was no feed on the hither bank, where we ourselves camped. The ferryman was a soldier in the employ of the Telegraphic Commission. His good-looking, pleasant-mannered wife, evidently of both Indian and negro blood, was with him, and was doing all she could do as a housekeeper, in the comfortless little cabin, with its primitive bareness of furniture and fittings.

Here we saw Captain Amilcar, who had come back to hurry up his rear-guard. We stood ankle-deep in mud and water, by the swollen river, while the rain beat on us, and enjoyed a few minutes' talk with the cool, competent officer who was doing a difficult job with such workmanlike efficiency. He had no poncho, and was wet through, but was much too busy in getting his laden oxen forward to think of personal discomfort. He had had a good deal of trouble with his mules, but his oxen were still in fair shape.

After leaving the Juruena the ground became somewhat more hilly, and the scrubby forest was less open, but otherwise there was no change in the monotonous, and yet to me rather attractive, landscape. The ant-hills, and the ant-houses in the trees—arboreal ant-hills, so to speak—were as conspicuous as ever. The architects of some were red ants, of others black ants; and others, which were on the whole the largest, had been built by the white ants, the termites. The latter were not infrequently taller than a horseman's head.

That evening round the camp-fire Colonel Rondon happened to mention how the brother of one of the soldiers with us—a Parecís Indian—had been killed by a jararaca snake. Cherrie told of a narrow escape he had from one while collecting in Guiana. At night he used to set traps in camp for small mammals. One night he heard one of these traps go off under his hammock. He reached down for it, and as he fumbled for the chain he felt a snake strike at him, just missing him in the darkness, but actually brushing his hand. He lit a light and saw that a big jararaca had been caught in the trap; and he preserved it as a specimen. Snakes frequently came into his camp after nightfall. He killed one rattlesnake which had swallowed the skinned bodies of four mice he had prepared as specimens; which shows that rattlesnakes do not always feed only on living prey. Another rattlesnake which he killed in Central America had just swallowed an opossum which proved to be of a species new to science. Miller told how once on the Orinoco he saw on the bank a small anaconda, some ten feet long, killing one of the iguanas, big, active, truculent, carnivorous lizards, equally at home on the land and in the water. Evidently the iguanas were digging out holes in the bank in which to lay their eggs; for there were several such holes, and iguanas working at them. The snake had crushed its prey to a pulp; and not more than a couple of feet away another iguana was still busily, and with entire unconcern, engaged in making its burrow. At Miller's approach the anaconda left the dead iguana and rushed into the water, and the live

The ant-hills were not infrequently taller than a horseman's head

From a photograph by Miller

iguana promptly followed it. Miller also told of the stone gods and altars and temples he had seen in the great Colombian forests, monuments of strange civilizations which flourished and died out ages ago, and of which all memory has vanished. He and Cherrie told of giant rivers and waterfalls, and of forests never penetrated, and mountains never ascended by civilized man; and of bloody revolutions that devastated the settled regions. Listening to them I felt that they could write "Tales of Two Naturalists" that would be worth reading.

They were short of literature, by the way—a party such as ours always needs books—and as Kermit's reading-matter consisted chiefly of Camoens and other Portuguese, or else Brazilian, writers, I strove to supply the deficiency with spare volumes of Gibbon. At the end of our march we were usually far ahead of the mule-train, and the rain was also usually falling. Accordingly we would sit about under trees, or under a shed or lean-to, if there was one, each solemnly reading a volume of Gibbon—and no better reading can be found. In my own case, as I had been having rather a steady course of Gibbon, I varied him now and then with a volume of Arsène Lupin lent me by Kermit.

There were many swollen rivers to cross at this point of our journey. Some we waded at fords. Some we crossed by rude bridges. The larger ones, such as the Juina, we crossed by ferry, and when the approaches were swampy, and the river broad and swift, many hours might be consumed in getting the mule-train, the loose bullocks, and the ox-cart over. We had few accidents, although we once lost a ferry-load of provisions, which was quite a misfortune in a country where they could not be replaced. The pasturage was poor, and it was impossible to make long marches with our weakened animals.

At one camp three Nhambiquaras paid us a visit at breakfast-time. They left their weapons behind them before they appeared, and shouted loudly while they were still hid by the forest, and it was only after repeated answering calls of welcome that they approached. Always in the wilderness friends proclaim their presence; a silent advance marks a foe. Our visitors were men, and stark naked, as usual. One seemed sick; he was thin, and his back was scarred with marks of the grub of the loathsome berni fly. Indeed, all of them showed scars, chiefly from insect wounds. But the other two were in good condition, and, although they ate greedily of the food offered them, they had with them a big mandioc cake, some honey, and a little fish. One of them wore a high helmet of puma-skin, with the tail hanging down his back—handsome head-gear, which he gladly bartered for several strings of bright coral-red beads. Around the upper arms of two of them were bands bound so tightly as to cut into and deform the muscles—a singular custom, seemingly not only purposeless but mischievous, which is common among this tribe and many others.

The Nhambiquaras are a numerous tribe, covering a large region. But they have no general organization. Each group of families acts for itself. Half a dozen years previously they had been very hostile, and Colonel Rondon had to guard his camp and exercise every precaution to guarantee his safety, while at the same time successfully endeavoring to avoid the necessity of himself shedding blood. Now they are, for the most part, friendly. But there are groups or individuals that are not. Several soldiers have been killed at these little lonely stations; and while in some cases the attack may have been due to the soldiers' having meddled with Nhambiquara women, in other cases the killing was entirely wanton and unprovoked. Sooner or later these criminals or outlaws will have to be brought to justice; it will not do to let their crimes go unpunished. Twice soldiers have deserted and fled to the Nhambiquaras. The runaways were well received, were given wives, and adopted into the tribe.

The country when opened will be a healthy abode for white settlers. But pioneering in the wilderness is grim work for both man and beast. Continually, as we journeyed onward, under the pitiless glare of the sun or through blinding torrents of rain, we passed desolate little graves by the roadside. They marked the last resting-places of men who had died by fever, or dysentery, or Nhambiquara arrows. We raised our hats as our mules plodded slowly by through the sand. On each grave was a frail wooden cross, and this and the paling round about were already stained by the weather as gray as the tree-trunks of the stunted forest that stretched endlessly on every side.

The skeletons of mules and oxen were frequent along the road. Now and then we came across a mule or ox which had been abandoned by Captain Amilcar's party, ahead of us. The animal had been left with the hope that when night came it would follow along the trail to water. Sometimes it did so. Sometimes we found it dead, or standing motionless waiting for death. From time to time we had to leave behind one of our own mules.

It was not always easy to recognize what pasturage the mules would accept as good. One afternoon we pitched camp by a tiny rivulet, in the midst of the scrubby upland forest; a camp, by the way, where the piums, the small, biting flies, were a torment during the hours of daylight, while after dark their places were more than taken by the diminutive gnats which the Brazilians expressively term "polvora," or powder, and which get through the smallest meshes of a mosquito-net. The feed was so scanty, and the cover so dense, at this spot that I thought we would have great difficulty in gathering the mules next morning. But we did not. A few hours later, in the afternoon, we camped by a beautiful open meadow; on one side ran a rapid brook, with a waterfall eight feet high, under which we bathed and swam. Here the feed looked so good that we all expressed pleasure. But the mules did not like it, and after nightfall they hiked back on the trail, and it was a long and arduous work to gather them next morning.

I have touched above on the insect pests. Men unused to the South American wilderness speak with awe of the danger therein from jaguars, crocodiles, and poisonous snakes. In reality, the danger from these sources is trivial, much less than the danger of being run down by an automobile at home. But at times the torment of insect plagues can hardly be exaggerated. There are many different species of mosquitoes, some of them bearers of disease. There are many different kinds of small, biting flies and gnats, loosely grouped together under various titles. The ones more especially called piums by my companions were somewhat like our northern black flies. They gorged themselves with blood. At the moment their bites did not hurt, but they left an itching scar. Head-nets and gloves are a protection, but are not very comfortable in stifling hot weather. It is impossible to sleep without mosquito-biers. When settlers of the right type come into a new land they speedily learn to take the measures necessary to minimize the annoyance caused by all these pests. Those that are winged have plenty of kinsfolk in so much of the northern continent as has not yet been subdued by man. But the most noxious of the South American ants have, thank Heaven, no representatives in North America. At the camp of the piums a column of the carnivorous foraging ants made its appearance before nightfall, and for a time we feared it might put us out of our tents, for it went straight through camp, between the kitchen-tent and our own sleeping-tents. However, the column turned neither to the right nor the left, streaming uninterruptedly past for several hours, and doing no damage except to the legs of any incautious man who walked near it.

On the afternoon of February 15 we reached Campos Novos. This place was utterly unlike the country we had been traversing. It was a large basin, several miles across, traversed by several brooks. The brooks ran in deep, swampy valleys, occupied by a matted growth of tall tropical forest. Between them the ground rose in bold hills, bare of forest and covered with grass, on which our jaded animals fed eagerly. On one of these rounded hills a number of buildings were ranged in a quadrangle, for the pasturage at this spot is so good that it is permanently occupied. There were milch cows, and we got delicious fresh milk; and there were goats, pigs, turkeys, and chickens. Most of the buildings were made of upright poles, with roofs of palm thatch. One or two were of native brick, plastered with mud, and before these there was an enclosure with a few ragged palms, and some pineapple plants. Here we halted. Our attendants made two kitchens: one was out in the open air, one was under a shelter of ox-hide. The view over the surrounding grassy hills, riven by deep wooded valleys, was lovely. The air was cool and fresh. We were not bothered by insects, although mosquitoes swarmed in every belt of timber. Yet there has been much fever at this beautiful and seemingly healthy place. Doubtless when settlement is sufficiently advanced a remedy will be developed. The geology of this neighborhood was interesting—Oliveira found fossil tree-trunks which he believed to be of cretaceous age.

Here we found Amilcar and Mello, who had waited for us with the rear-guard of their pack-train, and we enjoyed our meeting with the two fine fellows, than whom no military service of any nation could produce more efficient men for this kind of difficult and responsible work. Next morning they mustered their soldiers, muleteers, and pack-ox men, and marched off. Reinisch the taxidermist was with them. We followed in the late afternoon, camping after a few miles. We left the ox-cart at Campos Novos; from thence on the trail was only for pack-animals.

In this neighborhood the two naturalists found many birds which we had not hitherto met. The most conspicuous was a huge oriole, the size of a small crow, with a naked face, a black-and-red bill, and gaudily variegated plumage of green, yellow, and chestnut. Very interesting was the false bell-bird, a gray bird with loud, metallic notes. There was also a tiny soft-tailed woodpecker, no larger than a kinglet; a queer humming-bird with a slightly flexible bill; and many species of ant-thrush, tanager, manakin, and tody. Among these unfamiliar forms was a vireo looking much like our solitary vireo. At one camp Cherrie collected a dozen perching birds; Miller a beautiful little rail; and Kermit, with the small Lüger belt-rifle, a handsome curassow, nearly as big as a turkey—out of which, after it had been skinned, the cook made a delicious canja, the thick Brazilian soup of fowl and rice than which there is nothing better of its kind. All these birds were new to the collection—no naturalists had previously worked this region—so that the afternoon's work represented nine species new to the collection, six new genera, and a most excellent soup.

Two days after leaving Campos Novos we reached Vilhena, where there is a telegraph station. We camped once at a small river named by Colonel Rondon the "Twelfth of October," because he reached it on the day Columbus discovered America—I had never before known what day it was!—and once at the foot of a hill which he had named after Lyra, his companion in the exploration. The two days' march—really one full day and part of two others—was through beautiful country, and we enjoyed it thoroughly, although there were occasional driving rain-storms, when the rain came in almost level sheets and drenched every one and everything. The country was like that around Campos Novos, and offered a striking contrast to the level, barren, sandy wastes of the chapadão, which is a healthy region, where great industrial centres can arise, but not suited for extensive agriculture as are the lowland flats. For these forty-eight hours the trail climbed into and out of steep valleys and broad basins and up and down hills. In the deep valleys were magnificent woods, in which giant rubber-trees towered, while the huge leaves of the low-growing pacova, or wild banana, were conspicuous in the undergrowth. Great azure butterflies flitted through the open, sunny glades, and the bell-birds, sitting motionless, uttered their ringing calls from the dark stillness of the columned groves. The hillsides were grassy pastures or else covered with low, open forest.

A huge frog, brown above, with a light streak down each side, was found hiding under some sticks in a damp place in one of the improvised kitchens; and another frog, with disks on his toes, was caught on one of the tents. A coral-snake puzzled us. Some coral-snakes are harmless; others are poisonous, although not aggressive. The best authorities give an infallible recipe for distinguishing them by the pattern of the colors, but this particular specimen, although it corresponded exactly in color pattern with the description of the poisonous snakes, nevertheless had no poison-fangs that even after the most minute examination we could discover. Miller and one of the dogs caught a sariema, a big, long-legged, bustard-like bird, in rather a curious way. We were on the march, plodding along through as heavy a tropic downpour as it was our ill fortune to encounter. The sariema, evidently as drenched and uncomfortable as we were, was hiding under a bush to avoid the pelting rain. The dog discovered it, and after the bird valiantly repelled him, Miller was able to seize it. Its stomach contained about half a pint of grasshoppers and beetles and young leaves. At Vilhena there was a tame sariema, much more familiar and at home than any of the poultry. It was without the least fear of man or dog. The sariema (like the screamer and the curassow) ought to be introduced into our barnyards and on our lawns, at any rate in the Southern States; it is a good-looking, friendly, and attractive bird. Another bird we met is in some places far more intimate, and domesticates itself. This is the pretty little honey-creeper. In Colombia Miller found the honey-creepers habitually coming inside the houses and hotels at meal-times, hopping about the table, and climbing into the sugar-bowl.

Along this part of our march there was much of what at a hasty glance seemed to be volcanic rock; but Oliveira showed me that it was a kind of conglomerate, with bubbles or hollows in it, made of sand and iron-bearing earth. He said it was a superficial quaternary deposit, formed by erosion from the cretaceous rocks, and that there were here no tertiary deposits. He described the geological structure of the lands through which we had passed as follows: The pantanals were of pleistocene age. Along the upper Sepotuba, in the region of the rapids, there were sandstones, shales, and clays of permian age. The rolling country east of this contained eruptive rocks—a porphyritic diabase, with zeolite, quartz, and agate of triassic age. With the chapadão of the Parecís plateau we came to a land of sand and clay, dotted with lumps of sandstone and pieces of petrified wood; this, according to Oliveira, is of mesozoic age, possibly cretaceous and similar to the South African formation. There are geologists who consider it as of permian age.

At Vilhena we were on a watershed which drained into the Gy-Paraná, which itself runs into the Madeira nearly midway between its sources and its mouth. A little farther along and northward we again came to streams running ultimately into the Tapajos; and between them, and close to them, were streamlets which drained into the Dúvida and Ananás, whose courses and outlets were unknown. This point is part of the divide between the basins of the Madeira and Tapajos. A singular topographical feature of the Plan Alto, the great interior sandy plateau of Brazil, is that at its westernmost end the southward-flowing streams, instead of running into the Paraguay as they do farther east, form the headwaters of the Guaporé, which may, perhaps, be called the upper main stream of the Madeira. These westernmost streams from the southern edge of the plateau, therefore, begin by flowing south; then for a long stretch they flow southwest; then north, and finally northeast into the Amazon. According to some exceptionally good geological observers, this is probably due to the fact that in a remote geologic past the ocean sent in an arm from the south, between the Plan Alto and what is now the Andean chain. These rivers then emptied into the Andean Sea. The gradual upheaval of the soil has resulted in substituting dry land for this arm of the ocean and in reversing the course of what is now the Madeira, just as, according to these geologists, in somewhat familiar fashion the Amazon has been reversed, it having once been, at least for the upper two thirds of its course, an affluent of the Andean Sea.

From Vilhena we travelled in a generally northward direction. For a few leagues we went across the chapadão, the sands or clays of the nearly level upland plateau, grassy or covered with thin, stunted forest, the same type of country that had been predominant ever since we ascended the Parecís table-land on the morning of the third day after leaving the Sepotuba. Then, at about the point where the trail dipped into a basin containing the headsprings of the Ananás, we left this type of country and began to march through thick forest, not very high. There was little feed for the animals on the chapadão. There was less in the forest. Moreover, the continual heavy rains made the travelling difficult and laborious for them, and they weakened. However, a couple of marches before we reached Tres Burity, where there is a big ranch with hundreds of cattle, we were met by ten fresh pack-oxen, and our serious difficulties were over.

There were piums in plenty by day, but neither mosquitoes nor sand-flies by night; and for us the trip was very pleasant, save for moments of anxiety about the mules. The loose bullocks furnished us abundance of fresh beef, although, as was inevitable under the circumstances, of a decidedly tough quality. One of the biggest of the bullocks was attacked one night by a vampire bat, and next morning his withers were literally bathed in blood.

With the chapadão we said good-by to the curious, gregarious, and crepuscular or nocturnal spiders which we found so abundant along the line of the telegraph-wire. They have offered one of the small problems with which the Commission has had to deal. They are not common in the dry season. They swarm during the rains; and, when their tough webs are wet, those that lead from the wire to the ground sometimes effectually short-circuit the wire.

They have on various occasions caused a good deal of trouble in this manner.

The third night out from Vilhena we emerged for a moment from the endless close-growing forest in which our poor animals got such scanty pickings, and came to a beautiful open country, where grassy slopes, dotted with occasional trees, came down on either side of a little brook which was one of the headwaters of the Dúvida. It was a pleasure to see the mules greedily bury their muzzles in the pasturage. Our tents were pitched in the open, near a shady tree, which sent out its low branches on every side. At this camp Cherrie shot a lark, very characteristic of the open upland country, and Miller found two bats in the rotten wood of a dead log. He heard them squeaking and dug them out; he could not tell by what method they had gotten in.

Here Kermit, while a couple of miles from our tents, came across an encampment of Nhambiquaras. There were twenty or thirty of them—men, women, and a few children. Kermit, after the manner of honest folk in the wilderness, advanced ostentatiously in the open, calling out to give warning of his coming. Like surroundings may cause like manners. The early Saxons in England deemed it legal to kill any man who came through the woods without shouting or blowing a horn; and in Nhambiquara land at the present time it is against etiquette, and may be very unhealthy, to come through the woods toward strangers without loudly announcing one's presence. The Nhambiquaras received Kermit with the utmost cordiality, and gave him pineapple-wine to drink. They were stark naked as usual; they had no hammocks or blankets, and their huts were flimsy shelters of palm-branches. Yet they were in fine condition. Half a dozen of the men and a couple of boys accompanied Kermit back to our camp, paying no slightest heed to the rain which was falling. They were bold and friendly, good-natured—at least superficially—and very inquisitive. In feasting, the long reeds thrust through holes in their lips did not seem to bother them, and they laughed at the suggestion of removing them; evidently to have done so would have been rather bad manners—like using a knife as an aid in eating ice-cream. They held two or three dances, and we were again struck by the rhythm and weird, haunting melody of their chanting. After supper they danced beside the camp-fire; and finally, to their delight, most of the members of our own party, Americans and Brazilians, enthusiastically joined the dance, while the colonel and I furnished an appreciative and applauding audience. Next morning, when we were awakened by the chattering and screaming of the numerous macaws, parrots, and parakeets, we found that nearly all the Indians, men and women, were gathered outside the tent. As far as clothing was concerned, they were in the condition of Adam and Eve before the fall. One of the women carried a little squirrel monkey. She put it up the big tree some distance from the tents; and when she called, it came scampering to her across the grass, ran up her, and clung to her neck. They would have liked to pilfer; but as they had no clothes it was difficult for them to conceal anything. One of the women was observed to take a fork; but as she did not possess a rag of clothing of any kind all she could do was to try to bury the fork in the sand and then sit on it; and it was reclaimed without difficulty. One or two of the children wore necklaces and bracelets made of the polished wood of the tucum palm, and of the molars of small rodents.

Next day's march led us across a hilly country of good pastureland. The valleys were densely wooded, palms of several kinds being conspicuous among the other trees; and the brooks at the bottoms we crossed at fords or by the usual rude pole bridges. On the open pastures were occasional trees, usually slender bacaba palms, with heads which the winds had dishevelled until they looked like mops. It was evidently a fine natural cattle country, and we soon began to see scores, perhaps hundreds, of the cattle belonging to the government ranch at Tres Burity, which we reached in the early afternoon. It is beautifully situated: the view roundabout is lovely, and certainly the land will prove healthy when settlements have been definitely established. Here we revelled in abundance of good fresh milk and eggs; and for dinner we had chicken canja and fat beef roasted on big wooden spits; and we even had watermelons. The latter were from seeds brought down by the American engineers who built the Madeira-Marmoré Railroad—a work which stands honorably distinguished among the many great and useful works done in the development of the tropics of recent years.

Amilcar's pack-oxen, which were nearly worn out, had been left in these fertile pastures. Most of the fresh oxen which he took in their places were unbroken, and there was a perfect circus before they were packed and marched off; in every direction, said the gleeful narrators, there were bucking oxen and loads strewed on the ground. This cattle-ranch is managed by the colonel's uncle, his mother's

A Nhambiquara family

From a photograph by Kermit Roosevelt

Nhambiquara women and children

"Adam and Eve"

From photographs by Cherrie

brother, a hale old man of seventy, white-haired but as active and vigorous as ever; with a fine, kindly, intelligent face. His name is Miguel Evangalista. He is a native of Matto Grosso, of practically pure Indian blood, and was dressed in the ordinary costume of the caboclo—hat, shirt, trousers, and no shoes or stockings. Within the last year he had killed three jaguars, which had been living on the mules; as long as they could get mules they did not at this station molest the cattle.

It was with this uncle's father, Colonel Rondon's own grandfather, that Colonel Rondon as an orphan spent the first seven years of his life. His father died before he was born, and his mother when he was only a year old. He lived on his grandfather's cattle-ranch, some fifty miles from Cuyabá. Then he went to live in Cuyabá with a kinsman on his father's side, from whom he took the name of Rondon; his own father's name was Da Silva. He studied in the Cuyabá Government School, and at sixteen was inscribed as one of the instructors. Then he went to Rio, served for a year in the army as an enlisted man in the ranks, and succeeded finally in getting into the military school. After five years as pupil he served three years as professor of mathematics in this school; and then, as a lieutenant of engineers in the Brazilian army, he came back to his home in Matto Grosso and began his life-work of exploring the wilderness.

Next day we journeyed to the telegraph station at Bonofacio, through alternate spells of glaring sunshine and heavy rain. On the way we stopped at an aldea—village—of Nhambiquaras. We first met a couple of men going to hunt, with bows and arrows longer than themselves.

A rather comely young woman, carrying on her back a wickerwork basket, or creel, supported by a forehead band, and accompanied by a small child, was with them. At the village there were a number of men, women, and children. Although as completely naked as the others we had met, the members of this band were more ornamented with beads, and wore earrings made from the inside of mussel-shells or very big snail-shells. They were more hairy than the ones we had so far met. The women, but not the men, completely remove the hair from their bodies —and look more, instead of less, indecent in consequence. The chief, whose body was painted red with the juice of a fruit, had what could fairly be styled a mustache and imperial; and one old man looked somewhat like a hairy Ainu, or perhaps even more like an Australian black fellow. My companion told me that this probably represented an infusion of negro blood, and possibly of mulatto blood, from runaway slaves of the old days, when some of the Matto Grosso mines were worked by slave labor. They also thought it possible that this infiltration of African negroes might be responsible for the curious shape of the bigger huts, which were utterly unlike their flimsy, ordinary shelters, and bore no resemblance in shape to those of the other Indian tribes of this region; whereas they were not unlike the ordinary beehive huts of the agricultural African negroes. There were in this village several huts or shelters open at the sides, and two of the big huts. These were of closely woven thatch, circular in outline, with a rounded dome, and two doors a couple of feet high opposite each other, and no other opening. There were fifteen or twenty people to each hut. Inside were their implements and utensils, such as wicker baskets (some of them filled with pineapples), gourds, fire-sticks, wooden knives, wooden mortars, and a board for grating mandioc, made of a thick slab of wood inset with sharp points of a harder wood. From the Brazilians one or two of them had obtained blankets, and one a hammock; and they had also obtained knives, which they sorely needed, for they are not even in the stone age. One woman shielded herself from the rain by holding a green palm-branch down her back. Another had on her head what we at first thought to be a monkey-skin head-dress. But it was a little, live, black monkey. It stayed habitually with its head above her forehead, and its arms and legs spread so that it lay moulded to the shape of her head; but both woman and monkey showed some reluctance about having their photographs taken.

Bonofacio consisted of several thatched one-room cabins, connected by a stockade which was extended to form an enclosure behind them. A number of tame parrots and parakeets, of several different species, scrambled over the roofs and entered the houses. In the open pastures near by were the curious, extensive burrows of a gopher rat, which ate the roots of grass, not emerging to eat the grass but pulling it into the burrows by the roots. These burrows bore a close likeness to those of our pocket gophers. Miller found the animals difficult to trap. Finally, by the aid of Colonel Rondon, several Indians, and two or three of our men, he dug one out. From the central shaft several surface galleries radiated, running for many rods about a foot below the surface, with, at intervals of half a dozen yards, mounds where the loose earth had been expelled.

The central shaft ran straight down for about eight feet, and then laterally for about fifteen feet, to a kind of chamber. The animal dug hard to escape, but when taken and put on the surface of the ground it moved slowly and awkwardly. It showed vicious courage. In looks it closely resembled our pocket gophers, but it had no pockets. This was one of the most interesting small mammals that we secured.

After breakfast at Bonafacio a number of Nhambiquaras—men, women, and children—strolled in. The men gave us an exhibition of not very good archery; when the bow was bent, it was at first held so that the arrow pointed straight upwards and was then lowered so that the arrow was aimed at the target. Several of the women had been taken from other tribes, after their husbands or fathers had been killed; for the Nhambiquaras are light-hearted robbers and murderers. Two or three miserable dogs accompanied them, half-starved and mangy, but each decorated with a collar of beads. The headmen had three or four wives apiece, and the women were the burden-bearers, but apparently were not badly treated. Most of them were dirty, although well-fed looking, and their features were of a low type; but some, especially among the children, were quite attractive.

From Bonafacio we went about seven miles, across a rolling prairie dotted with trees and clumps of scrub. There, on February 24, we joined Amilcar, who was camped by a brook which flowed into the Dúvida. We were only some six miles from our place of embarkation on the Dúvida, and we divided our party and our belongings. Amilcar, Miller, Mello, and Oliveira were to march three

First position

Second position

Nhambiquara archer

From photographs by Kermit Roosevelt

days to the Gy-Paraná, and then descend it, and continue down the Madeira to Manaos. Rondon, Lyra, the doctor, Cherrie, Kermit, and I, with sixteen paddlers, in seven canoes, were to descend the Dúvida, and find out whether it led into the Gy-Paraná, into the Madeira, or into the Tapajos. If within a few days it led into the Gy-Paraná, our purpose was to return and descend the Ananás, whose outlet was also unknown. Having this in view, we left a fortnight's provisions for our party of six at Bonofacio. We took with us provisions for about fifty days; not full rations, for we hoped in part to live on the country—on fish, game, nuts, and palm-tops. Our personal baggage was already well cut down: Cherrie, Kermit, and I took the naturalist's fly to sleep under, and a very light little tent extra for any one who might fall sick. Rondon, Lyra, and the doctor took one of their own tents. The things that we carried were necessities—food, medicines, bedding, instruments for determining the altitude and longitude and latitude—except a few books, each in small compass: Lyra's were in German, consisting of two tiny volumes of Goethe and Schiller; Kermit's were in Portuguese; mine, all in English, included the last two volumes of Gibbon, the plays of Sophocles, More's "Utopia," Marcus Aurelius, and Epictetus, the two latter lent me by a friend, Major Shipton of the regulars, our military attaché at Buenos Aires.

If our canoe voyage was prosperous we would gradually lighten the loads by eating the provisions. If we met with accidents, such as losing canoes and men in the rapids, or losing men in encounters with Indians, or if we encountered overmuch fever and dysentery, the loads would lighten themselves. We were all armed. We took no cartridges for sport. Cherrie had some to be used sparingly for collecting specimens. The others were to be used—unless in the unlikely event of having to repel an attack—only to procure food. The food and the arms we carried represented all reasonable precautions against suffering and starvation; but, of course, if the course of the river proved very long and difficult, if we lost our boats over falls or in rapids, or had to make too many and too long portages, or were brought to a halt by impassable swamps, then we would have to reckon with starvation as a possibility. Anything might happen. We were about to go into the unknown, and no one could say what it held.

CHAPTER VIII

THE RIVER OF DOUBT

ON February 27, 1914, shortly after midday, we started down the River of Doubt into the unknown. We were quite uncertain whether after a week we should find ourselves in the Gy-Paranã, or after six weeks in the Madeira, or after three months we knew not where. That was why the river was rightly christened the Dúvida.

We had been camped close to the river, where the trail that follows the telegraph-line crosses it by a rough bridge. As our laden dugouts swung into the stream, Amilcar and Miller and all the others of the Gy-Paranã party were on the banks and the bridge to wave farewell and wish us good-by and good luck. It was the height of the rainy season, and the swollen torrent was swift and brown. Our camp was at about 12° 1′ latitude south and 60° 15′ longitude west of Greenwich. Our general course was to be northward toward the equator, by waterway through the vast forest.

We had seven canoes, all of them dugouts. One was small, one was cranky, and two were old, waterlogged, and leaky. The other three were good. The two old canoes were lashed together, and the cranky one was lashed to one of the others. Kermit with two paddlers went in the smallest of the good canoes; Colonel Rondon and Lyra with three other paddlers in the next largest; and the doctor, Cherrie, and I in the largest with three paddlers. The remaining eight camaradas—there were sixteen in all—were equally divided between our two pairs of lashed canoes. Although our personal baggage was cut down to the limit necessary for health and efficiency, yet on such a trip as ours, where scientific work has to be done and where food for twenty-two men for an unknown period of time has to be carried, it is impossible not to take a good deal of stuff; and the seven dugouts were too heavily laden.

The paddlers were a strapping set. They were expert river-men and men of the forest, skilled veterans in wilderness work. They were lithe as panthers and brawny as bears. They swam like water-dogs. They were equally at home with pole and paddle, with axe and machete; and one was a good cook and others were good men around camp. They looked like pirates in the pictures of Howard Pyle or Maxfield Parrish; one or two of them were pirates, and one worse than a pirate; but most of them were hard-working, willing, and cheerful. They were white,—or, rather, the olive of southern Europe,—black, copper-colored, and of all intermediate shades. In my canoe Luiz the steersman, the headman, was a Matto Grosso negro; Julio the bowsman was from Bahia and of pure Portuguese blood; and the third man, Antonio, was a Parecís Indian.

The actual surveying of the river was done by Colonel Rondon and Lyra, with Kermit as their assistant. Kermit went first in his little canoe with the sighting-rod, on which two disks, one red and one white, were placed a metre apart. He selected a place which commanded as long vistas as possible up-stream and down, and which therefore might be at the angle of a bend; landed; cut away the branches which obstructed the view; and set up the

"I did my writing in headnet and gauntlets"

From a photograph by Kermit Roosevelt

Colonel Roosevelt's canoe disappears down the River of Doubt

From a photograph by Miller

sighting-pole—incidentally encountering maribundi wasps and swarms of biting and stinging ants. Lyra, from his station up-stream, with his telemetre established the distance, while Colonel Rondon with the compass took the direction, and made the records. Then they moved on to the point Kermit had left, and Kermit established a new point within their sight. The first half-day's work was slow. The general course of the stream was a trifle east of north, but at short intervals it bent and curved literally toward every point of the compass. Kermit landed nearly a hundred times, and we made but nine and a third kilometres.

My canoe ran ahead of the surveying canoes. The height of the water made the going easy, for most of the snags and fallen trees were well beneath the surface. Now and then, however, the swift water hurried us toward ripples that marked ugly spikes of sunken timber, or toward uprooted trees that stretched almost across the stream. Then the muscles stood out on the backs and arms of the paddlers as stroke on stroke they urged us away from and past the obstacle. If the leaning or fallen trees were the thorny, slender-stemmed boritana palms, which love the wet, they were often, although plunged beneath the river, in full and vigorous growth, their stems curving upward, and their frond-crowned tops shaken by the rushing water. It was interesting work, for no civilized man, no white man, had ever gone down or up this river or seen the country through which we were passing. The lofty and matted forest rose like a green wall on either hand. The trees were stately and beautiful. The looped and twisted vines hung from them like great ropes. Masses of epiphytes grew both on the dead trees and the living; some had huge leaves like elephants' ears. Now and then fragrant scents were blown to us from flowers on the banks. There were not many birds, and for the most part the forest was silent; rarely we heard strange calls from the depths of the woods, or saw a cormorant or ibis.

My canoe ran only a couple of hours. Then we halted to wait for the others. After a couple of hours more, as the surveyors had not turned up, we landed and made camp at a spot where the bank rose sharply for a hundred yards to a level stretch of ground. Our canoes were moored to trees. The axemen cleared a space for the tents; they were pitched, the baggage was brought up, and fires were kindled. The woods were almost soundless. Through them ran old tapir trails, but there was no fresh sign. Before nightfall the surveyors arrived. There were a few piums and gnats, and a few mosquitoes after dark, but not enough to make us uncomfortable. The small stingless bees, of slightly aromatic odor, swarmed while daylight lasted and crawled over our faces and hands; they were such tame, harmless little things that when they tickled too much I always tried to brush them away without hurting them. But they became a great nuisance after a while. It had been raining at intervals, and the weather was overcast; but after the sun went down the sky cleared. The stars were brilliant overhead, and the new moon hung in the west. It was a pleasant night, the air almost cool, and we slept soundly.

Next morning the two surveying canoes left immediately after breakfast. An hour later the two pairs of lashed canoes pushed off. I kept our canoe to let Cherrie collect, for in the early hours we could hear a number of birds in the woods near by. The most interesting birds he shot were a cotinga, brilliant turquoise-blue with a magenta-purple throat, and a big woodpecker, black above and cinnamon below with an entirely red head and neck. It was almost noon before we started. We saw a few more birds; there were fresh tapir and paca tracks at one point where we landed; once we heard howler monkeys from the depth of the forest, and once we saw a big otter in midstream. As we drifted and paddled down the swirling brown current, through the vivid rain-drenched green of the tropic forest, the trees leaned over the river from both banks. When those that had fallen in the river at some narrow point were very tall, or where it happened that two fell opposite each other, they formed barriers which the men in the leading canoes cleared with their axes. There were many palms, both the burity with its stiff fronds like enormous fans, and a handsome species of bacaba, with very long, gracefully curving fronds. In places the palms stood close together, towering and slender, their stems a stately colonnade, their fronds an arched fretwork against the sky. Butterflies of many hues fluttered over the river. The day was overcast, with showers of rain. When the sun broke through rifts in the clouds, his shafts turned the forest to gold.

In mid-afternoon we came to the mouth of a big and swift affluent entering from the right. It was undoubtedly the Bandeira, which we had crossed well toward its head, some ten days before, on our road to Bonofacio. The Nhambiquaras had then told Colonel Rondon that it flowed into the Dúvida. After its junction, with the added volume of water, the river widened without losing its depth. It was so high that it had overflowed and stood among the trees on the lower levels. Only the higher stretches were dry. On the sheer banks where we landed we had to push the canoes for yards or rods through the branches of the submerged trees, hacking and hewing. There were occasional bays and ox-bows from which the current had shifted. In these the coarse marsh grass grew tall.

This evening we made camp on a flat of dry ground, densely wooded, of course, directly on the edge of the river and five feet above it. It was fine to see the speed and sinewy ease with which the choppers cleared an open space for the tents. Next morning, when we bathed before sunrise, we dived into deep water right from the shore, and from the moored canoes. This second day we made sixteen and a half kilometres along the course of the river, and nine kilometres in a straight line almost due north.

The following day, March 1, there was much rain—sometimes showers, sometimes vertical sheets of water. Our course was somewhat west of north and we made twenty and a half kilometres. We passed signs of Indian habitation. There were abandoned palm-leaf shelters on both banks. On the left bank we came to two or three old Indian fields, grown up with coarse fern and studded with the burned skeletons of trees. At the mouth of a brook which entered from the right some sticks stood in the water, marking the site of an old fish-trap. At one point we found the tough vine hand-rail of an Indian bridge running right across the river, a couple of feet above it. Evidently the bridge had been built at low water.

Colonel Roosevelt's and Colonel Rondon's canoes at the mouth of the Bandeira

In mid-afternoon we came to the mouth of a big and swift affluent. . . . It was undoubtedly the Bandeira

From a photograph by Kermit Roosevelt

Three stout poles had been driven into the stream-bed in a line at right angles to the current. The bridge had consisted of poles fastened to these supports, leading between them and from the support at each end to the banks. The rope of tough vines had been stretched as a hand-rail, necessary with such precarious footing. The rise of the river had swept away the bridge, but the props and the rope hand-rail remained. In the afternoon, from the boat, Cherrie shot a large dark-gray monkey with a prehensile tail. It was very good eating.

We camped on a dry level space, but a few feet above, and close beside, the river—so that our swimming-bath was handy. The trees were cleared and camp was made with orderly hurry. One of the men almost stepped on a poisonous coral-snake, which would have been a serious thing, as his feet were bare. But I had on stout shoes, and the fangs of these serpents—unlike those of the pit-vipers—are too short to penetrate good leather. I promptly put my foot on him, and he bit my shoe with harmless venom. It has been said that the brilliant hues of the coral-snake when in its native haunts really confer on it a concealing coloration. In the dark and tangled woods, and to an only less extent in the ordinary varied landscape, anything motionless, especially if partially hidden, easily eludes the eye. But against the dark-brown mould of the forest floor on which we found this coral-snake its bright and varied coloration was distinctly revealing; infinitely more so than the duller mottling of the jararaca and other dangerous snakes of the genus lachecis. In the same place, however, we found a striking example of genuine protective or mimetic coloration and shape. A rather large insect larva—at least we judged it to be a larval form, but we were none of us entomologists—bore a resemblance to a partially curled dry leaf which was fairly startling. The tail exactly resembled the stem or continuation of the midrib of the dead leaf. The flattened body was curled up at the sides, and veined and colored precisely like the leaf. The head, colored like the leaf, projected in front.

We were still in the Brazilian highlands. The forest did not teem with life. It was generally rather silent; we did not hear such a chorus of birds and mammals as we had occasionally heard even on our overland journey, when more than once we had been awakened at dawn by the howling, screaming, yelping, and chattering of monkeys, toucans, macaws, parrots, and parakeets. There were, however, from time to time, queer sounds from the forest, and after nightfall different kinds of frogs and insects uttered strange cries and calls. In volume and frequency these seemed to increase until midnight. Then they died away and before dawn everything was silent.

At this camp the carregadores ants completely devoured the doctor's undershirt, and ate holes in his mosquito-net; and they also ate the strap of Lyra's gun-case. The little stingless bees, of many kinds, swarmed in such multitudes, and were so persevering, that we had to wear our head-nets when we wrote or skinned specimens.

The following day was almost without rain. It was delightful to drift and paddle slowly down the beautiful tropical river. Until mid-afternoon the current was not very fast, and the broad, deep, placid stream bent and curved in every direction, although the general course was northwest. The country was flat, and more of the land was

The Rapids of Navaitê
There were many curls, and one or two regular falls
From a photograph by Cherrie

under than above water. Continually we found ourselves travelling between stretches of marshy forest where for miles the water stood or ran among the trees. Once we passed a hillock. We saw brilliantly colored parakeets and trogons. At last the slow current quickened. Faster it went, and faster, until it began to run like a mill-race, and we heard the roar of rapids ahead. We pulled to the right bank, moored the canoes, and while most of the men pitched camp two or three of them accompanied us to examine the rapids. We had made twenty kilometres.

We soon found that the rapids were a serious obstacle. There were many curls, and one or two regular falls, perhaps six feet high. It would have been impossible to run them, and they stretched for nearly a mile. The carry, however, which led through woods and over rocks in a nearly straight line, was somewhat shorter. It was not an easy portage over which to carry heavy loads and drag heavy dugout canoes. At the point where the descent was steepest there were great naked flats of friable sandstone and conglomerate. Over parts of these, where there was a surface of fine sand, there was a growth of coarse grass. Other parts were bare and had been worn by the weather into fantastic shapes—one projection looked like an old-fashioned beaver hat upside down. In this place, where the naked flats of rock showed the projection of the ledge through which the river had cut its course, the torrent rushed down a deep, sheer-sided, and extremely narrow channel. At one point it was less than two yards across, and for quite a distance not more than five or six yards. Yet only a mile or two above the rapids the deep, placid river was at least a hundred yards wide. It seemed extraordinary, almost impossible, that so broad a river could in so short a space of time contract its dimensions to the width of the strangled channel through which it now poured its entire volume.

This had for long been a station where the Nhambiquaras at intervals built their ephemeral villages and tilled the soil with the rude and destructive cultivation of savages. There were several abandoned old fields, where the dense growth of rank fern hid the tangle of burnt and fallen logs. Nor had the Nhambiquaras been long absent. In one trail we found what gypsies would have called a "pateran," a couple of branches arranged crosswise, eight leaves to a branch; it had some special significance, belonging to that class of signals, each with some peculiar and often complicated meaning, which are commonly used by many wild peoples. The Indians had thrown a simple bridge, consisting of four long poles, without a hand-rail, across one of the narrowest parts of the rock gorge through which the river foamed in its rapid descent. This subtribe of Indians was called the Navaïté; we named the rapids after them, Navaïté Rapids. By observation Lyra found them to be (in close approximation to) latitude 11° 44′ south and longitude 60° 18′ west from Greenwich.

We spent March 3 and 4 and the morning of the 5th in portaging around the rapids. The first night we camped in the forest beside the spot where we had halted. Next morning we moved the baggage to the foot of the rapids, where we intended to launch the canoes, and pitched our tents on the open sandstone flat. It rained heavily. The little bees were in such swarms as to be a nuisance. Many small stinging bees were with them, which stung badly.

Cherrie holding a rifle to show the width of the rapids at Navaïté
At one point it was less than two yards across
From a photograph by Kermit Roosevelt

We were bitten by huge horse-flies, the size of bumblebees. More serious annoyance was caused by the pium and boroshuda flies during the hours of daylight, and by the polvora, the sand-flies, after dark. There were a few mosquitoes. The boroshudas were the worst pests; they brought the blood at once, and left marks that lasted for weeks. I did my writing in head-net and gauntlets. Fortunately we had with us several bottles of "fly dope"—so named on the label—put up, with the rest of our medicine, by Doctor Alexander Lambert; he had tested it in the north woods and found it excellent. I had never before been forced to use such an ointment, and had been reluctant to take it with me; but now I was glad enough to have it, and we all of us found it exceedingly useful. I would never again go into mosquito or sand-fly country without it. The effect of an application wears off after half an hour or so, and under many conditions, as when one is perspiring freely, it is of no use; but there are times when minute mosquitoes and gnats get through head-nets and under mosquito-bars, and when the ointment occasionally renewed may permit one to get sleep or rest which would otherwise be impossible of attainment. The termites got into our tent on the sand-flat, ate holes in Cherrie's mosquito-net and poncho, and were starting to work at our duffel-bags, when we discovered them.

Packing the loads across was simple. Dragging the heavy dugouts was labor. The biggest of the two water-logged ones was the heaviest. Lyra and Kermit did the job. All the men were employed at it except the cook, and one man who was down with fever. A road was chopped through the forest and a couple of hundred stout six-foot poles, or small logs, were cut as rollers and placed about two yards apart. With block and tackle the seven dugouts were hoisted out of the river up the steep banks, and up the rise of ground until the level was reached. Then the men harnessed themselves two by two on the drag-rope, while one of their number pried behind with a lever, and the canoe, bumping and sliding, was twitched through the woods. Over the sandstone flats there were some ugly ledges, but on the whole the course was downhill and relatively easy. Looking at the way the work was done, at the good-will, the endurance, and the bull-like strength of the camaradas, and at the intelligence and the unwearied efforts of their commanders, one could but wonder at the ignorance of those who do not realize the energy and the power that are so often possessed by, and that may be so readily developed in, the men of the tropics. Another subject of perpetual wonder is the attitude of certain men who stay at home, and still more the attitude of certain men who travel under easy conditions, and who belittle the achievements of the real explorers of, the real adventurers in, the great wilderness. The impostors and romancers among explorers or would-be explorers and wilderness wanderers have been unusually prominent in connection with South America (although the conspicuous ones are not South Americans, by the way); and these are fit subjects for condemnation and derision. But the work of the genuine explorer and wilderness wanderer is fraught with fatigue, hardship, and danger. Many of the men of little knowledge talk glibly of portaging as if it were simple and easy. A portage over rough and unknown ground is always a work of difficulty and of some risk to the canoe;

Portaging around Navaïté Rapids

We spent March 3 and 4 and the morning of the 5th in portaging around the rapids

From a photograph by Kermit Roosevelt

and in the untrodden, or even in the unfrequented, wilderness risk to the canoe is a serious matter. This particular portage at Navaïté Rapids was far from being unusually difficult; yet it not only cost two and a half days of severe and incessant labor, but it cost something in damage to the canoes. One in particular, the one in which I had been journeying, was split in a manner which caused us serious uneasiness as to how long, even after being patched, it would last. Where the canoes were launched, the bank was sheer, and one of the water-logged canoes filled and went to the bottom; and there was more work in raising it.

We were still wholly unable to tell where we were going or what lay ahead of us. Round the camp-fire, after supper, we held endless discussions and hazarded all kinds of guesses on both subjects. The river might bend sharply to the west and enter the Gy-Paraná high up or low down, or go north to the Madeira, or bend eastward and enter the Tapajos, or fall into the Canumá and finally through one of its mouths enter the Amazon direct. Lyra inclined to the first, and Colonel Rondon to the second, of these propositions. We did not know whether we had one hundred or eight hundred kilometres to go, whether the stream would be fairly smooth or whether we would encounter waterfalls, or rapids, or even some big marsh or lake. We could not tell whether or not we would meet hostile Indians, although no one of us ever went ten yards from camp without his rifle. We had no idea how much time the trip would take. We had entered a land of unknown possibilities.

We started down-stream again early in the afternoon of March 5. Our hands and faces were swollen from the bites and stings of the insect pests at the sand-flat camp, and it was a pleasure once more to be in the middle of the river, where they did not come, in any numbers, while we were in motion. The current was swift, but the river was so deep that there were no serious obstructions. Twice we went down over slight riffles, which in the dry season were doubtless rapids; and once we struck a spot where many whirlpools marked the presence underneath of bowlders which would have been above water had not the river been so swollen by the rains. The distance we covered in a day going down-stream would have taken us a week if we had been going up. The course wound hither and thither, sometimes in sigmoid curves; but the general direction was east of north. As usual, it was very beautiful; and we never could tell what might appear around any curve. In the forest that rose on either hand were tall rubber-trees. The surveying canoes, as usual, went first, while I shepherded the two pairs of lashed cargo canoes. I kept them always between me and the surveying canoes—ahead of me until I passed the surveying canoes, then behind me until, after an hour or so, I had chosen a place to camp. There was so much overflowed ground that it took us some little time this afternoon before we found a flat place high enough to be dry. Just before reaching camp Cherrie shot a jacu, a handsome bird somewhat akin to, but much smaller than, a turkey; after Cherrie had taken its skin, its body made an excellent canja. We saw parties of monkeys; and the false bell-birds uttered their ringing whistles in the dense timber around our tents. The giant ants, an inch and a quarter long, were rather too plentiful around this camp; one stung Kermit; it was almost like the sting of a small scorpion, and pained severely for a couple of hours. This half-day we made twelve kilometres.

On the following day we made nineteen kilometres, the river twisting in every direction, but in its general course running a little west of north. Once we stopped at a bee-tree, to get honey. The tree was a towering giant, of the kind called milk-tree, because a thick milky juice runs freely from any cut. Our camaradas eagerly drank the white fluid that flowed from the wounds made by their axes. I tried it. The taste was not unpleasant, but it left a sticky feeling in the mouth. The helmsman of my boat, Luiz, a powerful negro, chopped into the tree, balancing himself with springy ease on a slight scaffolding. The honey was in a hollow, and had been made by medium-sized stingless bees. At the mouth of the hollow they had built a curious entrance of their own, in the shape of a spout of wax about a foot long. At the opening the walls of the spout showed the wax formation, but elsewhere it had become in color and texture indistinguishable from the bark of the tree. The honey was delicious, sweet and yet with a tart flavor. The comb differed much from that of our honey-bees. The honey-cells were very large, and the brood-cells, which were small, were in a single instead of a double row. By this tree I came across an example of genuine concealing coloration. A huge tree-toad, the size of a bullfrog, was seated upright—not squatted flat—on a big rotten limb. It was absolutely motionless; the yellow brown of its back, and its dark sides, exactly harmonized in color with the light and dark patches on the log; the color was as concealing, here in its natural surroundings, as is the color of our common wood-frog among the dead leaves of our woods. When

I stirred it up it jumped to a small twig, catching hold with the disks of its finger-tips, and balancing itself with unexpected ease for so big a creature, and then hopped to the ground and again stood motionless. Evidently it trusted for safety to escaping observation. We saw some monkeys and fresh tapir sign, and Kermit shot a jacu for the pot.

At about three o'clock I was in the lead, when the current began to run more quickly. We passed over one or two decided ripples, and then heard the roar of rapids ahead, while the stream began to race. We drove the canoe into the bank, and then went down a tapir trail, which led alongside the river, to reconnoitre. A quarter of a mile's walk showed us that there were big rapids, down which the canoes could not go; and we returned to the landing. All the canoes had gathered there, and Rondon, Lyra, and Kermit started down-stream to explore. They returned in an hour, with the information that the rapids continued for a long distance, with falls and steep pitches of broken water, and that the portage would take several days. We made camp just above the rapids. Ants swarmed, and some of them bit savagely. Our men, in clearing away the forest for our tents, left several very tall and slender accashy palms; the bole of this palm is as straight as an arrow and is crowned with delicate, gracefully curved fronds. We had come along the course of the river almost exactly a hundred kilometres; it had twisted so that we were only about fifty-five kilometres north of our starting-point. The rock was porphyritic.

The 7th, 8th, and 9th we spent in carrying the loads and dragging and floating the dugouts past the series of rapids at whose head we had stopped.

Rapids of the Dúvida

From a photograph by Kermit Roosevelt

The first day we shifted camp a kilometre and a half to the foot of this series of rapids. This was a charming and picturesque camp. It was at the edge of the river, where there was a little, shallow bay with a beach of firm sand. In the water, at the middle point of the beach, stood a group of three burity palms, their great trunks rising like columns. Round the clearing in which our tents stood were several very big trees; two of them were rubber-trees. Kermit went down-stream five or six kilometres, and returned, having shot a jacu and found that at the point which he had reached there was another rapids, almost a fall, which would necessitate our again dragging the canoes over a portage. Antonio, the Parecís, shot a big monkey; of this I was glad because portaging is hard work, and the men appreciated the meat. So far Cherrie had collected sixty birds on the Dúvida, all of them new to the collection, and some probably new to science. We saw the fresh sign of paca, agouti, and the small peccary, and Kermit with the dogs roused a tapir, which crossed the river right through the rapids; but no one got a shot at it.

Except at one or perhaps two points a very big dugout, lightly loaded, could probably run all these rapids. But even in such a canoe it would be silly to make the attempt on an exploring expedition, where the loss of a canoe or of its contents means disaster; and moreover such a canoe could not be taken, for it would be impossible to drag it over the portages on the occasions when the portages became inevitable. Our canoes would not have lived half a minute in the wild water.

On the second day the canoes and loads were brought down to the foot of the first rapids. Lyra cleared the path and laid the logs for rollers, while Kermit dragged the dugouts up the bank from the water with block and tackle, with strain of rope and muscle. Then they joined forces, as over the uneven ground it needed the united strength of all their men to get the heavy dugouts along. Meanwhile the colonel with one attendant measured the distance, and then went on a long hunt, but saw no game. I strolled down beside the river for a couple of miles, but also saw nothing. In the dense tropical forest of the Amazonian basin hunting is very difficult, especially for men who are trying to pass through the country as rapidly as possible. On such a trip as ours getting game is largely a matter of chance.

On the following day Lyra and Kermit brought down the canoes and loads, with hard labor, to the little beach by the three palms where our tents were pitched. Many pacovas grew round about. The men used their immense leaves, some of which were twelve feet long and two and a half feet broad, to roof the flimsy shelters under which they hung their hammocks. I went into the woods, but in the tangle of vegetation it would have been a mere hazard had I seen any big animal. Generally the woods were silent and empty. Now and then little troops of birds of many kinds passed—wood-hewers, ant-thrushes, tanagers, flycatchers; as in the spring and fall similar troops of warblers, chickadees, and nuthatches pass through our northern woods. On the rocks and on the great trees by the river grew beautiful white and lilac orchids—the sobralia, of sweet and delicate fragrance. For the moment my own books seemed a trifle heavy, and perhaps I would have found the day tedious if Kermit had not lent me the

Oxford Book of French Verse. Eustache Deschamp, Joachim du Bellay, Ronsard, the delightful La Fontaine, the delightful but appalling Villon, Victor Hugo's "Guitare," Madame Desbordes-Valmore's lines on the little girl and her pillow, as dear little verses about a child as ever were written—these and many others comforted me much, as I read them in head-net and gauntlets, sitting on a log by an unknown river in the Amazonian forest.

On the 10th we again embarked and made a kilometre and a half, spending most of the time in getting past two more rapids. Near the first of these we saw a small cayman, a jacaré-tinga. At each set of rapids the canoes were unloaded and the loads borne past on the shoulders of the camaradas; three of the canoes were paddled down by a couple of naked paddlers apiece; and the two sets of double canoes were let down by ropes, one of one couple being swamped but rescued and brought safely to shore on each occasion. One of the men was upset while working in the swift water, and his face was cut against the stones. Lyra and Kermit did the actual work with the camaradas. Kermit, dressed substantially like the camaradas themselves, worked in the water, and, as the overhanging branches were thronged with crowds of biting and stinging ants, he was marked and blistered over his whole body. Indeed, we all suffered more or less from these ants; while the swarms of biting flies grew constantly more numerous. The termites ate holes in my helmet and also in the cover of my cot. Every one else had a hammock. At this camp we had come down the river about 102 kilometres, according to the surveying records, and in height had descended nearly 100 metres, as shown by the aneroid—although the figure in this case is only an approximation, as an aneroid cannot be depended on for absolute accuracy of results.

Next morning we found that during the night we had met with a serious misfortune. We had halted at the foot of the rapids. The canoes were moored to trees on the bank, at the tail of the broken water. The two old canoes, although one of them was our biggest cargo-carrier, were water-logged and heavy, and one of them was leaking. In the night the river rose. The leaky canoe, which at best was too low in the water, must have gradually filled from the wash of the waves. It sank, dragging down the other; they began to roll, bursting their moorings; and in the morning they had disappeared. A canoe was launched to look for them; but, rolling over the bowlders on the rocky bottom, they had at once been riven asunder, and the big fragments that were soon found, floating in eddies, or along the shore, showed that it was useless to look farther. We called these rapids Broken Canoe Rapids.

It was not pleasant to have to stop for some days; thanks to the rapids, we had made slow progress, and with our necessarily limited supply of food, and no knowledge whatever of what was ahead of us, it was important to make good time. But there was no alternative. We had to build either one big canoe or two small ones. It was raining heavily as the men started to explore in different directions for good canoe trees. Three—which ultimately proved not very good for the purpose—were found close to camp; splendid-looking trees, one of them five feet in diameter three feet from the ground. The axemen immediately attacked this one under the superintendence of Colonel Rondon. Lyra and Kermit started in opposite di-

Dragging the canoes over a portage by means of ropes and logs

From a photograph by Kermit Roosevelt

rections to hunt. Lyra killed a jacu for us, and Kermit killed two monkeys for the men. Toward nightfall it cleared. The moon was nearly full, and the foaming river gleamed like silver.

Our men were "regional volunteers," that is, they had enlisted in the service of the Telegraphic Commission especially to do this wilderness work, and were highly paid, as was fitting, in view of the toil, hardship, and hazard to life and health. Two of them had been with Colonel Rondon during his eight months' exploration in 1909, at which time his men were regulars, from his own battalion of engineers. His four aides during the closing months of this trip were Lieutenants Lyra, Amarante, Alencarliense, and Pyrineus. The naturalist Miranda Ribeiro also accompanied him. This was the year when, marching on foot through an absolutely unknown wilderness, the colonel and his party finally reached the Gy-Paraná, which on the maps was then (and on most maps is now) placed in an utterly wrong course, and over a degree out of its real position. When they reached the affluents of the Gy-Paraná a third of the members of the party were so weak with fever that they could hardly crawl. They had no baggage. Their clothes were in tatters, and some of the men were almost naked. For months they had had no food except what little game they shot, and especially the wild fruits and nuts; if it had not been for the great abundance of the Brazil-nuts they would all have died. At the first big stream they encountered they built a canoe, and Alencarliense took command of it and descended to map the course of the river. With him went Ribeiro, the doctor Tanageira, who could no longer walk on account of the ulceration of one foot, three men whom the fever had rendered unable longer to walk, and six men who were as yet well enough to handle the canoe. By the time the remainder of the party came to the next navigable river eleven more fever-stricken men had nearly reached the end of their tether. Here they ran across a poor devil who had for four months been lost in the forest and was dying of slow starvation. He had eaten nothing but Brazil-nuts and the grubs of insects. He could no longer walk, but could sit erect and totter feebly for a few feet. Another canoe was built, and in it Pyrineus started down-stream with the eleven fever patients and the starving wanderer. Colonel Rondon kept up the morale of his men by still carrying out the forms of military discipline. The ragged bugler had his bugle. Lieutenant Pyrineus had lost every particle of his clothing except a hat and a pair of drawers. The half-naked lieutenant drew up his eleven fever patients in line; the bugle sounded; every one came to attention; and the haggard colonel read out the orders of the day. Then the dugout with its load of sick men started down-stream, and Rondon, Lyra, Amarante, and the twelve remaining men resumed their weary march. When a fortnight later they finally struck a camp of rubber-gatherers three of the men were literally and entirely naked. Meanwhile Amilcar had ascended the Jacyparaná a month or two previously with provisions to meet them; for at that time the maps incorrectly treated this river as larger, instead of smaller, than the Gy-Paraná, which they were in fact descending; and Colonel Rondon had supposed that they were going down the former stream. Amilcar returned after himself suffering much hardship and danger. The different parties finally met at the mouth of the Gy-Paraná, where it enters the Madeira. The lost man whom they had found seemed on the road to recovery, and they left him at a ranch, on the Madeira, where he could be cared for; yet after they had left him they heard that he had died.

On the 12th the men were still hard at work hollowing out the hard wood of the big tree, with axe and adze, while watch and ward were kept over them to see that the idlers did not shirk at the expense of the industrious. Kermit and Lyra again hunted; the former shot a curassow, which was welcome, as we were endeavoring in all ways to economize our food supply. We were using the tops of palms also. I spent the day hunting in the woods, for the most part by the river, but saw nothing. In the season of the rains game is away from the river and fish are scarce and turtles absent. Yet it was pleasant to be in the great silent forest. Here and there grew immense trees, and on some of them mighty buttresses sprang from the base. The lianas and vines were of every size and shape. Some were twisted and some were not. Some came down straight and slender from branches a hundred feet above. Others curved like long serpents around the trunks. Others were like knotted cables. In the shadow there was little noise. The wind rarely moved the hot, humid air. There were few flowers or birds. Insects were altogether too abundant, and even when travelling slowly it was impossible always to avoid them—not to speak of our constant companions the bees, mosquitoes, and especially the boroshudas or bloodsucking flies. Now while bursting through a tangle I disturbed a nest of wasps, whose resentment was active; now I heedlessly stepped among the outliers of a small party of the carnivorous foraging ants; now, grasping a branch as I stumbled, I shook down a shower of fire-ants; and among all these my attention was particularly arrested by the bite of one of the giant ants, which stung like a hornet, so that I felt it for three hours. The camaradas generally went barefoot or only wore sandals; and their ankles and feet were swollen and inflamed from the bites of the boroshudas and ants, some being actually incapacitated from work. All of us suffered more or less, our faces and hands swelling slightly from the boroshuda bites; and in spite of our clothes we were bitten all over our bodies, chiefly by ants and the small forest ticks. Because of the rain and the heat our clothes were usually wet when we took them off at night, and just as wet when we put them on again in the morning.

All day on the 13th the men worked at the canoe, making good progress. In rolling and shifting the huge, heavy tree-trunk every one had to assist now and then. The work continued until ten in the evening, as the weather was clear. After nightfall some of the men held candles and the others plied axe or adze, standing within or beside the great, half-hollowed logs, while the flicker of the lights showed the tropic forest rising in the darkness round about. The night air was hot and still and heavy with moisture. The men were stripped to the waist. Olive and copper and ebony, their skins glistened as if oiled, and rippled with the ceaseless play of the thews beneath.

On the morning of the 14th the work was resumed in a torrential tropic downpour. The canoe was finished, dragged down to the water, and launched soon after midday, and another hour or so saw us under way. The

Manner of dragging the canoes across a hilly portage

From a photograph by Cherrie

Making the big canoe which was soon afterward lost

The inside of the log has been hollowed out and the men are rolling it over to shape the bottom of the canoe

From a photograph by Kermit Roosevelt

descent was marked, and the swollen river raced along. Several times we passed great whirlpools, sometimes shifting, sometimes steady. Half a dozen times we ran over rapids, and, although they were not high enough to have been obstacles to loaded Canadian canoes, two of them were serious to us. Our heavily laden, clumsy dugouts were sunk to within three or four inches of the surface of the river, and, although they were buoyed on each side with bundles of burity-palm branch-stems, they shipped a great deal of water in the rapids. The two biggest rapids we only just made, and after each we had hastily to push ashore in order to bail. In one set of big ripples or waves my canoe was nearly swamped. In a wilderness, where what is ahead is absolutely unknown, alike in terms of time, space, and method—for we had no idea where we would come out, how we would get out, or when we would get out—it is of vital consequence not to lose one's outfit, especially the provisions; and yet it is of only less consequence to go as rapidly as possible lest all the provisions be exhausted and the final stages of the expedition be accomplished by men weakened from semi-starvation, and therefore ripe for disaster. On this occasion, of the two hazards, we felt it necessary to risk running the rapids; for our progress had been so very slow that unless we made up the time, it was probable that we would be short of food before we got where we could expect to procure any more except what little the country, in the time of the rains and floods, might yield. We ran until after five, so that the work of pitching camp was finished in the dark. We had made nearly sixteen kilometres in a direction slightly east of north. This evening the air was fresh and cool.

The following morning, the 15th of March, we started in good season. For six kilometres we drifted and paddled down the swift river without incident. At times we saw lofty Brazil-nut trees rising above the rest of the forest on the banks; and back from the river these trees grow to enormous proportions, towering like giants. There were great rubber-trees also, their leaves always in sets of threes. Then the ground on either hand rose into bowlder-strewn, forest-clad hills and the roar of broken water announced that once more our course was checked by dangerous rapids. Round a bend we came on them; a wide descent of white water, with an island in the middle, at the upper edge. Here grave misfortune befell us, and graver misfortune was narrowly escaped.

Kermit, as usual, was leading in his canoe. It was the smallest and least seaworthy of all. He had in it little except a week's supply of our boxed provisions and a few tools; fortunately none of the food for the camaradas. His dog Trigueiro was with him. Besides himself, the crew consisted of two men: João, the helmsman, or pilot, as he is called in Brazil, and Simplicio, the bowsman. Both were negroes and exceptionally good men in every way. Kermit halted his canoe on the left bank, above the rapids, and waited for the colonel's canoe. Then the colonel and Lyra walked down the bank to see what was ahead. Kermit took his canoe across to the island to see whether the descent could be better accomplished on the other side. Having made his investigation, he ordered the men to return to the bank he had left, and the dugout was headed up-stream accordingly. Before they had gone a dozen yards, the paddlers digging their paddles with all their strength into the swift current, one of the shifting whirlpools of which I have spoken came down-stream, whirled them around, and swept them so close to the rapids that no human power could avoid going over them. As they were drifting into them broadside on, Kermit yelled to the steersman to turn her head, so as to take them in the only way that offered any chance whatever of safety. The water came aboard, wave after wave, as they raced down. They reached the bottom with the canoe upright, but so full as barely to float, and the paddlers urged her toward the shore. They had nearly reached the bank when another whirlpool or whirling eddy tore them away and hurried them back to midstream, where the dugout filled and turned over. João, seizing the rope, started to swim ashore; the rope was pulled from his hand, but he reached the bank. Poor Simplicio must have been pulled under at once, and his life beaten out on the bowlders beneath the racing torrent. He never rose again, nor did we ever recover his body. Kermit clutched his rifle, his favorite 405 Winchester with which he had done most of his hunting both in Africa and America, and climbed on the bottom of the upset boat. In a minute he was swept into the second series of rapids, and whirled away from the rolling boat, losing his rifle. The water beat his helmet down over his head and face and drove him beneath the surface; and when he rose at last he was almost drowned, his breath and strength almost spent. He was in swift but quiet water, and swam toward an overhanging branch. His jacket hindered him, but he knew he was too nearly gone to be able to get it off, and, thinking with the curious calm one feels when death is but a moment away, he realized that the utmost his failing strength could do was to reach the branch. He reached, and clutched it, and then almost lacked strength to haul himself out on the land. Good Trigueiro had faithfully swum alongside him through the rapids, and now himself scrambled ashore. It was a very narrow escape. Kermit was a great comfort and help to me on the trip; but the fear of some fatal accident befalling him was always a nightmare to me. He was to be married as soon as the trip was over; and it did not seem to me that I could bear to bring bad tidings to his betrothed and to his mother.

Simplicio was unmarried. Later we sent to his mother all the money that would have been his had he lived. The following morning we put on one side of the post erected to mark our camping-spot the following inscription, in Portuguese:

"In These Rapids Died Poor Simplicio."

On an expedition such as ours death is one of the accidents that may at any time occur, and narrow escapes from death are too common to be felt as they would be felt elsewhere. One mourns sincerely, but mourning cannot interfere with labor. We immediately proceeded with the work of the portage. From the head to the tail of this series of rapids the distance was about six hundred yards. A path was cut along the bank, over which the loads were brought. The empty canoes ran the rapids without mishap, each with two skilled paddlers. One of the canoes almost ran into a swimming tapir at the head of the rapids; it went down the rapids, and then climbed out of the river. Kermit, accompanied by João, went three or four miles down the river, looking for the body of Simplicio and for the sunk canoe. He found neither. But he found a box of provisions and a paddle, and salvaged both by swimming into midstream after them. He also found that a couple of kilometres below there was another stretch of rapids, and following them on the left-hand bank to the foot he found that they were worse than the ones we had just passed, and impassable for canoes on this left-hand side.

We camped at the foot of the rapids we had just passed. There were many small birds here, but it was extremely difficult to see or shoot them in the lofty tree tops, and to find them in the tangle beneath if they were shot. However, Cherrie got four species new to the collection. One was a tiny hummer, one of the species known as woodstars, with dainty but not brilliant plumage; its kind is never found except in the deep, dark woods, not coming out into the sunshine. Its crop was filled with ants; when shot it was feeding at a cluster of long red flowers. He also got a very handsome trogon and an exquisite little tanager, as brilliant as a cluster of jewels; its throat was lilac, its breast turquoise, its crown and forehead topaz, while above it was glossy purple-black, the lower part of the back ruby-red. This tanager was a female; I can hardly imagine that the male is more brilliantly colored. The fourth bird was a queer hawk of the genus *ibycter*, black, with a white belly, naked red cheeks and throat and red legs and feet. Its crop was filled with the seeds of fruits and a few insect remains; an extraordinary diet for a hawk.

The morning of the 16th was dark and gloomy. Through sheets of blinding rain we left our camp of misfortune for another camp where misfortune also awaited us. Less than half an hour took our dugouts to the head of the rapids below. As Kermit had already explored the left-hand side, Colonel Rondon and Lyra went down the right-hand side and found a channel which led round the worst part, so that they deemed it possible to let down the canoes by ropes from the bank. The distance to the foot of the rapids was about a kilometre. While the loads were being brought down the left bank, Luiz and Antonio Correa, our two best watermen, started to take a canoe down the right side, and Colonel Rondon walked ahead to see anything he could about the river. He was accompanied by one of our three dogs, Lobo. After walking about a kilometre he heard ahead a kind of howling noise, which he thought was made by spider-monkeys. He walked in the direction of the sound and Lobo ran ahead. In a minute he heard Lobo yell with pain, and then, still yelping, come toward him, while the creature that was howling also approached, evidently in pursuit. In a moment a second yell from Lobo, followed by silence, announced that he was dead; and the sound of the howling, when near, convinced Rondon that the dog had been killed by an Indian, doubtless with two arrows. Probably the Indian was howling to lure the spider-monkeys toward him. Rondon fired his rifle in the air, to warn off the Indian or Indians, who in all probability had never seen a civilized man, and certainly could not imagine that one was in the neighborhood. He then returned to the foot of the rapids, where the portage was still going on, and, in company with Lyra, Kermit, and Antonio Parecís, the Indian, walked back to where Lobo's body lay. Sure enough he found him, slain by two arrows. One arrow-head was in him, and near by was a strange stick used in the very primitive method of fishing of all these Indians. Antonio recognized its purpose. The Indians, who were apparently two or three in number, had fled. Some beads and trinkets were left on the spot to show that we were not angry and were friendly.

Meanwhile Cherrie stayed at the head and I at the foot of the portage as guards. Luiz and Antonio Correa brought down one canoe safely. The next was the new canoe, which was very large and heavy, being made of wood that would not float. In the rapids the rope broke, and the canoe was lost, Luiz being nearly drowned.

It was a very bad thing to lose the canoe, but it was even worse to lose the rope and pulleys. This meant that it would be physically impossible to hoist big canoes up even small hills or rocky hillocks, such as had been so frequent beside the many rapids we had encountered. It was not wise to spend the four days necessary to build new canoes where we were, in danger of attack from the Indians. Moreover, new rapids might be very near, in which case the new canoes would hamper us. Yet the four remaining canoes would not carry all the loads and all the men, no matter how we cut the loads down; and we intended to cut everything down at once. We had been gone eighteen days. We had used over a third of our food. We had gone only 125 kilometres, and it was probable that we had at least five times, perhaps six or seven times, this distance still to go. We had taken a fortnight to descend rapids amounting in the aggregate to less than seventy yards of fall; a very few yards of fall makes a dangerous rapid when the river is swollen and swift and there are obstructions. We had only one aneroid to determine our altitude, and therefore could make merely a loose approximation to it, but we probably had between two and three times this descent in the aggregate of rapids ahead of us. So far the country had offered little in the way of food except palm-tops. We had lost four canoes and one man. We were in the country of wild Indians, who shot well with their bows. It behooved us to go warily, but also to make all speed possible, if we were to avoid serious trouble.

The best plan seemed to be to march thirteen men down along the bank, while the remaining canoes, lashed two and two, floated down beside them. If after two or three days we found no bad rapids, and there seemed a reasonable chance of going some distance at decent speed, we could then build the new canoes—preferably two small ones, this time, instead of one big one. We left all the baggage we could. We were already down as far as comfort would permit; but we now struck off much of the comfort. Cherrie, Kermit, and I had been sleeping under a very light fly; and there was another small light tent for one person, kept for possible emergencies. The last was given to me for my cot, and all five of the others swung their hammocks under the big fly. This meant that we left two big and heavy tents behind. A box of surveying instruments was also abandoned. Each of us got his personal belongings down to one box or duffel-bag—although there was only a small diminution thus made; because we had so little that the only way to make a serious diminution was to restrict ourselves to the clothes on our backs.

The biting flies and ants were to us a source of discomfort and at times of what could fairly be called torment.

But to the camaradas, most of whom went barefoot or only wore sandals—and they never did or would wear shoes —the effect was more serious. They wrapped their legs and feet in pieces of canvas or hide; and the feet of three of them became so swollen that they were crippled and could not walk any distance. The doctor, whose courage and cheerfulness never flagged, took excellent care of them. Thanks to him, there had been among them hitherto but one or two slight cases of fever. He administered to each man daily a half-gram—nearly eight grains—of quinine, and every third or fourth day a double dose.

The following morning Colonel Rondon, Lyra, Kermit, Cherrie, and nine of the camaradas started in single file down the bank, while the doctor and I went in the two double canoes, with six camaradas, three of them the invalids with swollen feet. We halted continually, as we went about three times as fast as the walkers; and we traced the course of the river. After forty minutes' actual going in the boats we came to some rapids; the unloaded canoes ran them without difficulty, while the loads were portaged. In an hour and a half we were again under way, but in ten minutes came to other rapids, where the river ran among islands, and there were several big curls. The clumsy, heavily laden dugouts, lashed in couples, were unwieldy and hard to handle. The rapids came just round a sharp bend, and we got caught in the upper part of the swift water and had to run the first set of rapids in consequence. We in the leading pair of dugouts were within an ace of coming to grief on some big bowlders against which we were swept by a cross current at the turn. All of us paddling hard—scraping and bumping—we got through by the skin of our teeth, and managed to make the bank and moor our dugouts. It was a narrow escape from grave disaster. The second pair of lashed dugouts profited by our experience, made the run—with risk, but with less risk—and moored beside us. Then all the loads were taken out, and the empty canoes were run down through the least dangerous channels among the islands.

This was a long portage, and we camped at the foot of the rapids, having made nearly seven kilometres. Here a little river, a rapid stream of volume equal to the Dúvida at the point where we first embarked, joined from the west. Colonel Rondon and Kermit came to it first, and the former named it Rio Kermit. There was in it a waterfall about six or eight feet high, just above the junction. Here we found plenty of fish. Lyra caught two pacu, good-sized, deep-bodied fish. They were delicious eating. Antonio the Parecís said that these fish never came up heavy rapids in which there were falls they had to jump. We could only hope that he was correct, as in that case the rapids we would encounter in the future would rarely be so serious as to necessitate our dragging the heavy dugouts overland. Passing the rapids we had hitherto encountered had meant severe labor and some danger. But the event showed that he was mistaken. The worst rapids were ahead of us.

While our course as a whole had been almost due north, and sometimes east of north, yet where there were rapids the river had generally, although not always, turned westward. This seemed to indicate that to the east of us there was a low northward projection of the central plateau across which we had travelled on mule-back. This is the kind of projection that appears on the maps of this region as a sierra. Probably it sent low spurs to the west, and the farthest points of these spurs now and then caused rapids in our course (for the rapids generally came where there were hills) and for the moment deflected the river westward from its general down-hill trend to the north. There was no longer any question that the Dúvida was a big river, a river of real importance. It was not a minor affluent of some other affluent. But we were still wholly in the dark as to where it came out. It was still possible, although exceedingly improbable, that it entered the Gy-Paraná, as another river of substantially the same size, near its mouth. It was much more likely, but not probable, that it entered the Tapajos. It was probable, although far from certain, that it entered the Madeira low down, near its point of junction with the Amazon. In this event it was likely, although again far from certain, that its mouth would prove to be the Aripuanan. The Aripuanan does not appear on the maps as a river of any size; on a good standard map of South America which I had with me its name does not appear at all, although a dotted indication of a small river or creek at about the right place probably represents it. Nevertheless, from the report of one of his lieutenants who had examined its mouth, and from the stories of the rubber-gatherers, or seringuerros, Colonel Rondon had come to the conclusion that this was the largest affluent of the Madeira, with such a body of water that it must have a big drainage basin. He thought that the Dúvida was probably one of its head streams—although every existing map represented the lay of the land to be such as to render impossible the existence of such a river system and drainage basin. The rubber-gatherers reported that they had gone many days' journey up the river, to a point where there was a series of heavy rapids with above them the junction-point of two large rivers, one entering from the west. Beyond this they had difficulties because of the hostility of the Indians; and where the junction-point was no one could say. On the chance Colonel Rondon had directed one of his subordinate officers, Lieutenant Pyrineus, to try to meet us, with boats and provisions, by ascending the Aripuanan to the point of entry of its first big affluent. This was the course followed when Amilcar had been directed to try to meet the explorers who in 1909 came down the Gy-Paraná. At that time the effort was a failure, and the two parties never met; but we might have better luck, and in any event the chance was worth taking.

On the morning following our camping by the mouth of the Rio Kermit, Colonel Rondon took a good deal of pains in getting a big post set up at the entry of the smaller river into the Dúvida. Then he summoned me, and all the others, to attend the ceremony of its erection. We found the camaradas drawn up in line, and the colonel preparing to read aloud "the orders of the day." To the post was nailed a board with "Rio Kermit" on it; and the colonel read the orders reciting that by the direction of the Brazilian Government, and inasmuch as the unknown river was evidently a great river, he formally christened it the Rio Roosevelt. This was a complete surprise to me. Both Lauro Müller and Colonel Rondon had spoken to me on the subject, and I had urged, and Kermit had urged, as strongly as possible that the name be kept as Rio da Dúvida. We felt that the "River of Doubt" was an unusually good name; and it is always well to keep a name of this character. But my kind friends insisted otherwise, and it would have been churlish of me to object longer. I was much touched by their action, and by the ceremony itself. At the conclusion of the reading Colonel Rondon led in cheers for the United States and then for me and for Kermit; and the camaradas cheered with a will. I proposed three cheers for Brazil and then for Colonel Rondon, and Lyra, and the doctor, and then for all the camaradas. Then Lyra said that everybody had been cheered except Cherrie; and so we all gave three cheers for Cherrie, and the meeting broke up in high good humor.

Immediately afterward the walkers set off on their march down-stream, looking for good canoe-trees. In a quarter of an hour we followed with the canoes. As often as we overtook them we halted until they had again gone a good distance ahead. They soon found fresh Indian sign, and actually heard the Indians; but the latter fled in panic. They came on a little Indian fishing village, just abandoned. The three low, oblong huts, of palm-leaves, had each an entrance for a man on all fours, but no other opening. They were dark inside, doubtless as a protection against the swarms of biting flies. On a pole in this village an axe, a knife, and some strings of red beads were left, with the hope that the Indians would return, find the gifts, and realize that we were friendly. We saw further Indian sign on both sides of the river.

After about two hours and a half we came on a little river entering from the east. It was broad but shallow, and at the point of entrance rushed down, green and white, over a sharply inclined sheet of rock. It was a lovely sight and we halted to admire it. Then on we went, until, when we had covered about eight kilometres, we came on a stretch of rapids. The canoes ran them with about a third of the loads, the other loads being carried on the men's shoulders. At the foot of the rapids we camped, as there were several good canoe-trees near, and we had decided to build two rather small canoes. After dark the stars came out; but in the deep forest the glory of the stars in the night of the sky, the serene radiance of the moon, the splendor of sunrise and sunset, are never seen as they are seen on the vast open plains.

The following day, the 19th, the men began work on the canoes. The ill-fated big canoe had been made of wood so hard that it was difficult to work, and so heavy that the chips sank like lead in the water. But these trees were araputangas, with wood which was easier to work and which floated. Great buttresses, or flanges, jutted out from their trunks at the base, and they bore big hard nuts or fruits which stood erect at the ends of the branches. The first tree felled proved rotten, and moreover it was chopped so that it smashed a number of lesser trees into the kitchen, overthrowing everything, but not inflicting serious damage. Hard-working, willing, and tough though the camaradas were, they naturally did not have the skill of northern lumberjacks.

We hoped to finish the two canoes in three days. A space was cleared in the forest for our tents. Among the taller trees grew huge-leafed pacovas, or wild bananas. We bathed and swam in the river, although in it we caught piranhas. Carregadores ants swarmed all around our camp. As many of the nearest of their holes as we could we stopped with fire; but at night some of them got into our tents and ate things we could ill spare. In the early morning a column of foraging ants appeared, and we drove them back, also with fire. When the sky was not overcast the sun was very hot, and we spread out everything to dry. There were many wonderful butterflies round about, but only a few birds. Yet in the early morning and late afternoon there was some attractive bird music in the woods. The two best performers were our old friend the false bell-bird, with its series of ringing whistles, and a shy, attractive ant-thrush. The latter walked much on the ground, with dainty movements, courtesying and raising its tail; and in accent and sequence, although not in tone or time, its song resembled that of our white-throated sparrow.

It was three weeks since we had started down the River of Doubt. We had come along its winding course about 140 kilometres, with a descent of somewhere in the neighborhood of 124 metres. It had been slow progress. We could not tell what physical obstacles were ahead of us, nor whether the Indians would be actively hostile. But a river normally describes in its course a parabola, the steep descent being in the upper part; and we hoped that in the future we should not have to encounter so many and such difficult rapids as we had already encountered, and that therefore we would make better time—a hope destined to failure.

CHAPTER IX

DOWN AN UNKNOWN RIVER INTO THE EQUATORIAL FOREST

THE mightiest river in the world is the Amazon. It runs from west to east, from the sunset to the sunrise, from the Andes to the Atlantic. The main stream flows almost along the equator, while the basin which contains its affluents extends many degrees north and south of the equator. This gigantic equatorial river basin is filled with an immense forest, the largest in the world, with which no other forests can be compared save those of western Africa and Malaysia. We were within the southern boundary of this great equatorial forest, on a river which was not merely unknown but unguessed at, no geographer having ever suspected its existence. This river flowed northward toward the equator, but whither it would go, whether it would turn one way or another, the length of its course, where it would come out, the character of the stream itself, and the character of the dwellers along its banks—all these things were yet to be discovered.

One morning while the canoes were being built Kermit and I walked a few kilometres down the river and surveyed the next rapids below. The vast still forest was almost empty of life. We found old Indian signs. There were very few birds, and these in the tops of the tall trees. We saw a recent tapir-track; and under a cajazeira-tree by the bank there were the tracks of capybaras which had been eating the fallen fruit. This fruit is delicious and would make a valuable addition to our orchards. The tree although tropical is hardy, thrives when domesticated, and propagates rapidly from shoots. The Department of Agriculture should try whether it would not grow in southern California and Florida. This was the tree from which the doctor's family name was taken. His paternal grandfather, although of Portuguese blood, was an intensely patriotic Brazilian. He was a very young man when the independence of Brazil was declared, and did not wish to keep the Portuguese family name; so he changed it to that of the fine Brazilian tree in question. Such change of family names is common in Brazil. Doctor Vital Brazil, the student of poisonous serpents, was given his name by his father, whose own family name was entirely different; and his brother's name was again different.

There were tremendous downpours of rain, lasting for a couple of hours and accompanied by thunder and lightning. But on the whole it seemed as if the rains were less heavy and continuous than they had been. We all of us had to help in building the canoes now and then. Kermit, accompanied by Antonio the Parecís and João, crossed the river and walked back to the little river that had entered from the east, so as to bring back a report of it to Colonel Rondon. Lyra took observations, by the sun and by the stars. We were in about latitude 11° 21′ south, and due north of where we had started. The river had wound so that we had gone two miles for every one we made northward. Our progress had been very slow; and until we got out of the region of incessant rapids, with their attendant labor and hazard, it was not likely that we should go much faster.

On the morning of March 22 we started in our six canoes. We made ten kilometres. Twenty minutes after starting we came to the first rapids. Here every one walked except the three best paddlers, who took the canoes down in succession—an hour's job. Soon after this we struck a bees' nest in the top of a tree overhanging the river; our steersman climbed out and robbed it, but, alas! lost the honey on the way back. We came to a small steep fall which we did not dare run in our overladen, clumsy, and cranky dugouts. Fortunately, we were able to follow a deep canal which led off for a kilometre, returning just below the falls, fifty yards from where it had started. Then, having been in the boats and in motion only one hour and a half, we came to a long stretch of rapids which it took us six hours to descend, and we camped at the foot. Everything was taken out of the canoes, and they were run down in succession. At one difficult and perilous place they were let down by ropes; and even thus we almost lost one.

We went down the right bank. On the opposite bank was an Indian village, evidently inhabited only during the dry season. The marks on the stumps of trees showed that these Indians had axes and knives; and there were old fields in which maize, beans, and cotton had been grown. The forest dripped and steamed. Rubber-trees were plentiful. At one point the tops of a group of tall trees were covered with yellow-white blossoms. Others bore red blossoms. Many of the big trees, of different kinds, were buttressed at the base with great thin walls of

The Upper Dúvida

Cherrie in his canoe

From photographs by Kermit Roosevelt

wood. Others, including both palms and ordinary trees, showed an even stranger peculiarity. The trunk, near the base, but sometimes six or eight feet from the ground, was split into a dozen or twenty branches or small trunks which sloped outward in tent-like shape, each becoming a root. The larger trees of this type looked as if their trunks were seated on the tops of the pole frames of Indian tepees. At one point in the stream, to our great surprise, we saw a flying-fish. It skimmed the water like a swallow for over twenty yards.

Although we made only ten kilometres we worked hard all day. The last canoes were brought down and moored to the bank at nightfall. Our tents were pitched in the darkness.

Next day we made thirteen kilometres. We ran, all told, a little over an hour and three-quarters. Seven hours were spent in getting past a series of rapids at which the portage, over rocky and difficult ground, was a kilometre long. The canoes were run down empty—a hazardous run, in which one of them upset.

Yet while we were actually on the river, paddling and floating down-stream along the reaches of swift, smooth water, it was very lovely. When we started in the morning the day was overcast and the air was heavy with vapor. Ahead of us the shrouded river stretched between dim walls of forest, half-seen in the mist. Then the sun burned up the fog, and loomed through it in a red splendor that changed first to gold and then to molten white. In the dazzling light, under the brilliant blue of the sky, every detail of the magnificent forest was vivid to the eye: the great trees, the network of bush ropes, the caverns of greenery, where thick-leaved vines covered all things else. Wherever there was a hidden bowlder the surface of the current was broken by waves. In one place, in midstream, a pyramidal rock thrust itself six feet above the surface of the river. On the banks we found fresh Indian sign.

At home in Vermont Cherrie is a farmer, with a farm of six hundred acres, most of it woodland. As we sat at the foot of the rapids, watching for the last dugouts with their naked paddlers to swing into sight round the bend through the white water, we talked of the northern spring that was just beginning. He sells cream, eggs, poultry, potatoes, honey, occasionally pork and veal; but at this season it was the time for the maple-sugar crop. He has a sugar orchard, where he taps twelve hundred trees and hopes soon to tap as many more in addition. Said Cherrie: "It's a busy time now for Fred Rice"—Fred Rice is the hired man, and in sugar time the Cherrie boys help him with enthusiasm, and, moreover, are paid with exact justice for the work they do. There is much wild life about the farm, although it is near Brattleboro. One night in early spring a bear left his tracks near the sugar-house; and now and then in summer Cherrie has had to sleep in the garden to keep the deer away from the beans, cabbages, and beets.

There was not much bird life in the forest, but Cherrie kept getting species new to the collection. At this camp he shot an interesting little ant-thrush. It was the size of a warbler, jet-black, with white under-surfaces of the wings and tail, white on the tail-feathers, and a large spot of white on the back, normally almost concealed, the feathers on the back being long and fluffy. When he shot the bird, a male, it was showing off before a dull-colored little bird, doubtless the female; and the chief feature of the display was this white spot on the back. The white feathers were raised and displayed so that the spot flashed like the "chrysanthemum" on a prongbuck whose curiosity has been aroused. In the gloom of the forest the bird was hard to see, but the flashing of this patch of white feathers revealed it at once, attracting immediate attention. It was an excellent example of a coloration mark which served a purely advertising purpose; apparently it was part of a courtship display. The bird was about thirty feet up in the branches.

In the morning, just before leaving this camp, a tapir swam across stream a little way above us; but unfortunately we could not get a shot at it. An ample supply of tapir beef would have meant much to us. We had started with fifty days' rations; but this by no means meant full rations, in the sense of giving every man all he wanted to eat. We had two meals a day, and were on rather short commons—both our mess and the camaradas'—except when we got plenty of palm-tops. For our mess we had the boxes chosen by Fiala, each containing a day's rations for six men, our number. But we made each box last a day and a half, or at times two days, and in addition we gave some of the food to the camaradas. It was only on the rare occasions when we had killed some monkeys or curassows, or caught some fish, that everybody had enough. We would have welcomed that tapir. So far the game, fish, and fruit had been too scarce to be an element of weight in our food supply. In an exploring trip like ours, through a difficult and utterly unknown country, especially if densely forested, there is little time to halt, and game cannot be counted on. It is only in lands like our own West thirty years ago, like South Africa in the middle of the last century, like East Africa to-day that game can be made the chief food supply. On this trip our only substantial food supply from the country hitherto had been that furnished by the palm-tops. Two men were detailed every day to cut down palms for food.

A kilometre and a half after leaving this camp we came on a stretch of big rapids. The river here twists in loops, and we had heard the roaring of these rapids the previous afternoon. Then we passed out of earshot of them; but Antonio Correa, our best waterman, insisted all along that the roaring meant rapids worse than any we had encountered for some days. "I was brought up in the water, and I know it like a fish, and all its sounds," said he. He was right. We had to carry the loads nearly a kilometre that afternoon, and the canoes were pulled out on the bank so that they might be in readiness to be dragged overland next day. Rondon, Lyra, Kermit, and Antonio Correa explored both sides of the river. On the opposite or left bank they found the mouth of a considerable river, bigger than the Rio Kermit, flowing in from the west and making its entrance in the middle of the rapids. This river we christened the Taunay, in honor of a distinguished Brazilian, an explorer, a soldier, a senator, who was also a writer of note. Kermit had with him two of his novels, and I had read one of his books dealing with a disastrous retreat during the Paraguayan war.

Next morning, the 25th, the canoes were brought down. A path was chopped for them and rollers laid; and half-way down the rapids Lyra and Kermit, who were overseeing the work as well as doing their share of the pushing and hauling, got them into a canal of smooth water, which saved much severe labor. As our food supply lowered we were constantly more desirous of economizing the strength of the men. One day more would complete a month since we had embarked on the Dúvida—as we had started in February, the lunar and calendar months coincided. We had used up over half our provisions. We had come only a trifle over 160 kilometres, thanks to the character and number of the rapids. We believed we had three or four times the distance yet to go before coming to a part of the river where we might hope to meet assistance, either from rubber-gatherers, or from Pyrineus, if he were really coming up the river which we were going down. If the rapids continued to be as they had been it could not be much more than three weeks before we were in straits for food, aside from the ever-present danger of accident in the rapids; and if our progress were no faster than it had been—and we were straining to do our best—we would in such event still have several hundreds of kilometres of unknown river before us. We could not even hazard a guess at what was in front. The river was now a really big river, and it seemed impossible that it could flow either into the Gy-Paraná or the Tapajos. It was possible that it went into the Canuma, a big affluent of the Madeira low down, and next to the Tapajos. It was more probable that it was the headwaters of the Aripuanan, a river which, as I have said, was not even named on the excellent English map of Brazil I carried. Nothing but the mouth had been known to any geographer; but the lower course had long been known to rubber-gatherers, and recently a commission from the government of Amazonas had part-way ascended one branch of it—not as far as the rubber-gatherers had gone, and, as it turned out, not the branch we came down.

Two of our men were down with fever. Another man, Julio, a fellow of powerful frame, was utterly worthless, being an inborn, lazy shirk with the heart of a ferocious cur in the body of a bullock. The others were good men, some of them very good indeed. They were under the immediate supervision of Pedrinho Craveiro, who was first-class in every way.

This camp was very lovely. It was on the edge of a bay, into which the river broadened immediately below the rapids. There was a beach of white sand, where we bathed and washed our clothes. All around us, and across the bay, and on both sides of the long water-street made by the river, rose the splendid forest. There were flocks of parakeets colored green, blue, and red. Big toucans called overhead, lustrous green-black in color, with white throats, red gorgets, red-and-yellow tail coverts, and huge black-and-yellow bills. Here the soil was fertile; it will be a fine site for a coffee-plantation when this region is open to settlement. Surely such a rich and fertile land cannot be permitted to remain idle, to lie as a tenantless wilderness, while there are such teeming swarms of human beings in the overcrowded, overpeopled countries of the Old World. The very rapids and waterfalls which now make the navigation of the river so difficult and dangerous would drive electric trolleys up and down its whole length and far out on either side, and run mills and fac-

Red-and-Yellow Macaw

Hyacinth Macaw

Egret

Toco Toucan

Curassow

tories, and lighten the labor on farms. With the incoming of settlement and with the steady growth of knowledge how to fight and control tropical diseases, fear of danger to health would vanish. A land like this is a hard land for the first explorers, and perhaps for their immediate followers, but not for the people who come after them.

In mid-afternoon we were once more in the canoes; but we had paddled with the current only a few minutes, we had gone only a kilometre, when the roar of rapids in front again forced us to haul up to the bank. As usual, Rondon, Lyra, and Kermit, with Antonio Correa, explored both sides while camp was being pitched. The rapids were longer and of steeper descent than the last, but on the opposite or western side there was a passage down which we thought we could get the empty dugouts at the cost of dragging them only a few yards at one spot. The loads were to be carried down the hither bank, for a kilometre, to the smooth water. The river foamed between great rounded masses of rock, and at one point there was a sheer fall of six or eight feet. We found and ate wild pineapples. Wild beans were in flower. At dinner we had a toucan and a couple of parrots, which were very good.

All next day was spent by Lyra in superintending our three best watermen as they took the canoes down the west side of the rapids, to the foot, at the spot to which the camp had meantime been shifted. In the forest some of the huge sipas, or rope vines, which were as big as cables, bore clusters of fragrant flowers. The men found several honey-trees, and fruits of various kinds, and small cocoanuts; they chopped down an ample number of palms, for the palm-cabbage; and, most important of all, they gathered a quantity of big Brazil-nuts, which when roasted tasted like the best of chestnuts and are nutritious; and they caught a number of big piranhas, which were good eating. So we all had a feast, and everybody had enough to eat and was happy.

By these rapids, at the fall, Cherrie found some strange carvings on a bare mass of rock. They were evidently made by men a long time ago. As far as is known, the Indians thereabouts make no such figures now. They were in two groups, one on the surface of the rock facing the land, the other on that facing the water. The latter were nearly obliterated. The former were in good preservation, the figures sharply cut into the rock. They consisted, upon the upper flat part of the rock, of four multiple circles with a dot in the middle (◉), very accurately made and about a foot and a half in diameter; and below them, on the side of the rock, four multiple m's or inverted w's (M). What these curious symbols represented, or who made them, we could not, of course, form the slightest idea. It may be that in a very remote past some Indian tribes of comparatively advanced culture had penetrated to this lovely river, just as we had now come to it. Before white men came to South America there had already existed therein various semicivilizations, some rude, others fairly advanced, which rose, flourished, and persisted through immemorial ages, and then vanished. The vicissitudes in the history of humanity during its stay on this southern continent have been as strange, varied, and inexplicable as paleontology shows to have been the case, on the same continent, in the history of the higher forms of animal life during the age of mammals. Colonel Rondon stated that such figures as these are not found anywhere else in Matto Grosso where he has been, and therefore it was all the more strange to find them in this one place on the unknown river, never before visited by white men, which we were descending.

Next morning we went about three kilometres before coming to some steep hills, beautiful to look upon, clad as they were in dense, tall, tropical forest, but ominous of new rapids. Sure enough, at their foot we had to haul up and prepare for a long portage. The canoes we ran down empty. Even so, we were within an ace of losing two, the lashed couple in which I ordinarily journeyed. In a sharp bend of the rapids, between two big curls, they were swept among the bowlders and under the matted branches which stretched out from the bank. They filled, and the racing current pinned them where they were, one partly on the other. All of us had to help get them clear. Their fastenings were chopped asunder with axes. Kermit and half a dozen of the men, stripped to the skin, made their way to a small rock island in the little falls just above the canoes, and let down a rope which we tied to the outermost canoe. The rest of us, up to our armpits and barely able to keep our footing as we slipped and stumbled among the bowlders in the swift current, lifted and shoved while Kermit and his men pulled the rope and fastened the slack to a half-submerged tree. Each canoe in succession was hauled up the little rock island, baled, and then taken down in safety by two paddlers. It was nearly four o'clock before we were again ready to start, having been delayed by a rain-storm so heavy that we could not see across the river. Ten minutes' run took us to the head of another series of rapids;

the exploring party returned with the news that we had an all day's job ahead of us; and we made camp in the rain, which did not matter much, as we were already drenched through. It was impossible, with the wet wood, to make a fire sufficiently hot to dry all our soggy things, for the rain was still falling. A tapir was seen from our boat, but, as at the moment we were being whisked round in a complete circle by a whirlpool, I did not myself see it in time to shoot.

Next morning we went down a kilometre, and then landed on the other side of the river. The canoes were run down, and the loads carried to the other side of a little river coming in from the west, which Colonel Rondon christened Cherrie River. Across this we went on a bridge consisting of a huge tree felled by Macario, one of our best men. Here we camped, while Rondon, Lyra, Kermit, and Antonio Correa explored what was ahead. They were absent until mid-afternoon. Then they returned with the news that we were among ranges of low mountains, utterly different in formation from the high plateau region to which the first rapids, those we had come to on the 2d of March, belonged. Through the first range of these mountains the river ran in a gorge, some three kilometres long, immediately ahead of us. The ground was so rough and steep that it would be impossible to drag the canoes over it and difficult enough to carry the loads; and the rapids were so bad, containing several falls, one of at least ten metres in height, that it was doubtful how many of the canoes we could get down them. Kermit, who was the only man with much experience of rope work, was the only man who believed we could get the canoes down at all; and it was, of course, possible that we should have to build new ones at the foot to supply the place of any that were lost or left behind. In view of the length and character of the portage, and of all the unpleasant possibilities that were ahead, and of the need of keeping every pound of food, it was necessary to reduce weight in every possible way and to throw away everything except the barest necessities.

We thought we had reduced our baggage before; but now we cut to the bone. We kept the fly for all six of us to sleep under. Kermit's shoes had gone, thanks to the amount of work in the water which he had been doing; and he took the pair I had been wearing, while I put on my spare pair. In addition to the clothes I wore, I kept one set of pajamas, a spare pair of drawers, a spare pair of socks, half a dozen handkerchiefs, my wash-kit, my pocket medicine-case, and a little bag containing my spare spectacles, gun-grease, some adhesive plaster, some needles and thread, the "fly-dope," and my purse and letter of credit, to be used at Manaos. All of these went into the bag containing my cot, blanket, and mosquito-net. I also carried a cartridge-bag containing my cartridges, head-net, and gauntlets. Kermit cut down even closer; and the others about as close.

The last three days of March we spent in getting to the foot of the rapids in this gorge. Lyra and Kermit, with four of the best watermen, handled the empty canoes. The work was not only difficult and laborious in the extreme, but hazardous; for the walls of the gorge were so sheer that at the worst places they had to cling to narrow shelves on the face of the rock, while letting the canoes down with ropes. Meanwhile Rondon surveyed and cut a trail for the burden-bearers, and superintended the portage of the loads. The rocky sides of the gorge were too steep for laden men to attempt to traverse them. Accordingly the trail had to go over the top of the mountain, both the ascent and the descent of the rock-strewn, forest-clad slopes being very steep. It was hard work to carry loads over such a trail. From the top of the mountain, through an opening in the trees on the edge of a cliff, there was a beautiful view of the country ahead. All around and in front of us there were ranges of low mountains about the height of the lower ridges of the Alleghanies. Their sides were steep and they were covered with the matted growth of the tropical forest. Our next camping-place, at the foot of the gorge, was almost beneath us, and from thence the river ran in a straight line, flecked with white water, for about a kilometre. Then it disappeared behind and between mountain ridges, which we supposed meant further rapids. It was a view well worth seeing; but, beautiful although the country ahead of us was, its character was such as to promise further hardships, difficulty, and exhausting labor, and especially further delay; and delay was a serious matter to men whose food supply was beginning to run short, whose equipment was reduced to the minimum, who for a month, with the utmost toil, had made very slow progress, and who had no idea of either the distance or the difficulties of the route in front of them.

There was not much life in the woods, big or little. Small birds were rare, although Cherrie's unwearied efforts were rewarded from time to time by a species new to the collection. There were tracks of tapir, deer, and agouti; and if we had taken two or three days to devote to nothing else than hunting them we might perchance have killed something; but the chance was much too uncertain, the work we were doing was too hard and wearing, and the need of pressing forward altogether too great to permit us to spend any time in such manner. The hunting had to come in incidentally. This type of well-nigh impenetrable forest is the one in which it is most difficult to get even what little game exists therein. A couple of curassows and a big monkey were killed by the colonel and Kermit. On the day the monkey was brought in Lyra, Kermit, and their four associates had spent from sunrise to sunset in severe and at moments dangerous toil among the rocks and in the swift water, and the fresh meat was appreciated. The head, feet, tail, skin, and entrails were boiled for the gaunt and ravenous dogs. The flesh gave each of us a few mouthfuls; and how good those mouthfuls tasted!

Cherrie, in addition to being out after birds in every spare moment, helped in all emergencies. He was a veteran in the work of the tropic wilderness. We talked together often, and of many things, for our views of life, and of a man's duty to his wife and children, to other men, and to women, and to the state in peace and war, were in all essentials the same. His father had served all through the Civil War, entering an Iowa cavalry regiment as a private and coming out as a captain; his breast-bone was shattered by a blow from a musket-butt, in hand-to-hand fighting at Shiloh.

During this portage the weather favored us. We were coming toward the close of the rainy season. On the last day of the month, when we moved camp to the foot of the gorge, there was a thunder-storm; but on the whole we were not bothered by rain until the last night, when it rained heavily, driving under the fly so as to wet my cot and bedding. However, I slept comfortably enough, rolled in the damp blanket. Without the blanket I should have been uncomfortable; a blanket is a necessity for health. On the third day Lyra and Kermit, with their daring and hard-working watermen, after wearing labor, succeeded in getting five canoes through the worst of the rapids to the chief fall. The sixth, which was frail and weak, had its bottom beaten out on the jagged rocks of the broken water. On this night, although I thought I had put my clothes out of reach, both the termites and the carregadores ants got at them, ate holes in one boot, ate one leg of my drawers, and riddled my handkerchief; and I now had nothing to replace anything that was destroyed.

Next day Lyra, Kermit, and their camaradas brought the five canoes that were left down to camp. They had in four days accomplished a work of incredible labor and of the utmost importance; for at the first glance it had seemed an absolute impossibility to avoid abandoning the canoes when we found that the river sank into a cataract-broken torrent at the bottom of a canyon-like gorge between steep mountains. On April 2 we once more started, wondering how soon we should strike other rapids in the mountains ahead, and whether in any reasonable time we should, as the aneroid indicated, be so low down that we should necessarily be in a plain where we could make a journey of at least a few days without rapids. We had been exactly a month going through an uninterrupted succession of rapids. During that month we had come only about 110 kilometres, and had descended nearly 150 metres—the figures are approximate but fairly accurate.* We had lost four of the canoes with which we started, and one other, which we had built, and the life of one man; and the life of a dog which by its death had in all probability saved the life of Colonel Rondon. In a straight line northward, toward our supposed destination, we had not made more than a mile and a quarter a day; at the cost of bitter toil for most of the party, of much risk for some of the party, and of some risk and some hardship for all the party. Most of the camaradas were downhearted, naturally enough, and occasionally asked one of us if we really believed that we should ever get out alive; and we had to cheer them up as best we could.

There was no change in our work for the time being. We made but three kilometres that day. Most of the party walked all the time; but the dugouts carried the luggage until we struck the head of the series of rapids which were to take up the next two or three days. The river rushed through a wild gorge, a chasm or canyon, between two mountains. Its sides were very steep, mere rock walls, although in most places so covered with the luxuriant growth of the trees and bushes that clung in the crevices, and with green moss, that the naked rock was hardly seen. Rondon, Lyra, and Kermit, who were in front, found a small level spot, with a beach of sand, and sent back word to camp there, while they spent several hours in exploring the country ahead. The canoes were

* The first four days, before we struck the upper rapids, and during which we made nearly seventy kilometres, are of course not included when I speak of our making our way down the rapids.

run down empty, and the loads carried painfully along the face of the cliffs; so bad was the trail that I found it rather hard to follow, although carrying nothing but my rifle and cartridge-bag. The explorers returned with the information that the mountains stretched ahead of us, and that there were rapids as far as they had gone. We could only hope that the aneroid was not hopelessly out of kilter, and that we should, therefore, fairly soon find ourselves in comparatively level country. The severe toil, on a rather limited food supply, was telling on the strength as well as on the spirits of the men; Lyra and Kermit, in addition to their other work, performed as much actual physical labor as any of them.

Next day, the 3d of April, we began the descent of these sinister rapids of the chasm. Colonel Rondon had gone to the summit of the mountain in order to find a better trail for the burden-bearers, but it was hopeless, and they had to go along the face of the cliffs. Such an exploring expedition as that in which we were engaged of necessity involves hard and dangerous labor, and perils of many kinds. To follow down-stream an unknown river, broken by innumerable cataracts and rapids, rushing through mountains of which the existence has never been even guessed, bears no resemblance whatever to following even a fairly dangerous river which has been thoroughly explored and has become in some sort a highway, so that experienced pilots can be secured as guides, while the portages have been pioneered and trails chopped out, and every dangerous feature of the rapids is known beforehand. In this case no one could foretell that the river would cleave its way through steep mountain chains, cutting narrow clefts in

The river rushed through a wild gorge, a chasm or canyon, between two mountains

From a photograph by Cherrie

which the cliff walls rose almost sheer on either hand. When a rushing river thus "canyons," as we used to say out West, and the mountains are very steep, it becomes almost impossible to bring the canoes down the river itself and utterly impossible to portage them along the cliff sides, while even to bring the loads over the mountain is a task of extraordinary labor and difficulty. Moreover, no one can tell how many times the task will have to be repeated, or when it will end, or whether the food will hold out; every hour of work in the rapids is fraught with the possibility of the gravest disaster, and yet it is imperatively necessary to attempt it; and all this is done in an uninhabited wilderness, or else a wilderness tenanted only by unfriendly savages, where failure to get through means death by disease and starvation. Wholesale disasters to South American exploring parties have been frequent. The first recent effort to descend one of the unknown rivers to the Amazon from the Brazilian highlands resulted in such a disaster. It was undertaken in 1889 by a party about as large as ours under a Brazilian engineer officer, Colonel Telles Peres. In descending some rapids they lost everything—canoes, food, medicine, implements—everything. Fever smote them, and then starvation. All of them died except one officer and two men, who were rescued months later. Recently, in Guiana, a wilderness veteran, André, lost two-thirds of his party by starvation. Genuine wilderness exploration is as dangerous as warfare. The conquest of wild nature demands the utmost vigor, hardihood, and daring, and takes from the conquerors a heavy toll of life and health.

Lyra, Kermit, and Cherrie, with four of the men,

worked the canoes half-way down the canyon. Again and again it was touch and go whether they could get by a given point. At one spot the channel of the furious torrent was only fifteen yards across. One canoe was lost, so that of the seven with which we had started only two were left. Cherrie labored with the other men at times, and also stood as guard over them, for, while actually working, of course no one could carry a rifle. Kermit's experience in bridge building was invaluable in enabling him to do the rope work by which alone it was possible to get the canoes down the canyon. He and Lyra had now been in the water for days. Their clothes were never dry. Their shoes were rotten. The bruises on their feet and legs had become sores. On their bodies some of the insect bites had become festering wounds, as indeed was the case with all of us. Poisonous ants, biting flies, ticks, wasps, bees were a perpetual torment. However, no one had yet been bitten by a venomous serpent, a scorpion, or a centiped, although we had killed all of the three within camp limits.

Under such conditions whatever is evil in men's natures comes to the front. On this day a strange and terrible tragedy occurred. One of the camaradas, a man of pure European blood, was the man named Julio, of whom I have already spoken. He was a very powerful fellow and had been importunately eager to come on the expedition; and he had the reputation of being a good worker. But, like so many men of higher standing, he had had no idea of what such an expedition really meant, and under the strain of toil, hardship, and danger his nature showed its true depths of selfishness, cowardice, and ferocity. He shirked all work. He shammed sickness. Nothing could make him do his share; and yet unlike his self-respecting fellows he was always shamelessly begging for favors. Kermit was the only one of our party who smoked; and he was continually giving a little tobacco to some of the camaradas, who worked especially well under him. The good men did not ask for it; but Julio, who shirked every labor, was always, and always in vain, demanding it. Colonel Rondon, Lyra, and Kermit each tried to get work out of him, and in order to do anything with him had to threaten to leave him in the wilderness. He threw all his tasks on his comrades; and, moreover, he stole their food as well as ours. On such an expedition the theft of food comes next to murder as a crime, and should by rights be punished as such. We could not trust him to cut down palms or gather nuts, because he would stay out and eat what ought to have gone into the common store. Finally, the men on several occasions themselves detected him stealing their food. Alone of the whole party, and thanks to the stolen food, he had kept in full flesh and bodily vigor.

One of our best men was a huge negro named Paixão—Paishon—a corporal and acting sergeant in the engineer corps. He had, by the way, literally torn his trousers to pieces, so that he wore only the tatters of a pair of old drawers until I gave him my spare trousers when we lightened loads. He was a stern disciplinarian. One evening he detected Julio stealing food and smashed him in the mouth. Julio came crying to us, his face working with fear and malignant hatred; but after investigation he was told that he had gotten off uncommonly lightly. The men had three or four carbines, which were sometimes carried by those who were not their owners.

On this morning, at the outset of the portage, Pedrinho discovered Julio stealing some of the men's dried meat. Shortly afterward Paishon rebuked him for, as usual, lagging behind. By this time we had reached the place where the canoes were tied to the bank and then taken down one at a time. We were sitting down, waiting for the last loads to be brought along the trail. Pedrinho was still in the camp we had left. Paishon had just brought in a load, left it on the ground with his carbine beside it, and returned on the trail for another load. Julio came in, put down his load, picked up the carbine, and walked back on the trail, muttering to himself but showing no excitement. We thought nothing of it, for he was always muttering; and occasionally one of the men saw a monkey or big bird and tried to shoot it, so it was never surprising to see a man with a carbine.

In a minute we heard a shot; and in a short time three or four of the men came up the trail to tell us that Paishon was dead, having been shot by Julio, who had fled into the woods. Colonel Rondon and Lyra were ahead; I sent a messenger for them, directed Cherrie and Kermit to stay where they were and guard the canoes and provisions, and started down the trail with the doctor—an absolutely cool and plucky man, with a revolver but no rifle—and a couple of the camaradas. We soon passed the dead body of poor Paishon. He lay in a huddle, in a pool of his own blood, where he had fallen, shot through the heart. I feared that Julio had run amuck, and intended merely to take more lives before he died, and that he would begin with

Pedrinho, who was alone and unarmed in the camp we had left. Accordingly I pushed on, followed by my companions, looking sharply right and left; but when we came to the camp the doctor quietly walked by me, remarking, "My eyes are better than yours, colonel; if he is in sight I'll point him out to you, as you have the rifle." However, he was not there, and the others soon joined us with the welcome news that they had found the carbine.

The murderer had stood to one side of the path and killed his victim, when a dozen paces off, with deliberate and malignant purpose. Then evidently his murderous hatred had at once given way to his innate cowardice; and, perhaps hearing some one coming along the path, he fled in panic terror into the wilderness. A tree had knocked the carbine from his hand. His footsteps showed that after going some rods he had started to return, doubtless for the carbine, but had fled again, probably because the body had then been discovered. It was questionable whether or not he would live to reach the Indian villages, which were probably his goal. He was not a man to feel remorse—never a common feeling; but surely that murderer was in a living hell, as, with fever and famine leering at him from the shadows, he made his way through the empty desolation of the wilderness. França, the cook, quoted out of the melancholy proverbial philosophy of the people the proverb: "No man knows the heart of any one"; and then expressed with deep conviction a weird ghostly belief I had never encountered before: "Paishon is following Julio now, and will follow him until he dies; Paishon fell forward on his hands and knees, and when a murdered man falls like that his ghost will follow the slayer as long as the slayer lives."

We did not attempt to pursue the murderer. We could not legally put him to death, although he was a soldier who in cold blood had just deliberately killed a fellow soldier. If we had been near civilization we would have done our best to bring him in and turn him over to justice. But we were in the wilderness, and how many weeks' journey were ahead of us we could not tell. Our food was running low, sickness was beginning to appear among the men, and both their courage and their strength were gradually ebbing. Our first duty was to save the lives and the health of the men of the expedition who had honestly been performing, and had still to perform, so much perilous labor. If we brought the murderer in he would have to be guarded night and day on an expedition where there were always loaded firearms about, and where there would continually be opportunity and temptation for him to make an effort to seize food and a weapon and escape, perhaps murdering some other good man. He could not be shackled while climbing along the cliff slopes; he could not be shackled in the canoes, where there was always chance of upset and drowning; and standing guard would be an additional and severe penalty on the weary, honest men already exhausted by overwork. The expedition was in peril, and it was wise to take every chance possible that would help secure success. Whether the murderer lived or died in the wilderness was of no moment compared with the duty of doing everything to secure the safety of the rest of the party. For the two days following we were always on the watch against his return, for he could have readily killed some one else by rolling rocks down on any of the men working on the cliff sides or in the bottom of the gorge. But we did not see him until the morning of the third day. We had passed the last of the rapids of the chasm, and the four boats were going down-stream when he appeared behind some trees on the bank and called out that he wished to surrender and be taken aboard; for the murderer was an arrant craven at heart, a strange mixture of ferocity and cowardice. Colonel Rondon's boat was far in advance; he did not stop nor answer. I kept on in similar fashion with the rear boats, for I had no intention of taking the murderer aboard, to the jeopardy of the other members of the party, unless Colonel Rondon told me that it would have to be done in pursuance of his duty as an officer of the army and a servant of the Government of Brazil. At the first halt Colonel Rondon came up to me and told me that this was his view of his duty, but that he had not stopped because he wished first to consult me as the chief of the expedition. I answered that for the reasons enumerated above I did not believe that in justice to the good men of the expedition we should jeopardize their safety by taking the murderer along, and that if the responsibility were mine I should refuse to take him; but that he, Colonel Rondon, was the superior officer of both the murderer and of all the other enlisted men and army officers on the expedition, and in return was responsible for his actions to his own governmental superiors and to the laws of Brazil; and that in view of this responsibility he must act as his sense of duty bade him. Accordingly, at the next camp he sent back two men, expert woodsmen, to find the murderer and bring him in. They failed to find him.*

*The above account of all the circumstances connected with the murder was read to and approved as correct by all six members of the expedition.

I have anticipated my narrative because I do not wish to recur to the horror more than is necessary. I now return to my story. After we found that Julio had fled, we returned to the scene of the tragedy. The murdered man lay with a handkerchief thrown over his face. We buried him beside the place where he fell. With axes and knives the camaradas dug a shallow grave while we stood by with bared heads. Then reverently and carefully we lifted the poor body which but half an hour before had been so full of vigorous life. Colonel Rondon and I bore the head and shoulders. We laid him in the grave, and heaped a mound over him, and put a rude cross at his head. We fired a volley for a brave and loyal soldier who had died doing his duty. Then we left him forever, under the great trees beside the lonely river.

That day we got only half-way down the rapids. There was no good place to camp. But at the foot of one steep cliff there was a narrow, bowlder-covered slope where it was possible to sling hammocks and cook; and a slanting spot was found for my cot, which had sagged until by this time it looked like a broken-backed centiped. It rained a little during the night, but not enough to wet us much. Next day Lyra, Kermit, and Cherrie finished their job, and brought the four remaining canoes to camp, one leaking badly from the battering on the rocks. We then went down-stream a few hundred yards, and camped on the opposite side; it was not a good camping-place, but it was better than the one we left.

The men were growing constantly weaker under the endless strain of exhausting labor. Kermit was having an attack of fever, and Lyra and Cherrie had touches of dys-

Rapids at the chasm

From a photograph by Cherrie

We bathed and swam in the river although in it we caught piranhas

From a photograph by Kermit Roosevelt

entery, but all three continued to work. While in the water trying to help with an upset canoe I had by my own clumsiness bruised my leg against a bowlder; and the resulting inflammation was somewhat bothersome. I now had a sharp attack of fever, but thanks to the excellent care of the doctor, was over it in about forty-eight hours; but Kermit's fever grew worse and he too was unable to work for a day or two. We could walk over the portages, however. A good doctor is an absolute necessity on an exploring expedition in such a country as that we were in, under penalty of a frightful mortality among the members; and the necessary risks and hazards are so great, the chances of disaster so large, that there is no warrant for increasing them by the failure to take all feasible precautions.

The next day we made another long portage round some rapids, and camped at night still in the hot, wet, sunless atmosphere of the gorge. The following day, April 6, we portaged past another set of rapids, which proved to be the last of the rapids of the chasm. For some kilometres we kept passing hills, and feared lest at any moment we might again find ourselves fronting another mountain gorge; with, in such case, further days of grinding and perilous labor ahead of us, while our men were disheartened, weak, and sick. Most of them had already begun to have fever. Their condition was inevitable after over a month's uninterrupted work of the hardest kind in getting through the long series of rapids we had just passed; and a long further delay, accompanied by wearing labor, would have almost certainly meant that the weakest among our party would have begun to die. There were already two of the camaradas who were too weak to help the others, their condition being such as to cause us serious concern.

However, the hills gradually sank into a level plain, and the river carried us through it at a rate that enabled us during the remainder of the day to reel off thirty-six kilometres, a record that for the first time held out promise. Twice tapirs swam the river while we passed, but not near my canoe. However, the previous evening Cherrie had killed two monkeys and Kermit one, and we all had a few mouthfuls of fresh meat; we had already had a good soup made out of a turtle Kermit had caught. We had to portage by one short set of rapids, the unloaded canoes being brought down without difficulty. At last, at four in the afternoon, we came to the mouth of a big river running in from the right. We thought it was probably the Ananás, but, of course, could not be certain. It was less in volume than the one we had descended, but nearly as broad; its breadth at this point being ninety-five yards as against one hundred and twenty for the larger river. There were rapids ahead, immediately after the junction, which took place in latitude 10° 58′ south. We had come 216 kilometres all told, and were nearly north of where we had started. We camped on the point of land between the two rivers. It was extraordinary to realize that here about the eleventh degree we were on such a big river, utterly unknown to the cartographers and not indicated by even a hint on any map. We named this big tributary Rio Cardozo, after a gallant officer of the commission who had died of beriberi just as our expedition began. We spent a day at this spot, determining our exact position by the sun, and afterward by the stars, and sending on two men to explore the rapids in advance. They returned with the news that there were big cataracts in them, and that they would form an obstacle to our progress. They had also caught a huge siluroid fish, which furnished an excellent meal for everybody in camp. This evening at sunset the view across the broad river, from our camp where the two rivers joined, was very lovely; and for the first time we had an open space in front of and above us, so that after nightfall the stars, and the great waxing moon, were glorious overhead, and against the rocks in midstream the broken water gleamed like tossing silver.

The huge catfish which the men had caught was over three feet and a half long, with the usual enormous head, out of all proportion to the body, and the enormous mouth, out of all proportion to the head. Such fish, although their teeth are small, swallow very large prey. This one contained the nearly digested remains of a monkey. Probably the monkey had been seized while drinking from the end of a branch; and once engulfed in that yawning cavern there was no escape. We Americans were astounded at the idea of a catfish making prey of a monkey; but our Brazilian friends told us that in the lower Madeira and the part of the Amazon near its mouth there is a still more gigantic catfish which in similar fashion occasionally makes prey of man. This is a grayish-white fish over nine feet long, with the usual disproportionately large head and gaping mouth, with a circle of small teeth; for the engulfing mouth itself is the danger, not the teeth. It is called the piraiba—pronounced in four syllables. While stationed at the small city of Itacoatiara, on the Amazon, at the mouth of the Madeira, the doctor had seen one of these monsters which had been killed by the two men it had attacked. They were fishing in a canoe when it rose from the bottom —for it is a ground fish—and raising itself half out of the water lunged over the edge of the canoe at them, with open mouth. They killed it with their *falcóns*, as machetes are called in Brazil. It was taken round the city in triumph in an ox-cart; the doctor saw it, and said it was three metres long. He said that swimmers feared it even more than the big cayman, because they could see the latter, whereas the former lay hid at the bottom of the water. Colonel Rondon said that in many villages where he had been on the lower Madeira the people had built stockaded enclosures in the water in which they bathed, not venturing to swim in the open water for fear of the piraiba and the big cayman.

Next day, April 8, we made five kilometres only, as there was a succession of rapids. We had to carry the loads past two of them, but ran the canoes without difficulty, for on the west side were long canals of swift water through the forest. The river had been higher, but was still very high, and the current raced round the many islands that at this point divided the channel. At four we made camp at the head of another stretch of rapids, over which the Canadian canoes would have danced without shipping a teaspoonful of water, but which our dugouts could only run empty. Cherrie killed three monkeys and Lyra caught two big piranhas, so that we were again all of us well provided with dinner and breakfast. When a number of men, doing hard work, are most of the time on half-rations, they grow to take a lively interest in any reasonably full meal that does arrive.

On the 10th we repeated the proceedings: a short quick run; a few hundred metres' portage, occupying, however, at least a couple of hours; again a few minutes' run; again other rapids. We again made less than five kilometres; in the two days we had been descending nearly a metre for every kilometre we made in advance; and it hardly seemed as if this state of things could last, for the aneroid showed that we were getting very low down. How I longed for a big Maine birch-bark, such as that in which I once went down the Mattawamkeag at high water! It would have slipped down these rapids as a girl trips through a country dance. But our loaded dugouts would have shoved their noses under every curl. The country was lovely. The wide river, now in one channel, now in several channels, wound among hills; the shower-freshened forest glistened in the sunlight; the many kinds of beautiful palm-fronds and the huge pacova-leaves stamped the peculiar look of the tropics on the whole landscape—it was like passing by water through a gigantic botanical garden. In the afternoon we got an elderly toucan, a piranha, and a reasonably edible side-necked river-turtle; so we had fresh meat again. We slept as usual in earshot of rapids. We had been out six weeks, and almost all the time we had been engaged in wearily working our way down and past rapid after rapid. Rapids are by far the most dangerous enemies of explorers and travellers who journey along these rivers.

Next day was a repetition of the same work. All the morning was spent in getting the loads to the foot of the rapids at the head of which we were encamped, down which the canoes were run empty. Then for thirty or forty minutes we ran down the swift, twisting river, the two lashed canoes almost coming to grief at one spot where a swirl of the current threw them against some trees on a small submerged island. Then we came to another set of rapids, carried the baggage down past them, and made camp long after dark in the rain—a good exercise in patience for those of us who were still suffering somewhat from fever. No one was in really buoyant health. For some weeks we had been sharing part of the contents of our boxes with the camaradas; but our food was not very satisfying to them. They needed quantity, and the mainstay of each of their meals was a mass of palmitas; but on this day they had no time to cut down palms. We finally decided to run these rapids with the empty canoes, and they came down in safety. On such a trip it is highly undesirable to take any save necessary risks, for the consequences of disaster are too serious; and yet if no risks are taken the progress is so slow that disaster comes anyhow; and it is necessary perpetually to vary the terms of the perpetual working compromise between rashness and overcaution. This night we had a very good fish to eat, a big silvery fellow called a pescada, of a kind we had not caught before.

One day Trigueiro failed to embark with the rest of us, and we had to camp where we were next day to find him. Easter Sunday we spent in the fashion with which we were altogether too familiar. We only ran in a clear course for ten minutes all told, and spent eight hours in portaging the loads past rapids down which the canoes were run; the balsa was almost swamped. This day we caught twenty-eight big fish, mostly piranhas, and everybody had

Castanho-tree
(Brazil-nut)

Pacova-tree
The huge pacova leaves stamped the peculiar look of the tropics on the whole landscape

From photographs by Cherrie

all he could eat for dinner, and for breakfast the following morning.

The forenoon of the following day was a repetition of this wearisome work; but late in the afternoon the river began to run in long quiet reaches. We made fifteen kilometres, and for the first time in several weeks camped where we did not hear the rapids. The silence was soothing and restful. The following day, April 14, we made a good run of some thirty-two kilometres. We passed a little river which entered on our left. We ran two or three light rapids, and portaged the loads by another. The river ran in long and usually tranquil stretches. In the morning when we started the view was lovely. There was a mist, and for a couple of miles the great river, broad and quiet, ran between the high walls of tropical forest, the tops of the giant trees showing dim through the haze. Different members of the party caught many fish, and shot a monkey and a couple of jacú-tinga—birds kin to a turkey, but the size of a fowl—so we again had a camp of plenty. The dry season was approaching, but there were still heavy, drenching rains. On this day the men found some new nuts of which they liked the taste; but the nuts proved unwholesome and half of the men were very sick and unable to work the following day. In the balsa only two were left fit to do anything, and Kermit plied a paddle all day long.

Accordingly, it was a rather sorry crew that embarked the following morning, April 15. But it turned out a red-letter day. The day before, we had come across cuttings, a year old, which were probably but not certainly made by pioneer rubber-men. But on this day—during which we made twenty-five kilometres—after running two hours and a half we found on the left bank a board on a post, with the initials J. A., to show the farthest-up point which a rubber-man had reached and claimed as his own. An hour farther down we came on a newly built house in a little planted clearing; and we cheered heartily. No one was at home, but the house, of palm thatch, was clean and cool. A couple of dogs were on watch, and the belongings showed that a man, a woman, and a child lived there, and had only just left. Another hour brought us to a similar house where dwelt an old black man, who showed the innate courtesy of the Brazilian peasant. We came on these rubber-men and their houses in about latitude 10° 24′.

In mid-afternoon we stopped at another clean, cool, picturesque house of palm thatch. The inhabitants all fled at our approach, fearing an Indian raid; for they were absolutely unprepared to have any one come from the unknown regions up-stream. They returned and were most hospitable and communicative; and we spent the night there. Said Antonio Correa to Kermit: "It seems like a dream to be in a house again, and hear the voices of men and women, instead of being among those mountains and rapids." The river was known to them as the Castanho, and was the main affluent, or rather the left or western branch, of the Aripuanan; the Castanho is a name used by the rubber-gatherers only; it is unknown to the geographers. We were, according to our informants, about fifteen days' journey from the confluence of the two rivers; but there were many rubber-men along the banks, some of whom had become permanent settlers. We had come over three hundred kilometres, in forty-eight days, over absolutely unknown ground; we had seen no human being, although we had twice heard Indians. Six weeks had been spent in steadily slogging our way down through the interminable series of rapids. It was astonishing before, when we were on a river of about the size of the upper Rhine or Elbe, to realize that no geographer had any idea of its existence. But, after all, no civilized man of any grade had ever been on it. Here, however, was a river with people dwelling along the banks, some of whom had lived in the neighborhood for eight or ten years; and yet on no standard map was there a hint of the river's existence. We were putting on the map a river, running through between five and six degrees of latitude—of between seven and eight if, as should properly be done, the lower Aripuanan is included as part of it—of which no geographer, in any map published in Europe, or the United States, or Brazil, had even admitted the possibility of the existence; for the place actually occupied by it was filled, on the maps, by other—imaginary—streams, or by mountain ranges. Before we started, the Amazonas Boundary Commission had come up the lower Aripuanan and then the eastern branch, or upper Aripuanan, to 8° 48′, following the course which for a couple of decades had been followed by the rubber-men, but not going as high. An employee, either of this commission or of one of the big rubber-men, had been up the Castanho, which is easy of ascent in its lower course, to about the same latitude, not going nearly as high as the rubber-men had gone; this we found out while we ourselves were descending the lower Castanho. The lower main stream, and the lower portion of its main affluent, the Castanho, had been commercial highways for rubber-men and settlers for nearly two decades, and, as we speedily found, were as easy to traverse as the upper stream, which we had just come down, was difficult to traverse; but the governmental and scientific authorities, native and foreign, remained in complete ignorance; and the rubber-men themselves had not the slightest idea of the headwaters, which were in country never hitherto traversed by civilized men. Evidently the Castanho was, in length at least, substantially equal, and probably superior, to the upper Aripuanan; it now seemed even more likely that the Ananás was the headwaters of the main stream than of the Cardozo.* For the first time this great river, the greatest affluent of the Madeira, was to be put on the map; and the understanding of its real position and real relationship, and the clearing up of the complex problem of the sources of all these lower right-hand affluents of the Madeira, was rendered possible by the seven weeks of hard and dangerous labor we had spent in going down an absolutely unknown river, through an absolutely unknown wilderness. At this stage of the growth of world geography I esteemed it a great piece of good fortune to be able to take part in such a feat—a feat which represented the capping of the pyramid which during the previous seven years had been built by the labor of the Brazilian Telegraphic Commission.

We had passed the period when there was a chance of

*I hope that this year the Ananás, or Pineapple, will also be put on the map. One of Colonel Rondon's subordinates is to attempt the descent of the river. We passed the headwaters of the Pineapple on the high plateau, very possibly we passed its mouth, although it is also possible that it empties into the Canama or Tapajos. But it will not be "put on the map" until some one descends and finds out where, as a matter of fact, it really does go.

peril, of disaster, to the whole expedition. There might be risk ahead to individuals, and some difficulties and annoyances for all of us; but there was no longer the least likelihood of any disaster to the expedition as a whole. We now no longer had to face continual anxiety, the need of constant economy with food, the duty of labor with no end in sight, and bitter uncertainty as to the future.

It was time to get out. The wearing work, under very unhealthy conditions, was beginning to tell on every one. Half of the camaradas had been down with fever and were much weakened; only a few of them retained their original physical and moral strength. Cherrie and Kermit had recovered; but both Kermit and Lyra still had bad sores on their legs, from the bruises received in the water work. I was in worse shape. The after effects of the fever still hung on; and the leg which had been hurt while working in the rapids with the sunken canoe had taken a turn for the bad and developed an abscess. The good doctor, to whose unwearied care and kindness I owe much, had cut it open and inserted a drainage tube; an added charm being given the operation, and the subsequent dressings, by the enthusiasm with which the piums and boroshudas took part therein. I could hardly hobble, and was pretty well laid up. But "there aren't no 'stop, conductor,' while a battery's changing ground." No man has any business to go on such a trip as ours unless he will refuse to jeopardize the welfare of his associates by any delay caused by a weakness or ailment of his. It is his duty to go forward, if necessary on all fours, until he drops. Fortunately, I was put to no such test. I remained in good shape until we had passed the last of the rapids of the chasms. When my serious trouble came we had only canoe-riding ahead of us. It is not ideal for a sick man to spend the hottest hours of the day stretched on the boxes in the bottom of a small open dugout, under the well-nigh intolerable heat of the torrid sun of the mid-tropics, varied by blinding, drenching downpours of rain; but I could not be sufficiently grateful for the chance. Kermit and Cherrie took care of me as if they had been trained nurses; and Colonel Rondon and Lyra were no less thoughtful.

The north was calling strongly to the three men of the north—Rocky Dell Farm to Cherrie, Sagamore Hill to me; and to Kermit the call was stronger still. After nightfall we could now see the Dipper well above the horizon—upside down, with the two pointers pointing to a north star below the world's rim; but the Dipper, with all its stars. In our home country spring had now come, the wonderful northern spring of long, glorious days, of brooding twilights, of cool delightful nights. Robin and bluebird, meadow-lark and song-sparrow, were singing in the mornings at home; the maple-buds were red; windflowers and blood-root were blooming while the last patches of snow still lingered; the rapture of the hermit-thrush in Vermont, the serene golden melody of the wood-thrush on Long Island, would be heard before we were there to listen. Each man to his home, and to his true love! Each was longing for the homely things that were so dear to him, for the home people who were dearer still, and for the one who was dearest of all.

CHAPTER X

TO THE AMAZON AND HOME; ZOOLOGICAL AND GEOGRAPHICAL RESULTS OF THE EXPEDITION

Our adventures and our troubles were alike over. We now experienced the incalculable contrast between descending a known and travelled river, and one that is utterly unknown. After four days we hired a rubber-man to go with us as guide. He knew exactly what channels were passable when we came to the rapids, when the canoes had to unload, and where the carry-trails were. It was all child's play compared to what we had gone through. We made long days' journeys, for at night we stopped at some palm-thatched house, inhabited or abandoned, and therefore the men were spared the labor of making camp; and we bought ample food for them, so there was no further need of fishing and chopping down palms for the palm-tops. The heat of the sun was blazing; but it looked as if we had come back into the rainy season, for there were many heavy rains, usually in the afternoon, but sometimes in the morning or at night. The mosquitoes were sometimes rather troublesome at night. In the daytime the piums swarmed, and often bothered us even when we were in midstream.

For four days there were no rapids we could not run without unloading. Then, on the 19th, we got a canoe from Senhor Barboso. He was a most kind and hospitable man, who also gave us a duck and a chicken and some mandioc and six pounds of rice, and would take no payment; he lived in a roomy house with his dusky, cigar-smoking wife and his many children. The new canoe was light and roomy, and we were able to rig up a low shelter under which I could lie; I was still sick. At noon we passed the mouth of a big river, the Rio Branco, coming in from the left; this was about in latitude 9° 38′. Soon afterward we came to the first serious rapids, the Panela. We carried the boats past, ran down the empty canoes, and camped at the foot in a roomy house. The doctor bought a handsome trumpeter bird, very friendly and confiding, which was thenceforth my canoe companion.

We had already passed many inhabited—and a still larger number of uninhabited—houses. The dwellers were rubber-men, but generally they were permanent settlers also, home-makers, with their wives and children. Some, both of the men and women, were apparently of pure negro blood, or of pure Indian or south European blood; but in the great majority all three strains were mixed in varying degrees. They were most friendly, courteous, and hospitable. Often they refused payment for what they could afford, out of their little, to give us. When they did charge, the prices were very high, as was but just, for they live back of the beyond, and everything costs them fabulously, save what they raise themselves. The cool, bare houses of poles and palm thatch contained little except hammocks and a few simple cooking-utensils; and often a clock or sewing-machine, or Winchester rifle, from our own country. They often had flowers planted, including fragrant roses. Their only live stock, except the dogs, were a few chickens and ducks. They planted patches of mandioc, maize, sugar-cane, rice, beans, squashes, pineapples, bananas, lemons, oranges, melons, peppers; and various purely native fruits and vegetables, such as the *kniabo*—a vegetable-fruit growing on the branches of a high bush—which is cooked with meat. They get some game from the forest, and more fish from the river. There is no representative of the government among them—indeed, even now their very existence is barely known to the governmental authorities; and the church has ignored them as completely as the state. When they wish to get married they have to spend several months getting down to and back from Manaos or some smaller city; and usually the first christening and the marriage ceremony are held at the same time. They have merely squatter's right to the land, and are always in danger of being ousted by unscrupulous big men who come in late, but with a title technically straight. The land laws should be shaped so as to give each of these pioneer settlers the land he actually takes up and cultivates, and upon which he makes his home. The small home-maker, who owns the land which he tills with his own hands, is the greatest element of strength in any country.

These are real pioneer settlers. They are the true wilderness-winners. No continent is ever really conquered, or thoroughly explored, by a few leaders, or exceptional men, although such men can render great service. The real conquest, the thorough exploration and settlement, is made by a nameless multitude of small men of whom the most important are, of course, the home-makers. Each treads most of the time in the footsteps of his predecessors, but for some few miles, at some time or other, he breaks new ground; and his house is built where no house has ever stood before. Such a man, the real pioneer, must have no strong desire for social life and no need, probably no knowledge, of any luxury, or of any comfort save of the most elementary kind. The pioneer who is always longing for the comfort and luxury of civilization, and especially of great cities, is no real pioneer at all. These settlers whom we met were contented to live in the wilderness. They had found the climate healthy and the soil fruitful; a visit to a city was a very rare event, nor was there any overwhelming desire for it.

In short, these men, and those like them everywhere on the frontier between civilization and savagery in Brazil, are now playing the part played by our backwoodsmen when over a century and a quarter ago they began the conquest of the great basin of the Mississippi; the part played by the Boer farmers for over a century in South Africa, and by the Canadians when less than half a century ago they began to take possession of their Northwest. Every now and then some one says that the "last frontier" is now to be found in Canada or Africa, and that it has almost vanished. On a far larger scale this frontier is to be found in Brazil—a country as big as Europe or the United States—and decades will pass before it vanishes. The first settlers came to Brazil a century before the first settlers came to the United States and Canada. For three hundred years progress was very slow—Portuguese colonial government at that time was almost as bad as Spanish. For the last half-century and over there has been a steady increase in the rapidity of the rate of development;

At the rubber-man's house

The canoe rigged with a cover under which Colonel Roosevelt travelled when sick

From photographs by Cherrie

and this increase bids fair to be constantly more rapid in the future.

The Paolistas, hunting for lands, slaves, and mines, were the first native Brazilians who, a hundred years ago, played a great part in opening to settlement vast stretches of wilderness. The rubber hunters have played a similar part during the last few decades. Rubber dazzled them, as gold and diamonds have dazzled other men and driven them forth to wander through the wide waste spaces of the world. Searching for rubber they made highways of rivers the very existence of which was unknown to the governmental authorities, or to any map-makers. Whether they succeeded or failed, they everywhere left behind them settlers, who toiled, married, and brought up children. Settlement began; the conquest of the wilderness entered on its first stage.

On the 20th we stopped at the first store, where we bought, of course at a high price, sugar and tobacco for the camaradas. In this land of plenty the camaradas overate, and sickness was as rife among them as ever. In Cherrie's boat he himself and the steersman were the only men who paddled strongly and continuously. The storekeeper's stock of goods was very low, only what he still had left from that brought in nearly a year before; for the big boats, or batelãos—batelons—had not yet worked as far up-stream. We expected to meet them somewhere below the next rapids, the Inferno. The trader or rubber-man brings up his year's supply of goods in a batelão, starting in February and reaching the upper course of the river early in May, when the rainy season is over. The parties of rubber-explorers are then equipped and provisioned;

and the settlers purchase certain necessities, and certain things that strike them as luxuries. This year the Brazil-nut crop on the river had failed, a serious thing for all explorers and wilderness wanderers.

On the 20th we made the longest run we had made, fifty-two kilometres. Lyra took observations where we camped; we were in latitude 8° 49′. At this camping-place the great, beautiful river was a little over three hundred metres wide. We were in an empty house. The marks showed that in the high water, a couple of months back, the river had risen until the lower part of the house was flooded. The difference between the level of the river during the floods and in the dry season is extraordinary.

On the 21st we made another good run, getting down to the Inferno rapids, which are in latitude 8° 19′ south. Until we reached the Cardozo we had run almost due north; since then we had been running a little west of north. Before we reached these rapids we stopped at a large, pleasant thatch house, and got a fairly big and roomy as well as light boat, leaving both our two smaller dugouts behind. Above the rapids a small river, the Madeirainha, entered from the left. The rapids had a fall of over ten metres, and the water was very wild and rough. Met with for the first time, it would doubtless have taken several days to explore a passage and, with danger and labor, get the boats down. But we were no longer exploring, pioneering, over unknown country. It is easy to go where other men have prepared the way. We had a guide; we took our baggage down by a carry three-quarters of a kilometre long; and the canoes were run through known channels the following morning. At the foot of the rapids was a big house and store; and camped at the head were a number of rubber-workers, waiting for the big boats of the head rubber-men to work their way up from below. They were a reckless set of brown daredevils. These men lead hard lives of labor and peril; they continually face death themselves, and they think little of it in connection with others. It is small wonder that they sometimes have difficulties with the tribes of utterly wild Indians with whom they are brought in contact, although there is a strong Indian strain in their own blood.

The following morning, after the empty canoes had been run down, we started, and made a rather short afternoon's journey. We had to take the baggage by one rapids. We camped in an empty house, in the rain. Next day we ran nearly fifty kilometres, the river making a long sweep to the west. We met half a dozen batelãos making their way up-stream, each with a crew of six or eight men, and two of them with women and children in addition. The crew were using very long poles, with crooks, or rather the stubs of cut branches which served as crooks, at the upper end. With these they hooked into the branches and dragged themselves up along the bank, in addition to poling where the depth permitted it. The river was as big as the Paraguay at Corumbá; but, in striking contrast to the Paraguay, there were few water-birds. We ran some rather stiff rapids, the Infernino, without unloading, in the morning. In the evening we landed for the night at a large, open, shed-like house, where there were two or three pigs, the first live stock we had seen other than poultry and ducks. It was a dirty place, but we got some eggs.

The following day, the 24th, we ran down some fifty kilometres to the Carupanan rapids, which by observation Lyra found to be in latitude 7° 47′. We met several batelãos, and the houses on the bank showed that the settlers were somewhat better off than was the case farther up. At the rapids was a big store, the property of Senhor Caripe, the wealthiest rubber-man who works on this river; many of the men we met were in his employ. He has himself risen from the ranks. He was most kind and hospitable, and gave us another boat to replace the last of our shovel-nosed dugouts. The large, open house was cool, clean, and comfortable.

With these began a series of half a dozen sets of rapids, all coming within the next dozen kilometres, and all offering very real obstacles. At one we saw the graves of four men who had perished therein; and many more had died whose bodies were never recovered; the toll of human life had been heavy. Had we been still on an unknown river, pioneering our own way, it would doubtless have taken us at least a fortnight of labor and peril to pass. But it actually took only a day and a half. All the channels were known, all the trails cut. Senhor Caripe, a first-class waterman, cool, fearless, and brawny as a bull, came with us as guide. Half a dozen times the loads were taken out and carried down. At one cataract the canoes were themselves dragged overland; elsewhere they were run down empty, shipping a good deal of water. At the foot of the cataract, where we dragged the canoes overland, we camped for the night. Here Kermit shot a big cayman. Our camp was alongside the graves of three men who at this point had perished in the swift water.

Senhor Caripe told us many strange adventures of rubber-workers he had met or employed. One of his men, working on the Gy-Paraná, got lost and after twenty-eight days found himself on the Madeirainha, which he thus discovered. He was in excellent health, for he had means to start a fire, and he found abundance of Brazil-nuts and big land-tortoises. Senhor Caripe said that the rubbermen now did not go above the ninth degree, or thereabouts, on the upper Aripuanan proper, having found the rubber poor on the reaches above. A year previously five rubbermen, Mundurucu Indians, were working on the Canumá at about that level. It is a difficult stream to ascend or descend. They made excursions into the forest for days at a time after caoutchouc. On one such trip, after fifteen days they, to their surprise, came out on the Aripuanan. They returned and told their "patron" of their discovery; and by his orders took their caoutchouc overland to the Aripuanan, built a canoe, and ran down with their caoutchouc to Manaos. They had now returned and were working on the upper Aripuanan. The Mundurucus and Brazilians are always on the best terms, and the former are even more inveterate enemies of the wild Indians than are the latter.

By mid-forenoon on April 26 we had passed the last dangerous rapids. The paddles were plied with hearty good will, Cherrie and Kermit, as usual, working like the camaradas, and the canoes went dancing down the broad, rapid river. The equatorial forest crowded on either hand to the water's edge; and, although the river was falling, it was still so high that in many places little islands were completely submerged, and the current raced among the trunks of the green trees. At one o'clock we came to the mouth of the Castanho proper, and in sight of the tent of Lieutenant Pyrineus, with the flags of the United States and Brazil flying before it; and, with rifles firing from the canoes and the shore, we moored at the landing of the neat, soldierly, well-kept camp. The upper Aripuanan, a river of substantially the same volume as the Castanho, but broader at this point, and probably of less length, here joined the Castanho from the east, and the two together formed what the rubber-men called the lower Aripuanan. The mouth of this was indicated, and sometimes named, on the maps, but only as a small and unimportant stream.

We had been two months in the canoes; from the 27th of February to the 26th of April. We had gone over 750 kilometres. The river from its source, near the thirteenth degree, to where it became navigable and we entered it, had a course of some 200 kilometres—probably more, perhaps 300 kilometres. Therefore we had now put on the map a river nearly 1,000 kilometres in length of which the existence was not merely unknown but impossible if the standard maps were correct. But this was not all. It seemed that this river of 1,000 kilometres in length was really the true upper course of the Aripuanan proper, in which case the total length was nearly 1,500 kilometres. Pyrineus had been waiting for us over a month, at the junction of what the rubber-men called the Castanho and of what they called the upper Aripuanan. (He had no idea as to which stream we would appear upon, or whether we would appear upon either.) On March 26 he had measured the volume of the two, and found that the Castanho, although the narrower, was the deeper and swifter, and that in volume it surpassed the other by 84 cubic metres a second. Since then the Castanho had fallen; our measurements showed it to be slightly smaller than the other; the volume of the river after the junction was about 4,500 cubic metres a second. This was in 7° 34′.

We were glad indeed to see Pyrineus and be at his attractive camp. We were only four hours above the little river hamlet of São João, a port of call for rubber-steamers, from which the larger ones go to Manaos in two days. These steamers mostly belong to Senhor Caripe. From Pyrineus we learned that Lauriadó and Fiala had reached Manaos on March 26. On the swift water in the gorge of the Papagaio Fiala's boat had been upset and all his belongings lost, while he himself had narrowly escaped with his life. I was glad indeed that the fine and gallant fellow had escaped. The Canadian canoe had done very well. We were no less rejoiced to learn that Amilcar, the head of the party that went down the Gy-Paraná, was also all right, although his canoe too had been upset in the rapids, and his instruments and all his notes lost. He had reached Manaos on April 10. Fiala had gone home. Miller was collecting near Manaos. He had been doing capital work.

The piranhas were bad here, and no one could bathe. Cherrie, while standing in the water close to the shore, was attacked and bitten; but with one bound he was on the bank before any damage could be done.

We spent a last night under canvas, at Pyrineus's encampment. It rained heavily. Next morning we all gathered at the monument which Colonel Rondon had erected, and he read the orders of the day. These recited just what had been accomplished: set forth the fact that we had now by actual exploration and investigation discovered that the river whose upper portion had been called the Dúvida on the maps of the Telegraphic Commission and the unknown major part of which we had just traversed, and the river known to a few rubber-men, but to no one else, as the Castanho, and the lower part of the river known to the rubber-men as the Aripuanan (which did not appear on the maps save as its mouth was sometimes indicated, with no hint of its size) were all parts of one and the same river; and that by order of the Brazilian Government this river, the largest affluent of the Madeira, with its source near the 13th degree and its mouth a little south of the 5th degree, hitherto utterly unknown to cartographers and in large part utterly unknown to any save the local tribes of Indians, had been named the Rio Roosevelt.

We left Rondon, Lyra, and Pyrineus to take observations, and the rest of us embarked for the last time on the canoes, and, borne swiftly on the rapid current, we passed over one set of not very important rapids and ran down to Senhor Caripe's little hamlet of São João, which we reached about one o'clock on April 27, just before a heavy afternoon rain set in. We had run nearly eight hundred kilometres during the sixty days we had spent in the canoes. Here we found and boarded Pyrineus's river steamer, which seemed in our eyes extremely comfortable. In the senhor's pleasant house we were greeted by the senhora, and they were both more than thoughtful and generous in their hospitality. Ahead of us lay merely thirty-six hours by steamer to Manaos. Such a trip as that we had taken tries men as if by fire. Cherrie had more than stood every test; and in him Kermit and I had come to recognize a

The camaradas, gathered around the monument erected by Colonel Rondon

From a photograph by Cherrie

friend with whom our friendship would never falter or grow less.

Early the following afternoon our whole party, together with Senhor Caripe, started on the steamer. It took us a little over twelve hours' swift steaming to run down to the mouth of the river on the upper course of which our progress had been so slow and painful; from source to mouth, according to our itinerary and to Lyra's calculations, the course of the stream down which we had thus come was about 1,500 kilometres in length—about 900 miles, perhaps nearly 1,000 miles—from its source near the 13th degree in the highlands to its mouth in the Madeira, near the 5th degree. Next morning we were on the broad sluggish current of the lower Madeira, a beautiful tropical river. There were heavy rain-storms, as usual, although this is supposed to be the very end of the rainy season. In the afternoon we finally entered the wonderful Amazon itself, the mighty river which contains one-tenth of all the running water of the globe. It was miles across, where we entered it; and indeed we could not tell whether the farther bank, which we saw, was that of the mainland or an island. We went up it until about midnight, then steamed up the Rio Negro for a short distance, and at one in the morning of April 30 reached Manaos.

Manaos is a remarkable city. It is only three degrees south of the equator. Sixty years ago it was a nameless little collection of hovels, tenanted by a few Indians and a few of the poorest class of Brazilian peasants. Now it is a big, handsome modern city, with opera-house, tramways, good hotels, fine squares and public buildings, and attractive private houses. The brilliant coloring and odd architecture give the place a very foreign and attractive flavor in northern eyes. Its rapid growth to prosperity was due to the rubber-trade. This is now far less remunerative than formerly. It will undoubtedly in some degree recover; and in any event the development of the immensely rich and fertile Amazonian valley is sure to go on, and it will be immensely quickened when closer connections are made with the Brazilian highland country lying south of it.

Here we found Miller, and glad indeed we were to see him. He had made good collections of mammals and birds on the Gy-Paraná, the Madeira, and in the neighborhood of Manaos; his entire collection of mammals was really noteworthy. Among them was the only sloth any of us had seen on the trip. The most interesting of the birds he had seen was the hoatzin. This is a most curious bird of very archaic type. Its flight is feeble, and the naked young have spurs on their wings, by the help of which they crawl actively among the branches before their feathers grow. They swim no less easily, at the same early age. Miller got one or two nests, and preserved specimens of the surroundings of the nests; and he made exhaustive records of the habits of the birds. Near Megasso a jaguar had killed one of the bullocks that were being driven along for food. The big cat had not seized the ox with its claws by the head, but had torn open its throat and neck.

Every one was most courteous at Manaos, especially the governor of the state and the mayor of the city. Mr. Robiliard, the British consular representative, and also the representative of the Booth line of steamers, was particularly kind. He secured for us passages on one of the cargo-boats of the line to Para, and thence on one of the regular cargo-and-passenger steamers to Barbadoes and New York. The Booth people were most courteous to us.

I said good-by to the camaradas with real friendship and regret. The parting gift I gave to each was in gold sovereigns; and I was rather touched to learn later that they had agreed among themselves each to keep one sovereign as a medal of honor and token that the owner had been on the trip. They were a fine set, brave, patient, obedient, and enduring. Now they had forgotten their hard times; they were fat from eating, at leisure, all they wished; they were to see Rio Janeiro, always an object of ambition with men of their stamp; and they were very proud of their membership in the expedition.

Later, at Belén, I said good-by to Colonel Rondon, Doctor Cajazeira, and Lieutenant Lyra. Together with my admiration for their hardihood, courage, and resolution, I had grown to feel a strong and affectionate friendship for them. I had become very fond of them; and I was glad to feel that I had been their companion in the performance of a feat which possessed a certain lasting importance.

On May 1 we left Manaos for Belén—Para, as until recently it was called. The trip was interesting. We steamed down through tempest and sunshine; and the towering forest was dwarfed by the giant river it fringed. Sunrise and sunset turned the sky to an unearthly flame of many colors above the vast water. It all seemed the embodiment of loneliness and wild majesty. Yet everywhere man was conquering the loneliness and wresting the majesty to his own uses. We passed many thriving, growing towns; at one we stopped to take on cargo. Everywhere there was growth and development. The change since the days when Bates and Wallace came to this then poor and utterly primitive region is marvellous. One of its accompaniments has been a large European, chiefly south European, immigration. The blood is everywhere mixed; there is no color line, as in most English-speaking countries, and the negro and Indian strains are very strong; but the dominant blood, the blood already dominant in quantity, and that is steadily increasing its dominance, is the olive-white.

Only rarely did the river show its full width. Generally we were in channels or among islands. The surface of the water was dotted with little islands of floating vegetation. Miller said that much of this came from the lagoons such as those where he had been hunting, beside the Solimoens—lagoons filled with the huge and splendid Victoria lily, and with masses of water hyacinths. Miller, who was very fond of animals and always took much care of them, had a small collection which he was bringing back for the Bronx Zoo. An agouti was so bad-tempered that he had to be kept solitary; but three monkeys, big, middle-sized, and little, and a young peccary formed a happy family. The largest monkey cried, shedding real tears, when taken in the arms and pitied. The middle-sized monkey was stupid and kindly, and all the rest of the company imposed on it; the little monkey invariably rode on its back, and the peccary used it as a head pillow when it felt sleepy.

Belén, the capital of the state of Para, was an admirable illustration of the genuine and almost startling progress which Brazil has been making of recent years. It is a beautiful city, nearly under the equator. But it is not merely beautiful. The docks, the dredging operations, the warehouses, the stores and shops, all tell of energy and success in commercial life. It is as clean, healthy, and well policed a city as any of the size in the north temperate zone. The public buildings are handsome, the private dwellings attractive; there are a fine opera-house, an excellent tramway system, and a good museum and botanical gardens. There are cavalry stables, where lights burn all night long to protect the horses from the vampire bats. The parks, the rows of palms and mango-trees, the open-air restaurants, the gay life under the lights at night, all give the city its own special quality and charm. Belén and Manaos are very striking examples of what can be done in the mid-tropics. The governor of Para and his charming wife were more than kind.

Cherrie and Miller spent the day at the really capital zoological gardens, with the curator, Miss Snethlage. Miss Snethlage, a German lady, is a first-rate field and closet naturalist, and an explorer of note, who has gone on foot from the Xingu to the Tapajos. Most wisely she has confined the Belén zoo to the animals of the lower Amazon valley, and in consequence I know of no better local zoological gardens. She has an invaluable collection of birds and mammals of the region; and it was a privilege to meet her and talk with her.

We also met Professor Farrabee, of the University of Pennsylvania, the ethnologist. He had just finished a very difficult and important trip, from Manaos by the Rio Branco to the highlands of Guiana, across them on foot, and down to the seacoast of British Guiana. He is an admirable representative of the men who are now opening South America to scientific knowledge.

On May 7 we bade good-by to our kind Brazilian friends and sailed northward for Barbadoes and New York.

Zoologically the trip had been a thorough success. Cherrie and Miller had collected over twenty-five hundred birds, about five hundred mammals, and a few reptiles, batrachians, and fishes. Many of them were new to science; for much of the region traversed had never previously been worked by any scientific collector.

Of course, the most important work we did was the geographic work, the exploration of the unknown river, undertaken at the suggestion of the Brazilian Government, and in conjunction with its representatives. No piece of work of this kind is ever achieved save as it is based on long-continued previous work. As I have before said, what we did was to put the cap on the pyramid that had been built by Colonel Rondon and his associates of the Telegraphic Commission during the six previous years. It was their scientific exploration of the chapadão, their mapping the basin of the Juruena, and their descent of the Gy-Paraná that rendered it possible for us to solve the mystery of the River of Doubt. On the map facing page vii I have given the outline route of my entire South American trip. The course of the new river is given separately.

The work of the commission, much the greatest work of the kind ever done in South America, is one of the many, many achievements which the republican government of

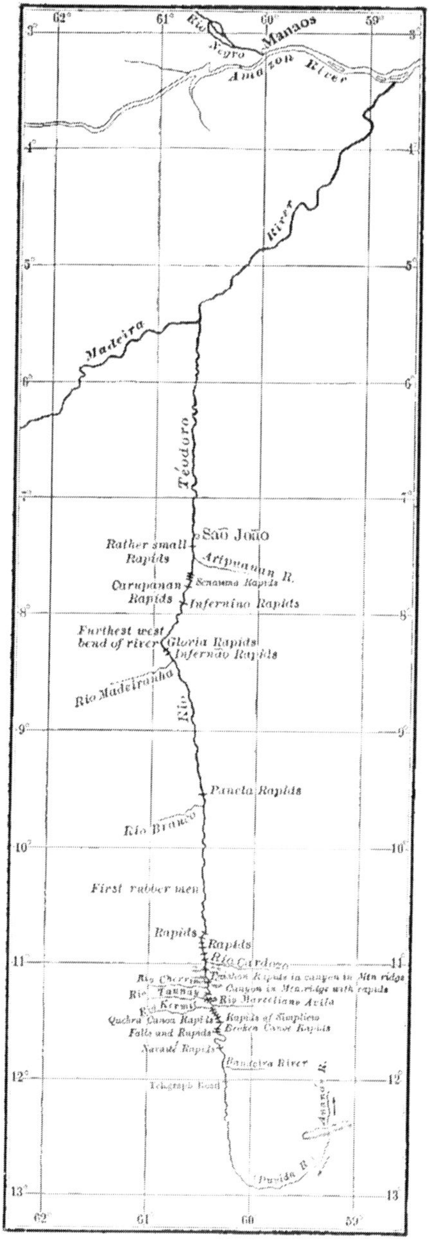

Sketch map of the unknown river christened Rio Roosevelt, and subsequently Rio Téodoro, by direction of the Brazilian Government

This map was prepared by Colonel Roosevelt from his journal and the diaries of Cherrie and of Kermit Roosevelt, the war having prevented the arrival of the map prepared by Lieutenant Lyra
The Ananás may be the headwaters of the Cardozo or of the Aripuanan, or it may flow into the Canuma or Tapajos; it will not be put on the map until it is actually descended

Brazil has to its credit. Brazil has been blessed beyond the average of her Spanish-American sisters because she won her way to republicanism by evolution rather than revolution. They plunged into the extremely difficult experiment of democratic, of popular, self-government, after enduring the atrophy of every quality of self-control, self-reliance, and initiative throughout three withering centuries of existence under the worst and most foolish form of colonial government, both from the civil and the religious standpoint, that has ever existed. The marvel is not that some of them failed, but that some of them have eventually succeeded in such striking fashion. Brazil, on the contrary, when she achieved independence, first exercised it under the form of an authoritative empire, then under the form of a liberal empire. When the republic came, the people were reasonably ripe for it. The great progress of Brazil—and it has been an astonishing progress—has been made under the republic. I could give innumerable examples and illustrations of this. The change that has converted Rio Janeiro from a picturesque pest-hole into a singularly beautiful, healthy, clean, and efficient modern great city is one of these. Another is the work of the Telegraphic Commission.

We put upon the map a river some fifteen hundred kilometres in length, of which the upper course was not merely utterly unknown to, but unguessed at by, anybody; while the lower course, although known for years to a few rubber-men, was utterly unknown to cartographers. It is the chief affluent of the Madeira, which is itself the chief affluent of the Amazon.

The source of this river is between the 12th and 13th

parallels of latitude south and the 59th and 60th degrees of longitude west from Greenwich. We embarked on it at about latitude 12° 1′ south, and about longitude 60° 15′ west. After that its entire course lay between the 60th and 61st degrees of longitude, approaching the latter most closely about latitude 8° 15′. The first rapids we encountered were in latitude 11° 44′, and in uninterrupted succession they continued for about a degree, without a day's complete journey between any two of them. At 11° 23′ the Rio Kermit entered from the left, at 11° 22′ the Rio Marciano Avila from the right, at 11° 18′ the Taunay from the left, at 10° 58′ the Cardozo from the right. In 10° 24′ we encountered the first rubber-men. The Rio Branco entered from the left at 9° 38′. Our camp at 8° 49′ was nearly on the boundary between Matto Grosso and Amazonas. The confluence with the Aripuanan, which joined from the right, took place at 7° 34′. The entrance into the Madeira was at about 5° 20′ (this point we did not determine by observation, as it is already on the maps). The stream we had followed down was from the river's highest sources; we had followed its longest course.

APPENDICES

APPENDIX A

THE WORK OF THE FIELD ZOOLOGIST AND FIELD GEOGRAPHER IN SOUTH AMERICA

PORTIONS of South America are now entering on a career of great social and industrial development. Much remains to be known, so far as the outside world is concerned, of the social and industrial conditions in the long-settled interior regions. More remains to be done, in the way of pioneer exploring and of scientific work, in the great stretches of virgin wilderness. The only two other continents where such work, of like volume and value, remains to be done are Africa and Asia; and neither Africa nor Asia offers a more inviting field for the best kind of field worker in geographical exploration and in zoological, geological, and paleontological investigation. The explorer is merely the most adventurous kind of field geographer; and there are two or three points worth keeping in mind in dealing with the South American work of the field geographer and field zoologist.

Roughly, the travellers who now visit (like those who for the past century have visited) South America come in three categories—although, of course, these categories are not divided by hard-and-fast lines.

First, there are the travellers who skirt the continent in comfortable steamers, going from one great seaport to another, and occasionally taking a short railway journey to some big interior city not too far from the coast. This is a trip well worth taking by all intelligent men and women who can afford it; and it is being taken by such men and women with increasing frequency. It entails no more difficulty than a similar trip to the Mediterranean—than such a trip as that which Mark Twain immortalized. It is a trip which to a learned and broad-minded observer offers the same chance for acquiring knowledge and, if he is himself gifted with wisdom, the same chance of imparting his knowledge to others that is offered by a trip of similar length through the larger cities of Europe or the United States. Probably the best instance of the excellent use to which such an observer can put his experience is afforded by the volume of Mr. Bryce. Of course, such a trip represents travelling of essentially the same kind as travelling by railroad from Atlanta to Calgary or from Madrid to Moscow.

Next there are the travellers who visit the long-settled districts and colonial cities of the interior, travelling over land or river highways which have been traversed for centuries but which are still primitive as regards the inns and the modes of conveyance. Such travelling is difficult in the sense that travelling in parts of Spain or southern Italy or the Balkan states is difficult. Men and women who have a taste for travel in out-of-the-way places and who, therefore, do not mind slight discomforts and inconveniences have the chance themselves to enjoy, and to make others profit by, travels of this kind in South America. In economic, social, and political matters the studies and observations of these travellers are essential in order to supplement, and sometimes to correct, those of travellers of the first category; for it is not safe to generalize overmuch about any country merely from a visit to its capital or its chief seaport. These travellers of the second category can give us most interesting and valuable information about quaint little belated cities; about backward country folk, kindly or the reverse, who show a mixture of the ideas of savagery with the ideas of an ancient peasantry; and about rough old highways of travel which in comfort do not differ much from those of mediæval Europe. The travellers who go up or down the highway rivers that have been travelled for from one to four hundred years—rivers like the Paraguay and Paraná, the Amazon, the Tapajos, the Madeira, the lower Orinoco—come in this category. They can add little to our geographical knowledge; but if they are competent zoologists or archæologists, especially if they live or sojourn long in a locality, their work may be invaluable from the scientific standpoint. The work of the archæologists among the immeasurably ancient ruins of the lowland forests and the Andean plateaux is of this kind. What Agassiz did for the fishes of the Amazon and what Hudson did for the birds of the Argentine are other instances of the work that can thus be done. Burton's writings on the interior of Brazil offer an excellent instance of the value of a sojourn or trip of this type, even without any especial scientific object.

Of course travellers of this kind need to remember that their experiences in themselves do not qualify them to speak as wilderness explorers.

Exactly as a good archæologist may not be competent to speak of current social or political problems, so a man who has done capital work as a tourist observer in little-visited cities and along remote highways must beware of regarding himself as being thereby rendered fit for genuine wilderness work or competent to pass judgment on the men who do such work. To cross the Andes on mule-back along the regular routes is a feat comparable to the feats of the energetic tourists who by thousands traverse the mule trails in out-of-the-way nooks of Switzerland. An ordinary trip on the highway portions of the Amazon, Paraguay, or Orinoco in itself no more qualifies a man to speak of or to take part in exploring unknown South American rivers than a trip on the lower Saint Lawrence qualifies a man to regard himself as an expert in a canoe voyage across Labrador or the Barren Grounds west of Hudson Bay.

A hundred years ago, even seventy or eighty years ago, before the age of steamboats and railroads, it was more difficult than at present to define the limits between this class and the next; and, moreover, in defining these limits I emphatically disclaim any intention of thereby attempting to establish a single standard of value for books of travel. Darwin's "Voyage of the Beagle" is to me the best book of the kind ever written; it is one of those classics which decline to go into artificial categories, and which stand by themselves; and yet Darwin, with his usual modesty, spoke of it as in effect a yachting voyage. Humboldt's work had a profound effect on the thought of the civilized world; his trip was one of adventure and danger; and yet it can hardly be called exploration proper. He visited places which had been settled and inhabited for centuries and traversed places which had been travelled by civilized men for years before he followed in their footsteps. But these places were in Spanish colonies, and access to them had been forbidden by the mischievous and intolerant tyranny—ecclesiastical, political, and economic—which then rendered Spain the most backward of European nations; and Humboldt was the first scientific man of intellectual independence who had permission to visit them. To this day many of his scientific observations are of real value. Bates came to the Amazon just before the era of Amazonian steamboats. He never went off the native routes of ordinary travel. But he was a devoted and able naturalist. He lived an exceedingly isolated, primitive, and laborious life for eleven years. Now, half a century after it was written, his

"Naturalist on the Amazon" is as interesting and valuable as it ever was, and no book since written has in any way supplanted it.

Travel of the third category includes the work of the true wilderness explorers who add to our sum of geographical knowledge and of the scientific men who, following their several bents, also work in the untrodden wilds. Colonel Rondon and his associates have done much in the geographical exploration of unknown country, and Cherrie and Miller have penetrated and lived for months and years in the wastes, on their own resources, as incidents to their mammalogical and ornithological work. Professor Farrabee, the anthropologist, is a capital example of the man who does this hard and valuable type of work.

An immense amount of this true wilderness work, geographical and zoological, remains to be done in South America. It can be accomplished with reasonable thoroughness only by the efforts of very many different workers, each in his own special field. It is desirable that here and there a part of the work should be done in outline by such a geographic and zoological reconnoissance as ours; we would, for example, be very grateful for such work in portions of the interior of the Guianas, on the headwaters of the Xingu, and here and there along the eastern base of the Andes.

But as a rule the work must be specialized; and in its final shape it must be specialized everywhere. The first geographical explorers of the untrodden wilderness, the first wanderers who penetrate the wastes where they are confronted with starvation, disease, and danger and death in every form, cannot take with them the elaborate equipment necessary in order to do the thorough scientific work demanded by modern scientific requirements. This is true even of exploration done along the courses of unknown rivers; it is more true of the exploration, which must in South America become increasingly necessary, done across country, away from the rivers.

The scientific work proper of these early explorers must be of a somewhat preliminary nature; in other words the most difficult and therefore ordinarily the most important pieces of first-hand exploration are precisely those where the scientific work of the accompanying cartographer, geologist, botanist, and zoologist must be furthest removed from finality. The zoologist who works to most advantage in the wilderness must take his time, and therefore he must normally follow in the footsteps of, and not accompany, the first explorers. The man who wishes to do the best scientific work in the wilderness must not try to combine incompatible types of work nor to cover too much ground in too short a time.

There is no better example of the kind of zoologist who does first-class field-work in the wilderness than John D. Haseman, who spent from 1907 to 1910 in painstaking and thorough scientific investigation over a large extent of South American territory hitherto only partially known or quite unexplored. Haseman's primary object was to study the characteristics and distribution of South American fishes, but as a matter of fact he studied at first hand many other more or less kindred subjects, as may be seen in his remarks on the Indians and in his excellent pamphlet on "Some Factors of Geographical Distribution in South America."

Haseman made his long journey with a very slender equipment, his extraordinarily successful field-work being due to his bodily health and vigor and his resourcefulness, self-reliance, and resolution. His writings are rendered valuable by his accuracy and common sense. The need of the former of these two attributes will be appreciated by whoever has studied the really scandalous fictions which have been published as genuine by some modern "explorers" and adventurers in South America; * and the need of the latter by whoever has studied some of the wild theories propounded in the name of science concerning the history

* It would be well if a geographical society of standing would investigate the formal and official charges made by Colonel Rondon, an officer and gentleman of the highest repute, against Mr. Savage Landor. Colonel Rondon, in an official report to the Brazilian Government, has written a scathing review of Mr. Landor. He states that Mr. Savage Landor did not perform, and did not even attempt to perform, the work he had contracted to do in exploration for the Brazilian Government. Mr. Landor had asserted and promised that he would go through unknown country along the line of eleven degrees latitude south, and, as Colonel Rondon states, it was because of this proposal of his that the Brazilian Government gave him material financial assistance in advance. However, Colonel Rondon sets forth that Mr. Landor did not keep his word or make any serious effort to fulfil his moral obligation to do as he had said he would do. In a letter to me under date of May 1, 1914—a letter which has been published in full in France—Colonel Rondon goes at length into the question of what territory Mr. Landor had traversed. Colonel Rondon states that—excepting on one occasion, when Mr. Landor, wandering off a beaten trail, immediately got lost and shortly returned to his starting-point without making any discoveries—he kept to old, well-travelled routes. One sentence of the colonel's letter to me runs as follows: "I can guarantee to you that in Brazil Mr. Landor did not cross a hand's breadth of land that had not been explored, the greater part of it many centuries ago." As regards Mr. Landor's sole and brief experience in leaving a beaten route, Colonel Rondon states that at São Manoel Mr. Landor engaged from Senhor José Sotero Barreto (the revenue officer of Matto Grosso, at São Manoel) a guide to lead him across a well-travelled trail which connects the Tapajos with the Madeira

of life on the South American continent. There is, however, one serious criticism to be made on Haseman: the extreme obscurity of his style—an obscurity mixed with occasional bits of scientific pedantry, which makes it difficult to tell whether or not on some points his thought is obscure also. Modern scientists, like modern historians and, above all, scientific and historical educators, should ever keep in mind that clearness of speech and writing is essential to clearness of thought and that a simple, clear, and, if possible, vivid style is vital to the production of the best work in either science or history. Darwin and Huxley are classics, and they would not have been if they had not written good English. The thought is essential, but ability to give it clear expression is only less essential. Ability to write well, if the writer has nothing to write about, entitles him to mere derision. But the greatest thought is robbed of an immense proportion of its value if expressed in a mean or obscure manner. Mr. Haseman has such excellent thought that it is a pity to make it a work of irritating labor to find out just what the thought is. Surely, if he will take as much pains with his writing as he has with the far more difficult business of exploring and collecting, he will become able to express his thought clearly and forcefully. At least he can, if he chooses, go over his sentences until he

via the Canama. The guide, however, got lost, and after a few days they all returned to the point of departure instead of going through to the Canama.

Senhor Barreto, a gentleman of high standing, related this last incident to Fiala when Fiala descended the Tapajos (and, by the way, Fiala's trip down the Papagaio, Juruena, and Tapajos was infinitely more important than all the work Mr. Landor did in South America put together). Lieutenants Pyrineus and Mello, mentioned in the body of this work, informed me that they accompanied Mr. Landor on most of his overland trip before he embarked on the Arinos, and that he simply followed the highroad or else the telegraph-line, and furthermore, Colonel Rondon states that the Indians whom Mr. Landor encountered and photographed were those educated at the missions.

Colonel Rondon's official report to the Brazilian Government and his letter to me are of interest to all geographers and other scientific men who have any concern with the alleged discoveries of Mr. Landor. They contain very grave charges, with which it is not necessary for me to deal. Suffice it to say that Mr. Landor's accounts of his alleged exploration cannot be considered as entitled to the slightest serious consideration until he has satisfactorily and in detail answered Colonel Rondon; and this he has thus far signally failed to do.

Fortunately, there are numerous examples of exactly the opposite type of work. From the days of Humboldt and Spix and Martius to the present time, German explorers have borne a conspicuous part in the exploration of South America. As representatives of the men and women who have done such capital work, who have fronted every hazard and hardship and labored in the scientific spirit, and who have added greatly to our fund of geographic, biologic, and ethnographic knowledge, I may mention Miss Snethlage and Herr Karl von den Steinen.

is reasonably sure that they can be parsed. He can take pains to see that his whole thought is expressed, instead of leaving vacancies which must be filled by the puzzled and groping reader. His own views and his quotations from the views of others about the static and dynamic theories of distribution are examples of an important principle so imperfectly expressed as to make us doubtful whether it is perfectly apprehended by the writer. He can avoid the use of those pedantic terms which are really nothing but offensive and, fortunately, ephemeral scientific slang. There has been, for instance, a recent vogue for the extensive misuse, usually tautological misuse, of the word "complexus"—an excellent word if used rarely and for definite purposes. Mr. Haseman drags it in continually when its use is either pointless and redundant or else serves purely to darken wisdom. He speaks of the "Antillean complex" when he means the Antilles, of the "organic complex" instead of the characteristic or bodily characteristics of an animal or species, and of the "environmental complex" when he means nothing whatever but the environment. In short, Mr. Haseman and those whose bad example he in this instance follows use "complexus" in much the same spirit as that displayed by the famous old lady who derived religious—instead of scientific—consolation from the use of "the blessed word Mesopotamia."

The reason that it is worth while to enter this protest against Mr. Haseman's style is because his work is of such real and marked value. The pamphlet on the distribution of South American species shows that to exceptional ability as a field worker he adds a rare power to draw, with both caution and originality, the necessary general conclusions from the results of his own observations and from the recorded studies of other men; and there is nothing more needed at the present moment among our scientific men than the development of a school of men who, while industrious and minute observers and collectors and cautious generalizers, yet do not permit the faculty of wise generalization to be atrophied by excessive devotion to labyrinthine detail.

Haseman upholds with strong reasoning the theory that since the appearance of all but the lowest forms of life on this globe there have always been three great continental masses, sometimes solid sometimes broken, extending southward from the northern hemisphere, and from time to time connected in the north, but not in the middle regions or the south since the carboniferous epoch. He holds that life has been intermittently distributed southward along these continental masses when there were no breaks in their southward connection, and intermittently exchanged between them when they were connected in the north; and he also upholds the view that from a common ancestral form the same species has been often developed in entirely disconnected localities when in these localities the conditions of environment were the same.

The opposite view is that there have been frequent connections between the great land masses, alike in the tropics, in the south temperate zone, and in the antarctic region. The upholders of this theory base it almost exclusively on the distribution of living and fossil forms of life; that is, it is based almost exclusively on biological and not geological considerations. Unquestionably, the distribution of many forms of life, past and present, offers problems which with our present paleontological knowledge we are wholly unable to solve. If we consider only the biological facts concerning some one group of animals it is not only easy but inevitable to conclude that its distribution must be accounted for by the existence of some former direct land bridge extending, for instance, between Patagonia and Australia, or between Brazil and South Africa, or between the West Indies and the Mediterranean, or between a part of the Andean region and northeastern Asia. The trouble is that as more groups of animals are studied from the standpoint of this hypothesis the number of such land bridges demanded to account for the existing facts of animal distribution is constantly and indefinitely extended. A recent book by one of the most learned advocates of this hypothesis calls for at least ten such land bridges between South America and all the other continents, present and past, of the world since a period geologically not very remote. These land bridges, moreover, must, many of them, have been literally bridges; long, narrow tongues of land thrust in every direction across the broad oceans. According to this view the continental land masses have been in a fairly fluid condition of instability. By parity of reasoning, the land bridges could be made a hundred instead of merely ten in number. The facts of distribution are in many cases inexplicable with our present knowledge; yet if the existence of widely separated but closely allied forms is habitually to be explained in accordance with the views of the extremists of this school we could, from the exclusive study of certain groups of animals, conclude that at different periods the United States and almost every other portion of the earth were connected by land and severed from all other regions by water—and, from the study of certain other groups of animals, arrive at directly opposite and incompatible conclusions.

The most brilliant and unsafe exponent of this school was Ameghino, who possessed and abused two gifts, both essential to the highest type of scientist, and both mischievous unless this scientist possess a rare and accurate habit of thought joined to industry and mastery of detail:—namely, the gift of clear and interesting writing, and the gift of generalization. Ameghino rendered marked services to paleontology. But he generalized with complete recklessness from the slenderest data; and even these data he often completely misunderstood or misinterpreted. His favorite thesis included the origin of mammalian life and of man himself in southernmost South America, with, as incidents, the belief that the mammalian-bearing strata of South America were of much greater age than the strata with corresponding remains elsewhere; that in South America various species and genera of men existed in tertiary times, some of them at least as advanced as fairly well advanced modern savages; that there existed various land bridges between South America and other southern continents, including Africa; and that the ancestral types of modern mammals and of man himself wandered across one of these bridges to the old world, and that thence their remote descendants, after ages of time, returned to the new. In addition to valuable investigations of fossil-bearing beds in the Argentine, he made some excellent general suggestions, such as that the pithecoid apes, like the baboons, do not stand in the line of man's ancestral stem but represent a divergence from it away from humanity and toward a retrogressive bestialization. But of his main theses he proves none, and what evidence we have tells against them. At the Museum of La Plata I found that the authorities were practically a unit in regarding his remains of tertiary men and proto-men as being either the remains of tertiary American monkeys or of American Indians from strata that were long post-tertiary. The extraordinary discovery, due to that eminent scientist and public servant Doctor Moreno, of the remains of man associated with the remains of the great extinct South American fauna, of the mylodon, of a giant ungulate, of a huge cat like the lion, and of an extraordinary aberrant horse (of a wholly different genus from the modern horse) conclusively shows that in its later stages the South American fauna consisted largely of types that elsewhere had already disappeared and that these types persisted into what was geologically a very recent period only some tens of thousands of years ago, when savage man of practically a modern type had already appeared in South America. The evidence we have, so far as it goes, tends to show that the South American fauna always has been more archaic in type than the arctogeal fauna of the same chronological level.

To loose generalizations, and to elaborate misinterpretations of paleontological records, the kind of work done by Mr. Haseman furnishes an invaluable antiscorbutic. To my mind, he has established a stronger presumption in favor of the theory he champions than has been established in favor of the theories of any of the learned and able scientific men from whose conclusions he dissents. Further research, careful, accurate, and long extended, can alone enable us to decide definitely in the matter; and this research, to be effective, must be undertaken by many men, each of whom shall in large measure possess Mr. Haseman's exceptional power of laborious work both in the field and in the study, his insight and accuracy of observation, and his determination to follow truth with inflexible rectitude wherever it may lead—one of the greatest among the many great qualities which lifted Huxley and Darwin above their fellows.

APPENDIX B

THE OUTFIT FOR TRAVELLING IN THE SOUTH AMERICAN WILDERNESS

South America includes so many different kinds of country that it is impossible to devise a scheme of equipment which shall suit all. A hunting-trip in the pantanals, in the swamp country of the upper Paraguay, offers a simple problem. An exploring trip through an unknown tropical forest region, even if the work is chiefly done by river, offers a very difficult problem. All that I can pretend to do is to give a few hints as the results of our own experience.

For bedding there should be a hammock, mosquito-net, and light blanket. These can be obtained in Brazil. For tent a light fly is ample; ours were brought with us from New York. In exploring only the open fly should be taken; but on trips where weight of luggage is no objection, there can be walls to the tent and even a canvas floor-cloth. Camp-chairs and a camp table should be brought—any good outfitter in the United States will supply them—and not thrown away until it becomes imperative to cut everything down. On a river trip, first-class pulleys and ropes—preferably steel, and at any rate very strong—should be taken. Unless the difficulties of transportation are insuperable, canvas-and-cement canoes, such as can be obtained from various firms in Canada and the United States, should by all means be taken. They are incomparably superior to the dugouts. But on different rivers wholly different canoes, of wholly different sizes, will be needed; on some steam or electric launches may be used; it is not possible to lay down a general rule.

As regards arms, a good plain 12-bore shotgun with a 30-30 rifle-barrel underneath the others is the best weapon to have constantly in one's hand in the South American forests, where big game is rare and yet may at any time come in one's path. When specially hunting the jaguar, marsh-deer, tapir, or big peccary, an ordinary light repeating rifle—the 30-30, 30-40, or 256—is preferable. No heavy rifle is necessary for South America. Tin boxes or trunks are the best in which to carry one's spare things. A good medicine-chest is indispensable. Nowadays doctors know so much of tropical diseases that there is no difficulty in fitting one out. It is better not to make the trip at all than to fail to take an ample supply of quinine pills. Cholera pills and cathartic pills come next in importance. In liquid shape there should be serum to inject for the stoppage of amœbic dysentery, and anti-snake-venom serum. Fly-dope should be taken in quantities.

For clothing Kermit and I used what was left over from our African trip. Sun helmets are best in the open; slouch-hats are infinitely preferable in the woods. There should be hobnailed shoes—the nails many and small, not few and large; and also moccasins or rubber-soled shoes; and light, flexible leggings. Tastes differ in socks; I like mine of thick wool. A khaki-colored shirt should be worn, or, as a better substitute, a khaki jacket with many pockets. Very light underclothes are good. If one's knees and legs are unfortunately tender, knickerbockers with long stockings and leggings should be worn; ordinary trousers tend to bind the knee. Better still, if one's legs will stand the exposure, are shorts, not coming down to the knee. A kilt would probably be best of all. Kermit wore shorts in the Brazilian forest, as he had already worn them in Africa, in Mexico, and in the New Brunswick woods. Some of the best modern hunters always wear shorts; as, for example, that first-class sportsman the Duke of Alva.

Mr. Fiala, after the experience of his trip down the Papagaio, the Juruena, and the Tapajos, gives his judgment about equipment and provisions as follows:

The history of South American exploration has been full of the losses of canoes and cargoes and lives. The native canoe made from the single trunk of a forest giant is the craft that has been used. It is durable and if lost can be readily replaced from the forest by good men with axes and adzes. But, because of its great weight and low free-board, it is unsuitable as a freight carrier and by reason of the limitations of its construction is not of the correct form to successfully run the rapid and bad waters of many of the South American rivers. The North American Indian has undoubtedly developed a vastly superior craft in the birch-bark canoe and with it will run rapids that a South American Indian with his log canoe would not think of attempting, though, as a general thing, the South American Indian is a wonderful waterman, the equal and, in some ways, the superior of his northern contemporary. At the many carries or portages the light birch-bark canoe or its modern representative, the canvas-covered canoe, can be picked up bodily and carried by from two to four men for several miles, if necessary, while the log canoe has to be hauled by ropes and back-breaking labor over rollers that have first to be cut from trees in the forest, or at great risk led along the edge of the rapids with ropes and hooks and poles, the men often up to their shoulders in the rushing waters, guiding the craft to a place of safety.

The native canoe is so long and heavy that it is difficult to navigate without some bumps on the rocks. In fact, it is usually dragged over the rocks in the shallow water near shore in preference to taking the risk of a plunge through the rushing volume of deeper water, for reasons stated above. The North American canoe can be turned with greater facility in critical moments in bad water. Many a time I heard my steersman exclaim with delight as we took a difficult passage between two rocks with our loaded Canadian canoe. In making the same passage the dugout would go sideways toward the rapid until by a supreme effort her three powerful paddlers and steersman would right her just in time. The native canoe would ship great quantities of water in places the Canadian canoe came through without taking any water on board. We did bump a few rocks under water, but the canoe was so elastic that no damage was done.

Our nineteen-foot *canvas*-covered freight canoe, a type especially built for the purpose on deep, full lines with high free-board, weighed about one hundred and sixty pounds and would carry a ton of cargo with ease—and also take it safely where the same cargo distributed among two or three native thirty or thirty-five foot canoes would be lost. The native canoes weigh from about nine hundred to two thousand five hundred pounds and more.

In view of the above facts the explorer-traveller is advised to take with him the North American canoe if he intends serious work. Two canoes would be a good arrangement for from five to seven men, with at least one steersman and two paddlers to each canoe. The canoes can be purchased in two sizes and nested for transportation, an arrangement which would save considerable expense in freight bills. At least six paddles should be packed with each boat, in length four and one half, four and three fourths, and five feet. Other paddles from six and one half feet to eight and one half feet should be provided for steering oars. The native paddler, after he has used the light Canadian paddle, prefers it to the best native make. My own paddlers lost or broke all of their own paddles so as to get the North American ones. which they marked with their initials and used most carefully.

To each canoe it would be well to have two copper air tanks, one fore, one aft, a hand-hole in each with a water-tight screw cover on hatch. In these tanks could be kept a small supply of matches, the chronometer or watch which is used for position, and the scientific records and diary. Of course, the fact should be kept in mind that these are air tanks, not to be used so as to appreciably diminish their buoyancy. Each canoe should also carry a small repair kit attached to one of the thwarts, containing cement, a piece of canvas same as cover of canoe, copper tacks, rivets, and some galvanized nails; a good hatchet and a hammer; a small can of canoe paint, spar varnish, and copper paint for worn places would be a protection against termites and torrential downpours. In concluding the subject of canoes I can state that the traveller in South America will find no difficulty in disposing of his craft at the end of his trip.

Motors.—We had with us a three and one half horse-power motor which could be attached to stern or gunwale of canoe or boat. It was made by the Evinrude Motor Company, who had a magneto placed in the fly-wheel of the engine so that we never had to resort to the battery to run the motor. Though the motor was left out in the rain and sun, often without a cover, by careless native help, it never failed us. We found it particularly valuable in going against the strong current of the Sepotuba River where several all-night trips were made up-stream, the motor attached to a heavy boat. For exploration up-stream it would be valuable, particularly as it is easily portable, weighing for the two horse-power motor fifty pounds, for three and one half horse-power one hundred pounds. If a carbureter could be attached so that kerosene could be used it would add to its value many times, for kerosene can be purchased almost anywhere in South America.

Tents.—There is nothing better for material than the light waterproof Sea Island cotton of American manufacture, made under the trade name of waterproof silk. It keeps out the heaviest rain and is very light. Canvas becomes water-soaked, and cravenetted material lets the water through. A waterproof canvas floor is a luxury, and, though it adds to the weight, it may with advantage be taken on ordinary trips. The tent should be eight by eight or eight by nine feet, large enough to swing a comfortable hammock. A waterproof canvas bag, a loose-fitting envelope for the tent should be provided. Native help is, as a rule, careless, and the bag would save wear and tear.

HAMMOCKS.—The hammock is the South American bed, and the traveller will find it exceedingly comfortable. After leaving the larger cities and settlements a bed is a rare object. All the houses are provided with extra hammock hooks. The traveller will be entertained hospitably and after dinner will be given two hooks upon which to hang his hammock, for he will be expected to have his hammock and, in insect time, his net, if he has nothing else. As a rule, a native hammock and net can be procured in the field. But it is best to take a comfortable one along, arranged with a fine-meshed net.

In regard to the folding cot: It is heavy and its numerous legs form a sort of highway system over which all sorts of insects can crawl up to the sleeper. The ants are special pests and some of them can bite with the enthusiastic vigor of beasts many times their size. The canvas floor in a tent obviates to a degree the insect annoyance.

The headwaters of the rivers are usually reached by pack-trains of mules and oxen. The primitive ox-cart also comes in where the trail is not too bad. One hundred and sixty to one hundred and eighty pounds is a good load for the pack-animals, and none of the cases should weigh more than fifty or sixty pounds. Each case should be marked with its contents and gross and net weight in kilos.

For personal baggage the light fibre sample case used by travelling men in the United States does admirably. The regulation fibre case with its metal binding sold for the purpose is too heavy and has the bad feature of swelling up under the influence of rain and dampness, often necessitating the use of an axe or heavy hammer to remove cover.

The ordinary fibre trunk is good for rail and steamer travel, but it is absolutely unpractical for mule-back or canoe. The fibre sample case could be developed into a container particularly fitted for exploration. The fibre should be soaked in hot paraffine and then hot-calendered or hot-pressed. This case could then be covered with waterproof canvas with throat opening like a duffel-bag.

The waterproof duffel-bags usually sold are too light in texture and wear through. A heavier grade should be used. The small duffel-bag is very convenient for hammock and clothing, but generally the thing wanted will be at the bottom of the bag! We took with us a number of small cotton bags. As cotton is very absorbent, I had them paraffined. Each bag was tagged and all were placed in the large duffel-bag. The light fibre case described above, made just the right size for mule pack, divided by partitions, and covered with a duffel-bag, would prove a great convenience.

The light steel boxes made in England for travellers in India and Africa would prove of value in South American exploration. They have the advantage of being insect and water proof and the disadvantage of being expensive.

It would be well if the traveller measured each case for personal equipment and computed the limit of weight that it could carry and still float. By careful distribution of light and heavy articles in the different containers, he could be sure of his belongings floating if accidentally thrown into the water.

It is not always possible to get comfortable native saddles. They are all constructed on heavy lines with thick padding which becomes water-soaked in the rainy season. A United States military saddle, with Whitman or McClellan tree, would be a positive luxury. Neither of them is padded, so would be the correct thing for all kinds of weather. The regulation army saddle-blanket is also advised as a protection for the mule's back. The muleteer should wash the saddle-blanket often. For a long mule-back trip through a game country, it would be well to have a carbine boot on the saddle (United States Army) and saddle-bags with canteen and cup. In a large pack-train much time and labor are lost every morning collecting the mules which strayed while grazing. It would pay in the long run to feed a little corn at a certain hour every morning in camp, always ringing a bell or blowing a horn at the time. The mules would get accustomed to receiving the feed and would come to camp for it at the signal.

All the rope that came to my attention in South America was three-strand hemp, a hard material, good for standing rigging but not good for tackle or for use aboard canoes. A four-ply bolt rope of best manilla, made in New Bedford, Mass., should be taken. It is the finest and most pliable line in the world, as any old whaler will tell you. Get a sailor of the old school to relay the coils before you go into the field so that the rope will be ready for use. Five eighths to seven eighths inch diameter is large enough. A few balls of marline come in conveniently as also does heavy linen fish-line.

A small-sized duffel-bag should be provided for each of the men as a container for hammock and net, spare clothing, and mess-kit. A very small waterproof pouch or bag should be furnished also for matches, tobacco, etc.

The men should be limited to one duffel-bag each. These bags should be numbered consecutively. In fact, every piece in the entire equipment should be thus numbered and a list kept in detail in a book.

The explorer should personally see that each of his men has a hammock, net, and poncho; for the native, if left unsupervised, will go into the field with only the clothing he has on.

FOOD.—Though South America is rich in food and food possibilities, she has not solved the problem of living economically on her frontiers. The prices asked for food in the rubber districts we passed through were amazing. Five milreis (one dollar and fifty cents) was cheap for a chicken, and eggs at five hundred reis (fifteen cents) apiece were a rarity. Sugar was bought at the rate of one to two milreis a kilo—in a country where sugar-cane grows luxuriantly. The main dependence is the mandioc, or farina, as it is called. It is the bread of the country and is served at every meal. The native puts it on his meat and in his soup and mixes it with his rice and beans. When he has nothing else he eats the farina, as it is called, by the handful. It is seldom cooked. The small mandioc tubers when boiled are very good and are used instead of potatoes. Native beans are nutritious and form one of the chief foods.

In the field the native cook wastes much time. Generally provided with an inadequate cooking equipment, hours are spent cooking beans after the day's work, and then, of course, they are often only partially cooked. A kettle or aluminum Dutch oven should be taken along, large enough to cook enough beans for both breakfast and dinner. The beans should be cooked all night, a fire kept burning for the purpose. It would only be necessary then to warm the beans for breakfast and dinner, the two South American meals.

For meat the rubber hunter and explorer depends upon his rifle and fish-hook. The rivers are full of fish which can readily be caught, and, in Brazil, the tapir, capybara, paca, agouti, two or three varieties of deer, and two varieties of wild pig can occasionally be shot; and most of the monkeys are used for food. Turtles and turtle eggs can be had in season and a great variety of birds, some of them delicious in flavor

Daily Ration for Five Men	Sun.	Mon.	Tues.	Wed.	Thur.	Fri.	Sat.
Rice	16	...	16	...	...	16	...
Oatmeal	...	13	...	...	13	...	13
Bread	100	100	100	100	100	100	100
Tea-biscuits	18	...	18	...	18	...	...
Gingersnaps	...	21	...	21	...	21	21
Dehydrated potatoes	11	11	11	11	11	11	...
Dehydrated onions	5	5	5	5	5	5	...
Erbswurst	...	8	...	8	...	8	...
Evaporated soups	6	...	6	...	...	...	6
Baked beans	...	...	...	...	25	...	25
Condensed milk	17	17	17	17	17	17	17
Bacon	44	44	44	44	44	44	44
Roast beef	...	56½	...	...	...	...	...
Braised beef	...	...	56	...	...	...	56
Corned beef	...	...	...	70	...	...	...
Ox tongue	...	...	...	...	78	...	...
Curry and chicken	...	...	...	...	...	71¼	...
Boned chicken	61	...	...	...	...	...	...
Fruits: evaporated berries	...	5	...	5	5	...	5
Figs	20	...	20	...	...	...	...
Dates	...	...	...	...	...	16	...
Sugar	32	32	32	32	32	32	32
Coffee	10½	10½	10½	10½	10½	10½	10½
Tea	5½	5½	5½	5½	5½	5½	5½
Salt	4	4	4	4	4	4	4
Sweet chocolate	...	...	...	16	...	...	...
Each box also contained							
Muslin, one yard	1	1	1	1	1	1	1
Matches, boxes	2	2	2	2	2	2	2
Soap, one cake	1	1	1	1	1	1	1

Above weights of food are net in avoirdupois ounces. Each complete ration with its tin container weighed nearly twenty-seven pounds. The five pounds over net weight of daily ration was taken up in tin necessary for protection of food. The weight of component parts of daily ration had to be governed to some extent by the size of the commercial package in which the food could be purchased on short notice. Austin, Nichols & Co. of New York, who supplied the food stores for my polar expedition, worked day and night to complete the packing of the rations on time.

and heavy in meat. In the hot, moist climate fresh meat will not keep and even salted meat has been known to spoil. For use on the Roosevelt expedition I arranged a ration for five men for one day packed in a tin box; the party which went down the Dúvida made each ration do for six men for a day and a half, and in addition gave over half the bread or hardtack to the camaradas. By placing the day's allowance of bread in this same box, it was lightened sufficiently to float if dropped into water. There were seven variations in the arrangement of food in these boxes and they were numbered from 1 to 7, so that a different box could be used every day of the week. In addition to the food, each box contained a cake of soap, a piece of cheese-cloth, two boxes of matches, and a box of table salt. These tin boxes were lacquered to protect from rust and enclosed in wooden cases for transportation. A number in large type was printed on each. No. 1 was cased separately; Nos. 2 and 3, 4 and 5, 6 and 7 were cased together. For canoe travel the idea was to take these wooden cases off. I did not have an opportunity personally to experience the management of these food cases. We had sent them all ahead by pack-train for the explorers of the Dúvida River. The exploration of the Papagaio was decided upon during the march over the plateau of Matto Grosso and was accomplished with dependence upon native food only.

The food cases described above were used on Colonel Roosevelt's descent of the Rio da Dúvida and also by the party who journeyed down the Gy-Paraná and Madeira Rivers. Leo Miller, the naturalist, who was a member of the last-named party, arrived in Manaos, Brazil, while I was there and, in answer to my question, told me that the food served admirably and was good, but that the native cooks had a habit of opening a number of cases at a time to satisfy their personal desire for special delicacies. Bacon was the article most sought for. Speaking critically, for a strenuous piece of work like the exploration of the Dúvida, the food was somewhat bulky. A ration arrangement such as I used on my sledge trips North would have contained more nutritious elements in a smaller space. We could have done without many of the luxuries. But the exploration of the Dúvida had not been contemplated and had no place in the itinerary mapped out in New York. The change of plan and the decision to explore the Dúvida River came about in Rio Janeiro, long after our rations had been made out and shipped.

"Matté," the tea of Brazil and Paraguay, used in most of the states of South America, should not be forgotten. It is a valuable beverage. With it a native can do a wonderful amount of work on little food. Upon the tired traveller it has a very refreshing effect.

Doctor Peckolt, celebrated chemist of Rio de Janeiro, has compared the analysis of matté with those of green tea, black tea, and coffee and obtained the following result:

In 1,000 parts of	Green Tea	Black Tea	Coffee	Matté
Natural oil	7.90	0.06	0.41	0.01
Chlorophyl	22.20	18.14	13.66	62.00
Resin	22.20	34.40	13.66	20.69
Tannin	178.09	128.80	16.39	12.28
Alkaloids:				
Mateina, Coffeina	4.50	4.30	2.66	2.50
Extractive substances	464.00	390.00	270.67	238.83
Cellulose and fibres	175.80	283.20	178.83	180.00
Ashes	85.60	25.61	25.61	38.11

Manner of preparation: The matté tea is prepared in the same manner as the Indian tea, that is to say, by pouring upon it boiling water during ten to fifteen minutes before using. To obtain a good infusion five spoonfuls of matté are sufficient for a litre of water.

Some experiments have been made lately with the use of matté in the German army, and probably it would be a valuable beverage for the use of our own troops. Two plates and a cup, knife, fork, and spoon should be provided for each member of the party. The United States Army mess-kit would serve admirably. Each man's mess-kit should be numbered to correspond with the number on his duffel-bag.

An aluminum (for lightness) cooking outfit, or the Dutch oven mentioned, with three or four kettles nested within, a coffee pot or a teapot would suffice. The necessary large spoons and forks for the cook, a small meat grinder, and a half dozen skinning knives could all be included in the fibre case. These outfits are usually sold with the cups, plates, etc., for the table. As before suggested, each member of the party should have his own mess-kit. It should not be carried with the general cooking outfit. By separating the eating equipments thus, one of the problems of hygiene and cleanliness is simplified.

Rifles—Ammunition.—A heavy rifle is not advised. The only animals that can be classed as dangerous are the jaguar and white-jawed peccary, and a 30-30 or 44 calibre is heavy enough for such game. The 44-calibre Winchester or Remington carbine is the arm generally used throughout South America, and 44 calibre is the only ammunition that one can depend upon securing in the field. Every man has his own preference for an arm. However, there is no need of carrying a nine or ten pound weapon when a rifle weighing only from six and three fourths to seven and one half pounds will do all that is necessary. I, personally, prefer the small-calibre rifle, as it can be used for birds also. The three-barrelled gun, combining a double shotgun and a rifle, is an excellent weapon, and it is particularly valuable for the collector of natural-history specimens. A new gun has just come on the market which may prove valuable in South America where there is such a variety of game, a four-barrel gun, weighing only eight and one fourth pounds. It has two shotgun barrels, one 30 to 44 calibre rifle and the rib separating the shotgun barrels is bored for a 22-calibre rifle cartridge. The latter is particularly adapted for the large food birds, which a heavy rifle-bullet might tear. Twenty-two-calibre ammunition is also very light and the long 22 calibre exceedingly powerful. Unless in practice it proves too complicated, it would seem to be a good arm for all-round use—sixteen to twenty gauge is large enough for the shotgun barrels. Too much emphasis cannot be placed upon the need of being provided with good weapons. After the loss of all our arms in the rapids we secured four poor, rusty rifles which proved of no value. We lost three deer, a tapir, and other game, and finally gave up the use of the rifles, depending upon hook and line. A 25 or 30 calibre high-power automatic pistol with six or seven inch barrel would prove a valuable arm to carry always on the person. It could be used for large game and yet would not be too large for food birds. It is to be regretted that there is nothing in the market of this character.

We had our rifle ammunition packed by the U. M. C. Co. in zinc cases of one hundred rounds each, a metallic strip with pull ring closing the two halves of the box. Shot-cartridge, sixteen gauge, were packed the same way, twenty-five to the box.

The explorer would do well always to have on his person a compass, a light waterproof bag containing matches, a waterproof box of salt, and a strong, light, linen or silk fish-line with several hooks, a knife, and an automatic at his belt, with several loaded magazines for the latter in his pocket. Thus provided, if accidentally lost for several days in the forest (which often happens to the rubber hunters in Brazil), he will be provided with the possibility of getting game and making himself shelter and fire at night.

Fish.—For small fish like the pacu and piranha an ordinary bass hook will do. For the latter, because of its sharp teeth, a hook with a long shank and phosphor-bronze leader is the best; the same character of leader is best on the hook to be used for the big fish. A tarpon hook will hold most of the great fish of the rivers. A light rod and reel would be a convenience in catching the pacu. We used to fish for the latter variety in the quiet pools while allowing the canoe to drift, and always saved some of the fish as bait for the big fellows. We fished for the pacu as the native does, kneading a ball of mandioc farina with water and placing it on the hook as bait. I should not be surprised, though, if it were possible, with carefully chosen flies, to catch some of the fish that every once in a while we saw rise to the surface and drag some luckless insect under.

Clothing.—Even the experienced traveller when going into a new field will commit the crime of carrying too much luggage. Articles which he thought to be camp necessities become camp nuisances which worry his men and kill his mules. The lighter one can travel the better. In the matter of clothing, before the actual wilderness is reached the costume one would wear to business in New York in summer is practical for most of South America, except, of course, the high mountain regions, where a warm wrap is necessary. A white or natural linen suit is a very comfortable garment. A light blue unlined serge is desirable as a change and for wear in rainy weather.

Strange to relate, the South American seems to have a fondness for stiff collars. Even in Corumbá, the hottest place I have ever been in, the native does not think he is dressed unless he wears one of these stiff abominations around his throat. A light negligee shirt with interchangeable or attached soft collars is vastly preferable. In the frontier regions and along the rivers the pajama seems to be the conventional garment for day as well as night wear. Several such suits of light material should be carried—the more ornamented and beautifully colored the greater favor will they find along the way. A light cravenetted mackintosh is necessary for occasional cool evenings and as a protection against the rain. It should have no cemented rubber seams to open up in the warm, moist climate. Yachting oxfords and a light pair of leather slippers complete the outfit for steamer travel. For the field, two or three light woollen khaki-colored shirts, made with two breast pockets with buttoned flaps, two pairs of long khaki trousers, two pairs of riding breeches, a khaki coat cut military fashion with four pockets with buttoned flaps, two suits of pajamas, handkerchiefs, socks, etc., would be necessary. The poncho should extend to below the knees and should be provided with a hood large enough to cover the helmet. It should have no cemented seams; the material recently adopted by the United States Army for ponchos seems to be the best. For foot-gear the traveller needs two pairs of stout, high hunting shoes, built on the moccasin form with soles. Hobnails should be taken along to insert if the going is over rocky places. It is also advisable to provide a pair of very light leather slipper boots to reach to just under the knee for wear in camp. They protect the legs and ankles from insect stings and bites. The traveller who enters tropical South America should protect his head with a wide-brimmed soft felt hat with ventilated head-band, or the best and lightest pith helmet that can be secured, one large enough to shade the face and back of neck. There should be a ventilating space all around the head-band; the wider the space the better. These helmets can be secured in Rio and Buenos Aires. Head-nets with face plates of horsehair are the best protection against small insect pests. They are generally made too small and the purchaser should be careful to get one large enough to go over his helmet and come down to the breast. Several pairs of loose gloves rather long in the wrist will be needed as protection against the flies, piums and boroshudas which draw blood with every bite and are numerous in many parts of South America. A waterproof sun umbrella, with a jointed handle about six feet long terminating in a point, would be a decided help to the scientist at work in the field. A fine-meshed net fitting around the edge of the umbrella would make it insect proof. When folded it would not be bulky and its weight would be negligible. Such an umbrella could also be attached, with a special clamp, to the thwart of a canoe and so prove a protection from both sun and rain.

There are little personal conveniences which sometimes grow into necessities. One of these in my own case was a little electric flash-light taken for the purpose of reading the verniers of a theodolite or sextant in star observations. It was used every night and for many purposes. As a matter of necessity, where insects are numerous one turns to the protection of his hammock, and net immediately after the evening meal. It was at such times that I found the electric lamp so helpful. Reclining in the hammock, I held the stock of the light under my left arm and with diary in my lap wrote up my records for the day. I sometimes read by its soft, steady light. One charge of battery, to my surprise, lasted nearly a month. When forced to pick out a camping spot after dark, an experience which comes to every traveller in the tropics in the rainy season, we found its light very helpful. Neither rain nor wind could put it out and the light could be directed wherever needed. The charges should be calculated on the plan of one for every three weeks. The acetylene lamp for camp illumination is an advance over the kerosene lantern. It has been found that for equal weight the carbide will give more light than kerosene or candle. The carbide should be put in small containers, for each time a box is opened some of the contents turns into gas from contact with the moist air.

TOOLS.—Three or four good axes, several bill-hooks, a good hatchet with hammer head and nail-puller should be in the tool kit. In addition, each man should be provided with a belt knife and a machete with sheath. Collins makes the best machetes. His axes, too, are excellent. The bill-hook, called *foice* in Brazil, is a most valuable tool for clearing away small trees, vines, and undergrowths. It is marvellous how quickly an experienced hand can clear the ground in a forest with one of these instruments. All of these tools should have handles of second-growth American hickory of first quality; and several extra handles should be taken along. The list of tools should be completed with a small outfit of pliers, tweezers, files, etc.—the character, of course, depending upon the mechanical ability of the traveller and the scientific instruments he has with him that might need repairs.

SURVEY INSTRUMENTS.—The choice of instruments will depend largely upon the character of the work intended. If a compass survey will suffice, there is nothing better than the cavalry sketching board used in the United States Army for reconnoissance. With a careful hand it approaches the high degree of perfection attained by the plane-table method. It is particularly adapted for river survey and, after one gets accustomed to its use, it is very simple. If the prismatic compass is preferred, nothing smaller than two and one half inches in diameter should be used. In the smaller sizes the magnet is not powerful enough to move the dial quickly or accurately.

Several good pocket compasses must be provided. They should all have good-sized needles with the north end well marked and degrees engraved in metal. If the floating dial is preferred it should be of aluminum and nothing smaller than two and one-half inches, for the same reason as mentioned above regarding the prismatic compass.

Expense should not be spared if it is necessary to secure good compasses. Avoid paper dials and leather cases which absorb moisture. The compass case should allow taking apart for cleaning and drying.

The regular chronometer movement, because of its delicacy, is out of the question for rough land or water travel. We had with us a small-sized half-chronometer movement recently brought out by the Waltham Company as a yacht chronometer. It gave a surprisingly even rate under the most adverse conditions. I was sorry to lose it in the rapids of the Papagaio when our canoes went down.

The watches should be waterproof with strong cases, and several should be taken. It would be well to have a dozen cheap but good watches and the same number of compasses for use around camp and for gifts or trade along the line of travel. Money is of no value after one leaves the settlements. I was surprised to find that many of the rubber hunters were not provided with compasses, and I listened to an American who told of having been lost in the depths of the great forest where for days he lived on monkey meat secured with his rifle until he found his way to the river. He had no compass and could not get one. I was sorry I had none to give; I had lost mine in the rapids.

For the determination of latitude and longitude there is nothing better than a small four or five inch theodolite not over fifteen pounds in weight. It should have a good prism eyepiece with an angle tube attached so it would not be necessary to break one's neck in reading high altitudes. For days we travelled in the direction the sun was going, with altitudes varying from 88° to 90°. Because of these high altitudes of the sun the sextant with artificial horizon could not be used unless one depended upon star observations altogether, an uncertain dependence because of the many cloudy nights.

Barometers.—The Goldsmith form of direct-reading aneroid is the most accurate portable instrument and, of course, should be compared with a standard mercurial at the last weather-bureau station.

Thermometers.—A swing thermometer, with wet and dry bulbs for determination of the amount of moisture in the air, and the maximum and minimum thermometer of the signal-service or weather-bureau type should be provided, with a case to protect them from injury.

A tape measure with metric scale of measurements on one side and feet and inches on the other is most important. Two small, light waterproof cases could be constructed and packed with scientific instruments, data, and spare clothing and yet not exceed the weight limit of flotation. In transit by pack-train these two cases would form but one mule load.

Photographic.—From the experience gained in several fields of exploration it seems to me that the voyager should limit himself to one small-sized camera, which he can always have with him, and then carry a duplicate of it, soldered in tin, in the baggage. The duplicate need not be equipped with as expensive a lens and shutter as the camera carried for work; 3¼ x 4¼ is a good size. Nothing larger than 3¼ x 5½ is advised. We carried the 3A special Kodak and found it a light, strong, and effective instrument. It seems to me that the ideal form of instrument would be one with a front board large enough to contain an adapter fitted for three lenses. For the 3¼ x 4¼:

One lens............................4 or 4½ focus
One lens............................6 or 7 focus
One lens telephoto or telecentric......9 to 12 focus

The camera should be made of metal and fitted with focal-plane shutter and direct view-finder.

A sole-leather case with shoulder-strap should contain the camera and lenses, with an extra roll of films, all within instant reach, so that a lens could be changed without any loss of time.

Plates, of course, are the best, but their weight and frailty, with difficulty of handling, rule them out of the question. The roll film is the best, as the film pack sticks together and the stubs pull off in the moist, hot climate. The films should be purchased in rolls of six exposures, each roll in a tin, the cover sealed with surgical tape. Twelve of these tubes should be soldered in a tin box. In places where the air is charged with moisture a roll of films should not be left in a camera over twenty-four hours.

Tank development is best for the field. The tanks provided for developing by the Kodak Company are best for fixing also. A nest of tanks would be a convenience; one tank should be kept separate for the fixing-bath. As suggested in the Kodak circular, for tropical development a large-size tank can be used for holding the freezing mixture of hypo. This same tank would become the fixing tank after development. In the rainy season it is a difficult matter to dry films. Development in the field, with washing water at 80° F., is a patience-trying operation. It has occurred to me that a small air-pump with a supply of chloride of calcium in small tubes might solve the problem of preserving films in the tropics. The air-pump and supply of chloride of calcium would not be as heavy or bulky as the tanks and powders needed for development. By means of the air-pump the films could be sealed in tin tubes free from moisture and kept thus until arrival at home or at a city where the air was fairly dry and cold water for washing could be had.

While I cordially agree with most of the views expressed by Mr. Fiala, there are some as to which I disagree; for instance, we came very strongly to the conclusion, in descending the Dúvida, where bulk was of great consequence, that the films should be in rolls of ten or twelve exposures. I doubt whether the four-barrel gun would be practical; but this is a matter of personal taste.

APPENDIX C

MY LETTER OF MAY 1 TO GENERAL LAURO MÜLLER

THE first report on the expedition, made by me immediately after my arrival at Manaos, and published in Rio Janeiro upon its receipt, is as follows:

MAY 1st, 1914.

TO HIS EXCELLENCY THE MINISTER OF
FOREIGN AFFAIRS,
RIO-DE-JANEIRO.

MY DEAR GENERAL LAURO MÜLLER:

I wish first to express my profound acknowledgments to you personally and to the other members of the Brazilian Government whose generous courtesy alone rendered possible the Expedicao Scientifica Roosevelt-Rondon. I wish also to express my high admiration and regard for Colonel Rondon and his associates who have been my colleagues in this work of exploration. In the third place I wish to point out that what we have just done was rendered possible only by the hard and perilous labor of the Brazilian Telegraphic Commission in the unexplored western wilderness of Matto Grosso during the last seven years. We have had a hard and somewhat dangerous but very successful trip. No less than six weeks were spent in slowly and with peril and exhausting labor forcing our way down through what seemed a literally endless succession of rapids and cataracts. For forty-eight days we saw no human being. In passing these rapids we lost five of the seven canoes with which we started and had to build others. One of our best men lost his life in the rapids. Under the strain one of the men went completely bad, shirked all his work, stole his comrades' food and when punished by the sergeant he with cold-blooded deliberation murdered the sergeant and fled into the wilderness. Colonel Rondon's dog running ahead of him while hunting, was shot by two Indians; by his death he in all probability saved the life of his master. We have put on the map a river about 1500 kilometers in length running from just south of the 13th. degree to north of the 5th. degree and the biggest affluent of the Madeira. Until now its upper course has been utterly unknown to every one, and its lower course although known for years to the rubber men utterly unknown to all cartographers. Its source is between the 12th. and 13th. parallels of latitude south, and between longitude 59 degrees and longitude 60 degrees west from Greenwich. We embarked on it about at latitude 12 degrees 1 minute south and longitude 60 degrees 18 west. After that its entire course was between the 60th. and 61st. degrees of longitude approaching the latter most closely about in latitude 8 degrees 15 minutes. The first rapids were at Navaité in 11 degrees 44 minutes and after that they were continuous and very difficult and dangerous until the rapids named after the murdered sergeant Paishon in 11 degrees 12 minutes. At 11 degrees 23 minutes the river received the Rio Kermit from the left. At 11 degrees 22 minutes the Marciano Avila entered it from the right. At 11 degrees 18 minutes the Taunay entered from the left. At 10 degrees 58 minutes the Cardozo entered from the right. At 10 degrees 24 minutes we encountered the first rubber man. The Rio Branco entered from the left at 9 degrees 38 minutes. We camped at 8 degrees 49 minutes or approximately the boundary line between Matto Grosso and Amazonas. The confluence with the upper Aripuanan, which entered from the right, was in 7 degrees 34 minutes. The mouth where it entered the Madeira was in about 5 degrees 30 minutes. The stream we have followed down is that which rises farthest away from the mouth and its general course is almost due north.

My dear Sir, I thank you from my heart for the chance to take part in this great work of exploration.

With high regard and respect, believe me

Very sincerely yours,

THEODORE ROOSEVELT.

INDEX

"African Game Trails," 22.
Agassiz, 344.
Agouti, 168, 336.
Alencarliense, Lieutenant, 263.
Alligator, 77.
Alva, Duke of, Appendix B, 354.
Amarante, Lieutenant, 263, 264.
Amazon, 7, 282, 333.
Amazonas, Boundary Commission of, 317, 340.
Ameghino, Doctor, 27; Appendix A, 351.
American Museum of Natural History, 2, 7, 65, 142, 182.
Amilcar, Captain, 153, 154, 166, 183, 203, 215, 221, 228, 240, 264; loss of his notes and instruments, 331; arrives at Manaos, 331.
Ammunition, Appendix B, 363.
Anaconda, 53, 222.
Ananás River, 182, 233, 241, 310; note, 318.
Andes, 6.
André, 301.
Aneroid, 262, 274, 313.
Animals, wild, curious local change in habits of, 28; ignorance of some hunters concerning, 84.
Ant-eater, giant, tamanduá bandeira, 65, 66, 73.
Ant-hills, giant, 88, 89, 185, 186, 221.
Ants, 159, 245; poisonous, 53, 89; fire-ants, 105, 110, 114, 116, 117, 146; foraging, 162, 163, 164, 227, 281; leaf-carrying, 186, 250, 280; giant, 256, 266.
Ants, socks and mosquito-netting eaten by, 159, 245, 298.
Argentina, 2.
Argentine, 9, 26.
Aripuanan, the, 277, 278, 289, 316, 317, 318, 329, 330, 331, 340.
Armadillos, 87, 88, 168, 200.
Arms, 5, 65, 242; Fox, 65; Springfield rifle, 79, 90; Lüger, 90, 229; Winchester, 81, 206, 322; Appendix B, 353, 363.
Arneberg, Mr., 30.
Arrows, 272.
Asuncion, 8; leave, 38; 43.
Automobile, a querulous traveller in the, 207, 208.
Ayolas, the Spanish explorer, 58.

Baggage, rearrangement of, 209; cutting down of, 241; further reduction of, 274; final reduction of, 295; personal, Appendix B, 357, 358.
Balsa, or ferry, 205, 214.
Bandeira, the, 247, 248.
Barbados, sail for, 338.
Barboso, Senhor, 321, 322.
Barilloche, 35.
Barometers, Appendix B, 368.
Barros, Senhor de, 64.
Bates, H. W., 116, 336; Appendix A, 345, 346.
Bats, 135; blood-sucking, 167, 168, 233, 234.
Bedding, Appendix B, 353.
Bees, 206, 246, 250, 252, 257.
Belén (formerly Para), 335, 336, 337; zoological gardens at, 337.
Benedetto, 144–147, 149.
Beriberi, 154, 197, 218, 310.
Birds, songs of, 32, 33, 281; bientevido, 34; tyrant flycatchers, 34, 35, 36; advertising coloration of, 36; habits of, 36; survival factors in species of, 37; water-fowl, 38, 49, 58, 64, 68; difference in bird fauna, 68, 71; "Jesus Christ," 72; wealth of bird life, 72; nests of, 72, 334; need for work of careful observer of, 72, 78; ants attack nestling, 89; extraordinary collection of, 89, 91; oven-birds,

92, 96, 97; owl, 96, 157, 168; Puan, 98, 101; sickle-billed humming, 104, 105; egrets, 107; toucan, grotesque attitudes of, 108, 160; finfoots, 108; herons, 108; troupials, 117; opportunity for study of, 120; parakeets, 120; screamers, 121; curassows, 122, 297; snake, 126; cormorants, 126; spurred lapwing, 126; contrasts in habits between closely allied species of, 126; manakin, 133; 145; whip-poorwill, 164; honey-creeper, 164; nunlets, 164; waxbill, 165; trogons, 174; false bell-bird, 174; woodpecker 197; some new, 212; breeding season of, 212; macaws, 213; old and new kinds of, 213; valuable addition to collection of, 215; unfamiliar, 228, 229; sariema, 230, 231; cotinga, 247; sixty new, 259, 260; four new species of, 271; ant-thrush, 287; 290, 313; jacaré-tinga, 315; trumpeter, 322; few water, 327; hoatzin, archaic type of, 334.

Boats, house, 99; their use as stores, 99.

Bonofacio, José, station of, 130, 237, 239; provisions left at, 241.

Books, 157, 223, 241, 261; of travel, Appendix A, 345, 346.

Booth Line, 334, 335.

Borah, Jake, 115.

Brazil, invitation of Government of, 2; arrival at boundary of, 48, 49; intellectual and spiritual liberty of, 50; healthiness of inland region of, 100; invaluable reports of explorations published by Government of, 130; educational needs of, 152; silver-mounted saddle and bridle presented to Colonel Roosevelt by Government of, 165; suggestion to combine the two expeditions made by Government of, 182; first explorers of, 183; houses of laborers in, 190; healthy region for settlement offered by high interior of western, 211; courtesy of peasants of, 316; "last frontier" still exists in, 324; development of, 324, 325; Government of, orders Dúvida River to be named Rio Roosevelt, 332; achievements of Government of, 338, 339; Colonel Rondon's report of Savage Landor to Government of, Appendix A, note, 347, 348.

Brazil, Doctor Vital, 14, 15, 18, 19, 20, 21, 22, 23, 24, 41, 283.

Brazil Land and Cattle Company, headquarters of, 121, 122.

Bridge, an Indian, 248, 249.

Bronx Zoo, 336.

Bryce, James, 172; Appendix A, 344.

Buenos Aires, 9, 31.

Bullets, umbrella-pointed, 137.

Bullock-train, 215.

Butterflies, 164, 230.

Burity River, camp at, 205, 206, 207.

Burton, 344.

Caboclos, 187, 237.

Caetano, Lieutenant, 183.

Caeté flags, 104.

Cajazeira, Doctor, 166, 183, 203, 275, 283, 304, 305, 312, 319; good-by to, 335.

Camaradas, 103, 104; skilful riding of, 104; 113, 114, 134; wilderness work disliked by, 155; 244, 261, 275; discouragement of, 299; tragedy among the, 302, 308; fever among, 309; share food with, 314; lose strength, 319; ill from overeating, 325; parting gift to, 335.

Camp chairs and table, Appendix B, 353.

Campos Novos, 227, 228.

Canama River, 255, 289, 329.

Canja, 165, 229.

Canoes, 134; Canadian, 165, 241, 243, 244; portaging the, 253, 255, 260, 261; loss of two, 262; building new, 265, 266; 267; lose another, 273; 275; build two more, 280; 293, 295; rocks break, 298; 299, 302, 313, 314, 321; obtain boat to replace, 328; two months in, 330; last trip in, 332; Appendix B, 353, 354, 355, 356.

Capricorn, Tropic of, 39.
Capybaras, or tapirs, 78, 80, 83, 85, 86, 87, 107, 113.
Cardozo, Captain, 154.
Caripe, Senhor, 328; his stories of rubber-workers, 329, 331, 332, 333.
"Carregadores," 186, 250, 280, 281.
Cartucho, the puppy, 186, 187.
Carvings, rock, 292.
"Cashada," the Brazilian name for peccary, 141, 144.
Castanho, the, 316, 317, 318, 330.
Cataracts, 311.
Catfish, 311.
Cattle, 70; jaguars attack, 83; branding of, 92, 93; regions of extraordinary possibilities for raising, 119, 122, 151.
Caymans, 39, 52, 53, 57, 58; jacarés, usual name for, 64, 65; interesting incident of truculence of, 85, 86; astonishing tameness of, 110, 312.
Centiped, 302.
Chaco, the, 39, 40.
Chapadão, 210, 229, 231, 233, 338.
Chapman, Frank, 2, 3.
Chasm, a, 299, 300.
Cherrie, George K., 3, 5, 9, 39, 61, 96, 99, 100, 148; good citizenship of, 152; good work done by, 161; 162, 168; widely varied experiences of, 179, 180; 183, 199, 203, 205, 209, 212, 213, 222; interesting tales told by, 223; 229, 234, 241, 249, 256, 259, 271, 273, 275; home life of, 286; helpfulness of, 297; 302, 304, 308, 312, 319, 320, 329; piranha attacks, 331; friendship inspired by, 333; 337, 338, 346.
Cherrie River, 294.
Chile, 9.
Cicadas, 63, 64.
Climate, difficulties of working in a damp, 201, 202.
Clothing, Appendix B, 354, 359, 364, 365.
Coati, 47, 110, 111.
Coimbra, 58, 59.
Coloration, advertising, of birds, 36, 287; theories concerning concealing, 97; concealing, not universal among big game, 118, 119, 123, 124, 125; coral-snake possesses revealing, 249; examples of protective, 250, 257.
Compass, necessity for a, 158, 175; Appendix B, 367.
Concepcion, 40, 41, 43, 45; visit to barracks at, 46; breakfast at City Hall at, 47.
Cooking, 155; equipment for, Appendix B, 359, 362.
Correa, Antonio, 272, 273, 288, 291, 294, 316.
Corumbá, 9, 60, 61, 62, 63; arrival at, 94; 119, 327.
Cougar, or puma, 26, 27, 28; man attacked by, 29, 30, 31, 53; 122, 123; deer preyed on by, 175.
Craveiro, Pedrinho, 290, 304.
Crops, 39, 326.
Cruz, Doctor, 41.
Cuyabá River, 98; party leaves the, 109; 119.

Da Cunha, Commander, 85.
Dance, an Indian, 200, 201; Nhambiquara, 219, 235.
Darwin, his "Voyage of the Beagle," 345; 348, 352.
Deer, bush, 111, 136, 137, 138, 150.
Deer, marsh, 76, 97; revealing coloration of, 118.
Deer, pampas, 175, 177.
Deer, whitetail, 111, 112, 118.
Dipper, the, 320.
Diseases, 197, 198.
Ditmars, R. L., 18.
Dogs, 65, 74, 77, 80, 105, 106, 113, 114; jaguar hunt exhausts, 115; need for good, 115; worthlessness of the, 136; custom of gelding hunting, 151; heat tries, 213.
Ducks, muscovy, 49; tree, 121.
Duffel-bags, Appendix B, 358, 359.

Easter Sunday, 314.
Education, need of, 151, 152.

Egan, Maurice Francis, 1.
Electric flashlight, Appendix B, 365, 366.
Enoerey, the god, 204.
Equipment, 5, 6, 209, 210; compass a necessary part of, 158, 175; for trip down unknown river, 241; blankets a necessary of, 298; Colonel Roosevelt's suggestion for, Appendix B, 353, 354; Fiala's suggestion for, 354–369.
Evangalista, Miguel, 236, 237.
Expedition, the, origin of, 1; members of, 3, 4, 5; ground to be covered by, 6, 7, 8; scientific character of, 26; arrival of Brazilian members of, 49, 50, 51; division of the, 166; primary purpose of, 182; official title of, 182, 183; individual work done by members of, 183; begin difficult part of, 203; final division of belongings and members of, 240, 241; perilous state of, 306; a good doctor essential on, 309; ill health of members of, 314; a red-letter day for, 315; no longer fear of disaster to, 319; complete zoological success of, 338; most important work done by, 338.
Explorers, dangers to pioneer, 53, 154, 171–173; work of Brazilian, 212; disasters to parties of, 301; much work in South America for, Appendix A, 343, 346; need for accuracy and common sense in writings of, 347, 348, 349; note, 348; useful articles which should always be carried by, 363, 364.

Farrabee, Professor, 172, 337, 338, Appendix A, 346.
Fauna, 7; pleistocene, 26, 27; bird, 68; mammalian, 68; South America rich in bird, 108; an interesting, 213; extinct South American, Appendix A, 351, 352.
Fazendas, 157, 158.
Fazendeiros, 134, 144.
Ferry, the, 188.
Fiala, Anthony, 4, 5, 9; outfit assembled by, 62; takes moving picture, 107; efficiency of, 161; 166, 179, 183, 203; loses baggage and provisions, 215; rations chosen by, 287; goes home, 331; his suggestions for equipment and provisions, Appendix B, 354–369.
Fish, best hooks and rods for, Appendix B, 364.
Fishing stick, 273.
Flies, horse, 126, 253; pium, 184, 253; polvora, 253; boroshuda, 253; berni, 146, 147, 224.
Floating islands, 336.
"Fly-dope," 253, Appendix B, 354.
Flying-fish, 285.
Food, 181; oxen for, 204, 233; 242; monkeys as, 249; economizing, 265; palm-tops used for, 274; shortage of, 287; country furnishes scant supply of, 287, 288; toucan and parrots as, 291; high prices for, 322; vegetables and fruits raised by settlers for, 323; Appendix B, 359; itemized list of, 360, 361.
Football, extraordinary game of, 192, 193.
Forage, scarcity of, 209, 210, 222, 226, 227.
Forests, 7, 58, 68, 132, 133; multitudes of insects inhabit, 147; 173, 174; absolute necessity for a compass in, 158, 175; 210, 245; difficulty of hunting in, 260; 265, 266, 297.
Fort Bourbon, 55.
França, the cook, ghostly belief of, 305.
Franco, Ricardo, 183, 184, 214.
Frogs, peculiar cries of, 205, 230.
Fungi, 164.

Game, big, inadequate knowledge of life histories of, 116.
Gauchos, 92, 93.
Geographer, work of field, in South America, Appendix A, 343, 346.
Geological structure of land, 231, 232.
Goff, Johnny, 115.
Gopher rat, 239, 240.

Graves, forlorn, 197, 205, 225.
Guaporé, the, 183.
Guarany, 43, 44.
Guiana, 337.
Gy-Paraná, the, 129, 130; descent of the, 153; boat, men, and provisions lost ascending the, 154; 241, 263, 264, 338.

Hammocks, Appendix B, 353, 357.
Harper, Frank, 4, 5, 161; specimens and unnecessary baggage returned to New York in care of, 166.
Haseman, John D., 172, Appendix A, 347, 348; theories of, 349, 350, 351.
Headball, 192, 193, 198.
Head-nets, 215, 227.
Herford, Oliver, nonsense rhymes of, 192.
Hoehne, the botanist, 167.
Honey, 257.
Honey-creeper, 231.
Horses, 67, 74; curious relations of tapirs and, 143.
Houses, native, 214, 238, 239.
Huatsui, camp at, 207.
Hudson, Mr., author of "Naturalist on the Plata," 28, 33, 84; Appendix A, 344.
Huguen, Marcelino, 30.
Humboldt, 345.
Hunters, native, 75; one christened "Nips," 76; curious ignorance regarding habits of animals of native and other, 84; riding costume of, 144; lack of sense of direction of, 175.
Huxley, 348, 352.

Ibis, turtles' nests plundered by, 99.
Iguanas, 222.
Indians, 47, 48; civilization of tribes of, 50; fishing village of, 101; governmental treatment of the, 152; wages paid the, 188; Colonel Rondon's treatment of, 188; telegraph-line patrolled by, 188; dog killed by, 272, 273; 279.
Indian mounds, 101.
Insects, 39, 40; man's worst animal foes, 40, 41; a menace to wilderness travel, 53, 67, 98; perpetuation of species of, 116, 117; atrocious suffering caused by, 147, 170, 171; many queer, 178; 187, 206, 207; torments from, 226; danger from wild animals less than from, 226, 227; 253, 256, 261, 266, 274, 298; festering wounds caused by bites of, 302; 321. *See* Mosquitoes, Flies, Wasps, Ants.
"Instituto serum-thérapico," 13, 14.
Irala, the Spanish explorer, 58.
Itacoatiara, 311.

Jabiru storks, 49, 64, 67, 90, 91; Fiala takes a moving picture of, 107; 151.
Jacanas, 72.
Jacaré-tinga. *See* Caymans.
Jacu, a, 256, 258.
Jacyparaná, the, 264.
Jaguar, 26, 31, 32, 53; hunt for, 77–82; cattle preyed on by, 83; spears and rifles used in hunting, 102; unsuccessful hunt for, 113, 114; melanism common among, 123; trees refuge of, 137; kills bullock, 334.
Jaguarundi, 122, 123.
Jararaca, 11, 12, 20, 21, 22; mussurama fights, 23, 24, 25; man bitten by, 53; 133; stories of, 222.
Jesuits, missions of the, 43.
João, Kermit's helmsman, 268, 269, 283.
Johnston, Sir Harry, 40.
Juina, the, 223.
Julio, 244, 290; story of tragedy caused by, 302–308.
Jungle, man strayed in, 158.
Juruena, the, 129, 130, 182, 203, 211; arrival at, 214; 338.

Kipling, poems of, 198.

Lambert, Doctor Alexander, 253.
Lamps, Appendix B, 36.

Landor, Savage, 173; Colonel Rondon's scathing review of, note, Appendix A, 347, 348.
Languages, Guarany, 43, 44; 54; 157.
La Plata Museum, 31; Appendix A, 351.
"Las Palmeiras," visit to ranch of, 64, 67; cattle at, 70; delightful stay at, 87; leave, 109.
"Last Frontier," in Brazil, 324.
Lauriadó, Lieutenant, 176, 203, 215, 331.
Lecture engagements, 2, 9.
Lobo, 272.
Long Island, spring on, 168, 320.
Lowell, 172.
Luiz, steersman, 244, 257, 272, 273.
Lyra, Lieutenant, João, 50, 128, 153, 154, 166, 179, 181, 183, 203, 204, 205, 229, 241, 243, 244, 252, 253, 255, 260, 261, 262, 263, 264, 265, 272, 275, 283, 288, 289, 291, 295, 297, 298, 299, 300, 302, 303, 308, 312, 319, 320, 326, 332, 335.

Macario, 294.
MacGahan, Januarius Aloysius, 1.
Machetes, 114, 144, 174; *falcóns*, Brazilian name for, 312.
Mackenzie, Murdo, 121.
Madeira, the, 128, 129, 183, 241, 265, 318, 333, 340.
Madeira-Marmoré Railroad, 236.
Madeirainha River, 326, 329.
Magalhães, Captain Amilcar de, 50.
Mammals, 68; variety in fecundity of different families of, 74; 96, 108, 161; noteworthy collection of, 334.
Manaos, 241, 329, 331, 332, 333, 334, 337.
Mandioc, 188.
Mantes, Praying, 186, 187.
Marino, Lieutenant, 214.
Marques, Dom João, the younger, 102; his gift to Colonel Roosevelt, 109, 110.
Marques, Senhor João da Costa, 100; noteworthy family of, 102.
Marsh, difficult swim across, 114.
Marsh plants, 104, 114.
Matté, 45, 181; Appendix B, 362.
Matto Grosso, 8, 100; largest ranch-house in, 109; 128, 129; future possibilities of interior of, 151, 152, 153; beginnings of province of, 184; 340.
McLean, —, 121.
Meat, Appendix B, 359, 360.
Medicines, Appendix B, 354.
Mello Filho, Lieutenant Joaquin, 51, 176, 203, 228, 240.
Merriam, Hart, 81.
Mess-kit, Appendix B, 362.
Mice, new varieties of, 108.
Miller, Leo E., 3, 5, 9, 39, 42, 61, 62, 71, 96, 99; good work done by, 161; 162, 168, 180, 183, 199, 203, 205, 209, 213, 222; interesting tales told by, 223; 229, 230, 234, 239, 240, 331; rejoins party, 334; 336, 337, 338; Appendix A, 346.
Monkeys, black howler, 105; 110, 112; nocturnal, 117; 121, 239, 247; flesh of, good eating, 249, 297; fish eats, 311; 336.
Montes, Captain Vicente, 31.
Montevideo, 13.
Moreno, Doctor Francisco P., 26; extraordinary discoveries of, 26, 27, 28; puma attacks, 29, 30, 31; Appendix A, 351, 352.
Mosquito-biers, 227.
Mosquitoes, 99, 100, 110, 114, 119; few, 158; absence of, 181; 228, 321.
Motors, Appendix B, 356.
Motor-trucks, 176, 180.
Mountains, 294, 296.
Mules, pack, 160, 169; weather exhausts, 199; loads for the, 209; weakness of, 209, 210; abandoned, 225; pasturage for, 226; loads for, Appendix B, 357.
Müller, General Lauro, 8, 49, 278; Colonel Roosevelt's letter to, Appendix B, 370, 371.
Mundurucu Indians, 329.
Museums, trained observers should be sent into wilderness by, 161.

Music, 141, 200, 201, 219, 235.
Mussurama, 14, 17, 18, 19, 22; jararaca fights, 23, 24, 25.

Natives, 134.
Naturalists, outdoor, possibilities for useful work of, 72, 73, 91; slight experience of big game possessed by most, 115, 116; ideal place for work of field, 120; museums should send into the wilderness trained, 161.
Navaïté Rapids, 252–255.
Nests, communal, 120; troupials', 159.
Nhambiquara Indians, 194; land of the, 203, 206; Colonel Rondon's just treatment of the, 216, 217; no wilder savages than the, 217; life and habits of, 217, 218; improvised dance of the, 219; dog stolen by, 220; a visit from three, 224; former hostility of, 224, 225; an encampment of, 234, 235; their lack of clothing, 235; ornaments of, 238; probable strain of negro blood in, 238; archery of, 240; the Navaïté, a sub-tribe of the, 252.
"Nips," a native hunter, 76.
North, the call of the, 320.
Nunlet, 164.
Nuts, Brazil, 292; crop of, fails, 326.
Nuts, unwholesome, 315.
Nyoac, the, the river boat, 95.

Ocelot, 122, 123.
Oliveira, Doctor Euzebio de, the geologist, 51, 183, 203, 228, 231.
Onelli, Doctor, 31.
Opossum, 96, 168.
Orchids, 132, 151, 158, 159; sobralia, 260.
Orioles, wasps surround nests of, 99.
Ornithology, Sclater and Hudson's, 35.
Osborn, Henry Fairfield, 2.
Otter, 247.
Outfit for South American wilderness, Appendix B, 353–369.
Outlook, The, 27.
Overland, trip begun, 160.
Owl, Moses, the tame, 96, 157, 168.
Ox-carts, 93, 94.
Oxen, pack, 160; difficulty in loading, 169; clothes eaten by, 193; 199, 215; secure some fresh, 233; loads for, Appendix B, 357.

Paca, 247.
Pacu, 276.
Paddlers, 241, 244.
Paixão (Paishon), 303, 304; Julio kills, 304; burial of, 308, 371.
Paleontological knowledge, our present, 350.
Palms, nacury, 81; Dr. Rodriguez's book on, 109; fig-trees kill, 145; wawasa, 145, 158; burity, 146, 174; bacaba, 236; boritana, 245, 247; accashy, 258.
"Pantanals," or swamps, 71.
Paolistas, the, 212, 325.
Papyrus swamps, 134, 136.
Para, 335, 336, 337.
Paraguay, 39; language and people of, 43, 44; development ahead of, 45; military service introduced in, 46, 47.
Paraguay, the, 6, 7, 8, 38, 39 *et seq.*; early knowledge of the, 55; American flag first seen on the upper, 58; 95; renewed ascent of the, 117; junction of São Lourenço and, 119; 183, 329.
Paraná, 33.
Parecís, Antonio, 144, 147, 149, 150, 244, 259, 272, 276.
Parecís Indians, 187, 190, 191; extraordinary game of football played by, 192, 193; Colonel Rondon holds a council with the, 194, 195; settlement of, 195, 196, 197; presents for the, 200; dance of the, 200, 201; ferry run by, 205, 206.
Parecís plateau, 174.
Park, Mungo, 184.
Patagonia, 26.
"Pateran," a, 252.
Peccary, white-lipped, 76, 89, 105, 106, 113, 141, 143, 148, 149, 150, 336.
Peckolt, Doctor, Appendix B, 362.
Peonage, 152.

Peons, 48, 65, 71.
Peres, Colonel Telles, 301.
Pescada, a, 314.
Photographic supplies, Appendix B, 368, 369.
Pineapples, wild, 291.
Pioneers, 323, 324.
Pipes, natives dance to, 200.
Piraiba, 311, 312.
Piranha, or cannibal fish, 41, 42, 43; stories of attacks by, 51, 52; Miller's study of the, 62, 63; 86; dogs' tails bitten off by, 133; 280; flesh of, good eating, 292; 310, 313, 314; attack Cherrie, 331.
Plan Alto, the, 119, 169; healthy region of, 174–176; 177; singular topographical feature of, 232.
Plantains, or pacovas, 174, 260.
Portages, 251, 254, 293, 296, 309, 314.
Porto Campo, 132, 140, 141.
Porto Martinho, 54.
Positivists, the, 49.
Pranchas, native trading-boats, 132, 160.
Provisions, 6, 41, 155; tin cases of, 165, 166; loss of ferry-load of, 233; 241, 242; half supply of, consumed, 289; Fiala's suggestions for, Appendix B, 359, 362.
Puma. *See* Cougar.
Puma-skin helmet, a, 224.
Pyrineus, Lieutenant, 52, 263, 264, 278, 289, 330, 331, 332.

"Queixada," the, 141.
Quinine, 275.

Rain, severe storm of, 107; beginning of rainy season, 109, 110; forty-eight hour fall of, 113; 174, 184, 196, 199; difficulties of travelling in rainy season, 215; 220, 221, 229, 230, 248, 283; end of rainy season, 297, 321.
Rainey, Paul, hounds used by, 115.
Ramsey, 121.
Ranches, 156, 157, 159, 160.
Rapids, 160; a mishap in the, 215; form serious obstacle, 251; 252, 255, 256, 258, 259, 261; Broken Canoe, 262; 267, 268, 269, 270, 273, 275, 284, 285, 289, 291, 293, 294, 295; time spent in going through, 298; note on, 299; 300, 309, 312, 313, 314; Panela, 322; Inferno, 325, 326; Infernino, 327; Carupanan, 328; last of the, 329.
"Regional Volunteers," 263.
Regions, healthy, 189, 190, 197; enter wilder, 203; rich and fertile, 290, 291; beautiful, 313.
Reinisch, Colonel Rondon's taxidermist, 109, 228.
Religions, 5, 56, 57; need for churches of all, 56, 57; liberty for all, 57.
Rheas, ostriches, 175.
Ribeiro, Miranda, 263.
Rickard, Tex, 40, 45.
Rifles, 5, 206, 229, 269; Appendix B, 353, 363.
Rio Branco, 322.
Rio Cardozo, 310, 318, 326.
Rio de Janeiro, 8, 339.
Rio Grande do Sul, 214.
Rio Kermit, 276, 278, 340.
Rio Marciano Avila, 340.
Rio Negro, 333.
Rio Papagaio, 180, 195, 203; Fiala's loss on, 215; 216, 331.
Rio Sacre, 184, 188.
River of Doubt (Rio da Dúvida), 8, 130, 181, 182; preparations for descent of the, 241, 242; start down, 243; probable direction of, 255; importance of the, 277; possible course of, 277; formally christened Rio Roosevelt, 278; conjectures as to, 289; losses in rapids of, 299; junction of Rio Cardozo and, 310; is put upon the map, 317, 318; length of the, 330, 333, 339; source of, 339, 340.
Rivers, 6, 7, 211; hazards of descending unknown, 216; 300, 301; methods of crossing, 223; 229; courses and outlets of, 232.
Robiliard, Mr., 334.
Rodéo, or round-up, 102.

Rodriguez, Doctor Barboso, 109.
Rogaciano, Lieutenant, 113–115.
Rondon, Colonel Candido Mariano da Silva, 8, 9, 49, 50, 51, 52, 53; outfit inspected by, 62; characteristics of, 75; 77, 95, 110, 113, 115; explorations of, 128, 129, 130; 147, 150, 151; people of Matto Grosso befriended by, 152; Indian service of Brazil headed by, 152; Sepotuba River explored and northwestern wilderness of Matto Grosso opened by, 153; most important exploring trip of, 153, 154; 166, 175; his stories of past experiences, 179, 181, 182, 183, 184; holds a council with the Indians, 194; Utiarity Falls discovered by, 195; gives presents to the Indians, 200, 203–206; work of, 212; friendship of Nhambiquaras for, 216, 217, 220; 222, 224; early life and education of, 237; 241, 243, 244, 255, 262; his eight months' exploration, 263, 264; 272, 275, 276, 277, 278; formally christens Rio Roosevelt, 278, 279; 288, 291, 293, 294; trail cut by, 296; 297, 299, 300, 303; his decision as to murderer, 307, 308; 312, 320; reads record of party's accomplishments, 331; 332; good-by to, 335, 338; Appendix A, 346; charges made against Mr. Savage Landor by, 347, 348.
Roosevelt, Kermit, 4, 5, 65, 66, 71, 73, 76, 77, 78, 80, 81, 90, 110, 113; speed and endurance of, 113, 114, 115; 152, 157, 168, 177, 183, 198, 203, 229, 234, 241, 243, 244, 253, 259, 260, 262, 265, 268; accident befalls, 269, 270; 272, 275; river called after, 276; 279, 283, 288, 289, 291, 293; his experience of rope work, 294, 295; 297, 298, 299, 300, 302; his bridge-building experience, 302; 303, 304; fever attacks, 308, 309, 315; 319, 320, 328, 329; Appendix B, 354.
Roosevelt, Theodore, is invited to attempt descent of unknown river, 8; reception to, 45, 47; Dom João's gift to, 109; receives silver-mounted saddle and bridle, 165; unknown river formally christened for, 278; injures his leg, 309; has an attack of fever, 309; his illness increases, 319, 320; quotation from Colonel Rondon's letter to, Appendix A, note, 347, 348; his suggestions for outfits in South American wilderness, 351, 352, 369; his report to General Lauro Müller, 370, 371.
Rope, Appendix B, 358, 359.
Rubber-gatherers, 212, 316, 318; act as guide, 321; homes of, 322, 323, 324; work of, in opening wilderness, 325; hard lives of, 327; adventures of, 329.

Saddles, Appendix B, 358.
Salto Bello waterfall, 188, 189; future value of, 189; splendid opportunities for settlement in region of, 189, 190; breakfast at the, 193, 194.
São João fazenda, arrival at, 100, 101; near hamlet of, 331, 332.
São Lourenço, 109–117; junction of Paraguay and, 119.
São Luis de Cáceres, 8, 119; arrival at, 127; fine government school at, 127; 194.
São Paulo, 13, 14, 127.
Scents, 164.
Scorpion, a, 302.
Sepotuba, the, or River of Tapirs, 132; fine cattle country along the, 151; exploration and first maps of, 153; camp beside, 170; 194.
Sequoia, 44.
Serpents, 302.
"Sertão," or wilderness, note, 204.
Serums, anti-venom, 10, 12, 13, 15, Appendix B, 354.
"Shenzi," one of the dogs, 65.
Shipton, Major, 241.
Sigg, Jacob, 4, 5, 9; motor-boat improvised by, 127; 161, 180, 199; return to Tapirapoan, 202.
Simplicio, 268; death of, 269.
Skobeloff, 1.
Sloth, a, 334.

Smith, Mr. Lord, 28.

Snakes, 9, 10, 11; poison of, 12, 13–20; some mammals immune to bites of, 21, 22; 133; stories of, 222; 230, 249, 250.

Snethlage, Miss, 172, 337.

Solimoens, 336.

South America, topography of, 6, 7; ceremony of public functions in, 46; Christianity in, 50; education in, 57; mammalian and avifauna of, 68, 69, 70; need for work of collector in, 72; rich bird fauna of, 108; field for work of big-game hunter and faunal naturalist in, 116; ferocity of certain small animals in, 168; much exploring work to be done in, 172; two great waterfalls of, 194; impostors among explorers of, 254; early semicivilizations in, 292; social and industrial development of, Appendix A, 343; travellers in, 343, 345, 346; wilderness work to be done in, 346.

Southern Cross, the, 48, 77.

Sparrows, 168.

Spear, jaguar, 103.

Spiders, a colony of, 178, 208, 209, 233.

Squirrels, 133.

Stilts, 195.

Stirrups, ornamental, 103.

Stockton, Frank, stories by, 186.

Store, the first, 325, 326.

Sunsets, contrasted, 198.

Surveying, method of, 244, 245; instruments for, Appendix B, 366, 367.

"Swiss Family Robinson," 75.

Tamanduá bandeira. *See* Ant-eater.

Tanageira, Doctor, 264.

Tapajos, the, 128, 129, 182, 183, 211, 241, 337.

Tapirapoan, 153; start up-stream for, 155; arrival at, 160; party divides at, 165; 167.

Tapirs, 134, 136, 138, 139, 140, 142; curious relation of horse and, 143.

Tapirs, River of. *See* Sepotuba.

Taquary, the, 62, 64.

Taunay River, 288, 340.

Telegraph, establishment of, 153; high wages paid for work on wilderness lines of, 154, 187; spiders swarm on, 233.

Telegraphic Commission, 160, 176, 206; work of, 212; Juruena first mapped by, 214; labor of, 318; solution of River of Doubt mystery made possible by previous work of, 33[illegible] 339.

Tents, 209, 241; Appendix B, 353.

Thermometers, Appendix B, 368.

Tools, Appendix B, 366.

Tragedy, a terrible, 302–308, note, 307.

Transportation, 183.

Travellers, status of the ordinary, 171, 172, 173; ignorance of certain, 254; three categories of, Appendix A, 343, 344, 345, 346.

Trees, 48, 49, 71; taruman, 78, 97; flowers on, 97, 135; fig, 145, 156, 158, 159; fruit and flowers on, 159, 174, 185; fossil trunk of, 228; 230, 246; barriers formed by, 247; bee, 257; rubber, 268, 284; araputanga, 280; fruit of cajazeira, 283; peculiarity of, 285; 291. *See* Palm.

Tree-toad, 257, 258.

Tres Burity, government ranch at, 236, 237.

"Trigueiro," one of the dogs, 65, 268, 270, 314.

Tropics, entered the, 47; iron cruelty of life in the, 147.

Turtle, a land, 155, 156, 313.

"Twelfth of October," 229.

University of Pennsylvania, a Paraguayan graduate of the, 47.

Uruguay, 9.

Utensils, Indians, 204, 239.

Utiarity Falls, 180; arrival at, 195; telegraph station at, 195; beauty of the, 196, 200.

Vaqueiros, 103, 121, 140.

Viedma, Lake, 28.

Vilhena, 229, 231, 232.

Vines, 110, 111.

Wallace, 336.
Wasp, orioles' nests surrounded by, 99; dangerous sting of red, 114; spiders preyed on by, 117; maribundi, 133, 146, 245; ants plunder nests of, 163.
Weapons, Indian, 204, 239.
Weasel, tayra, 96.
Weather, 58, 62, 93, 109, 155, 164.
Wilderness, party enters the, 204; difficulties of travel in, 210; etiquette of the, 234; first stage of conquest of the, 325; geographical and zoological work still to be done in the, Appendix A, 346.
Wolf, red, 122.
Woods, 230.
Wrens, ant, 162.

Xingu, 183, 337.

Zahm, Father, 1, 2, 5; children baptized by, 55; 128; Colonel Roosevelt reminded of his wish to shoot tapir and jaguar by, 140; 157, 180, 199; returns to Tapirapoan, 202.
Zoologist, work of field, in South America, Appendix A, 343, 346.

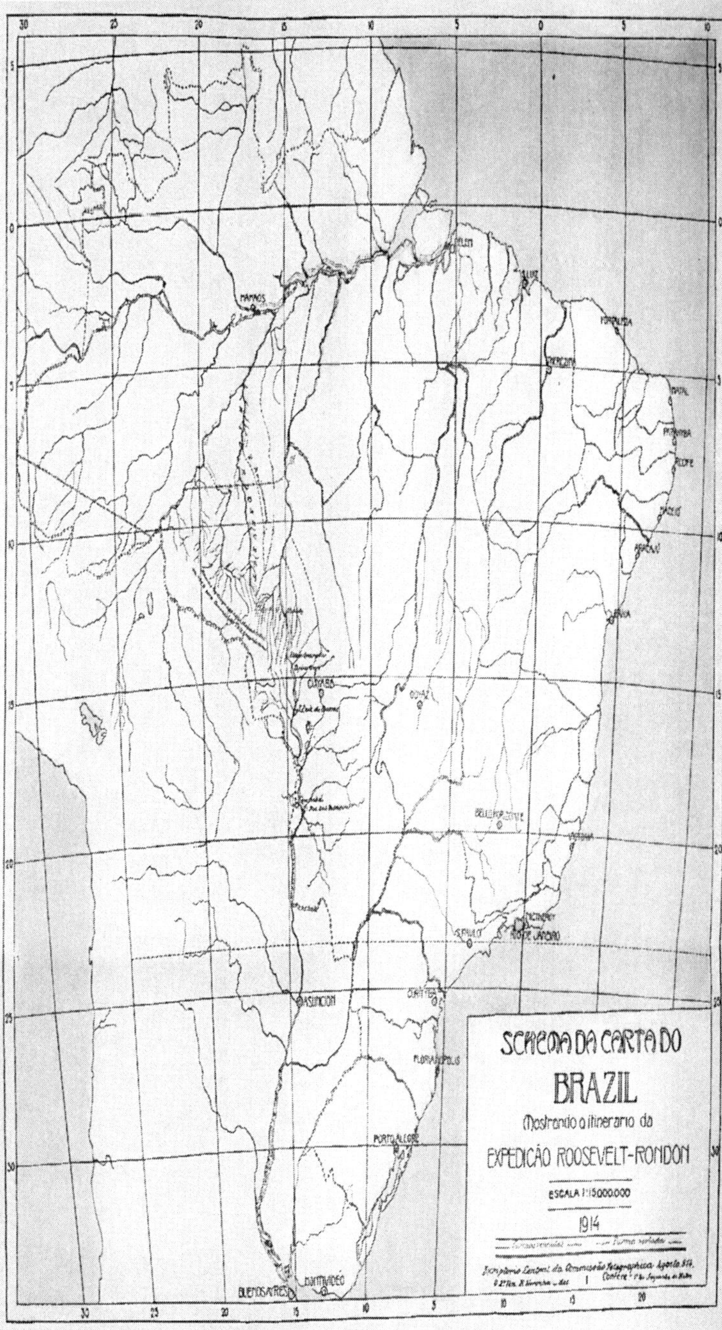

Map forwarded by Lieutenant Lyra, and received just after the completion of this book

Showing the route of the expedition, and the positions of the new river and of the Gy Paraná and of the upper tributaries of the Juruena